ILLNESS, IMMUNITY,
AND SOCIAL INTERACTION

ILLNESS, IMMUNITY, AND SOCIAL INTERACTION

THE DYNAMICS OF BIOSOCIAL RESONATION

GORDON ERVIN MOSS

Eastern Michigan University

A WILEY-INTERSCIENCE PUBLICATION

JOHN WILEY AND SONS, New York · London · Sydney · Toronto

Library of Congress Cataloging in Publication Data

Moss, Gordon Ervin, 1937–
    Illness, immunity, and social interaction.

    "A Wiley-Interscience publication."
    Bibliography: p.
    1. Medicine, Psychosomatic.   2. Stress (Physiology).
    3. Social interaction.   I. Title. [DNLM: 1. Disease—
    Etiology.   2. Social medicine.   3. Stress, Psychologic.

WA 30 M913i   1973]
RC49.M67   616.08   72-11782
ISBN 0-471-61925-6

Printed in the United States of America

10-9 8 7 6 5 4 3 2 1

To Carolee, Michelle, and Nicole

Preface

Science is growing in many directions, including a growing together. Consequently, a need to examine the knowledge of various disciplines has emerged in order to develop concepts that encourage and assist interdisciplinary cooperation.

This need is especially acute in the area of social stress. Frequently, medical researchers discover that examination of social dimensions are required for satisfactory explanation of their findings. Unfortunately, there is no suitable theory that links social behavior to physiological processes and disease, and the existing sociological theories are difficult to relate to biomedical problems. This deficiency severely limits the usefulness of sociology for medical research. Often one interesting sociological concept, such as status inconsistency, is related to disease without regard to other properties of the social milieu that might offer alternative explanations, and without any attempt to explain how the social variable could produce physiological changes and illness. By default, the greater activity of psychologists in this area has led to an overreliance on intrapsychic explanations of social and biological relations.

In this study I present a broad theoretical framework linking social behavior and disease. I hope it aids medical researchers in using sociological concepts and encourages sociologists to consider biological processes in their work.

I must acknowledge a considerable debt to the many scientists whose work has contributed to the evolution of my ideas to their current form. I owe much to the classic behavioral scientists, but especially to Durkheim, Weber, Mead, and William James. A number of contemporary sociologists such as Parsons, Buckley, and Blumer have influenced my thinking considerably. My orientation toward the physiological aspects of social behavior and the relations of these to health have been shaped by many physiologists, physicians, epidemiologists and psychologists, but especially by John Cassel, Lawrence Hinkle, James and Eleanor Gibson, Ernst Gellhorn, and Stanley Schachter.

I especially appreciate the work of Hans Selye. His conceptualization of stress has provided a powerful tool with which to study an important aspect of human existence. His research on the endocrinology of the adrenals and other glands continues to enlighten scientists concerning the body's adaptation to the environment. His book *From Dream to Discovery* was a comfort to me during the period in which the bulk of this theory was constructed, when I was much in need of some understanding of how one goes about getting the kinds of insights on which a simple but strong concept is founded.

Ultimately, were it not for my good fortune to have associated with some outstanding teachers and helpful colleagues, I might never have appreciated the richness of our intellectual heritage and current scientific developments. I am grateful to Harry Bredemeier, who introduced me to the delights of sociological theory; to Matilda Riley, who showed me that theory and methodology are indispensable to each other; and to Glenn Vernon, who helped me develop a feeling for the symbolic-interaction perspective. I am grateful to Saxon Graham, whose persistent skepticism, coupled with genuine concern for me, served to temper many of the ideas that have gone into this work, and to Edward Marra, who provided valuable advice on the medical and physiological portions of this study. I am deeply grateful to Llewellyn Gross, with whom I have spent many pleasant hours in wide-ranging discussions that have helped guide me around some of the pitfalls of theory development and have provided me with most of whatever intuitive sensitivity for sound theoretical conceptualization I may have. And finally I wish to express my deepest thanks to my wife Carolee for typing and assisting in the editing of the many drafts of this book, for her understanding and her ability to share my many moments of enthusiasm.

GORDON ERVIN MOSS

Ypsilanti, Michigan
August 1972

Acknowledgments

We are grateful to the following authors and publishers for permission to quote from their work: to M. Appley, R. Trumbull, J. Lacey, R. Lazurus, G. Ruff, and S. Korchin in *Psychological Stress: Issues in Research,* edited by Mortimer H. Appley and Richard Trumbull, copyright 1967, by permission of Appleton-Century-Crofts, Educational Division, Meredith Corporation; to H. Basowitz, H. Persky, S. Korchin, and R. Grinker, *Anxiety and Stress: An Interdisciplinary Study of a Life Situation,* copyright 1955 and used with permission of McGraw-Hill Book Company; D. Bindra, in *Physiological Correlates of Emotion,* edited by P. Black, copyright 1970 and used with permission of Academic Press; to W. Buckley, editor, *Modern Systems Research for the Behavioral Scientist,* copyright 1968 and used with permission of Aldine Publishing Company; to W. Cannon, *The Wisdom of the Body,* revised and enlarged edition copyright 1939 by Walter B. Cannon, renewed 1966, 1967 by Cornelia B. Cannon, used with permission of the publisher, W. W. Norton; to W. Caudill, *Effects of Social and Cultural Systems in Reactions to Stress,* copyright 1958, used with permission of Social Science Research Council.

Also to J. Cassel, E. Gross, R. Scott, and A. Howard in *Social Stress,* edited by Sol Levine and Norman A. Scotch, copyright 1970 by Aldine Publishing Company, reprinted by permission of the authors and Aldine-Atherton, Inc.; to P. Chauchard, *The Brain,* copyright 1970, Grove Press, by permission of *Editions du Seuil;* to Bruce P. Dohrenwend and the *Journal of Abnormal and Social Psychology,* copyright 1961 by the American Psychological Association and reproduced by permission; to J. Spaulding and G. Simpson, translators of *Suicide* by E. Durkheim, copyright 1951 by The Free Press and Routledge & Kegan Paul, Ltd., London; to A. Etzioni, *The Active Society,* copyright 1962 and used with permission of The Free Press; to J. Gibson, *The Senses Considered as Perceptual Systems,* copyright 1966 and used with permission of Houghton Mifflin and George Allen and Unwin, Ltd., London; to L. E. Hinkle, Jr., and *Archives of Environmental Health,* copyright 1968 by the American Medical Association; to H. Hughes, *Consciousness and Society,* copyright 1961 and used with permission of Alfred A. Knopf, Inc.; to S. Kety, C. Pfaffmann, and S. Schachter in *Neurophysiology and Emotion,* edited by D. Glass, copyright 1967 and used with permission of The Rockefeller University Press; to D. Krech and J. Singer in *William James: Unfinished Business,* edited by R. B. MacLeod, copyright 1969 by the American Psychological Association and reproduced with permission.

Also to R. Marks and A. Payne in *Social Stress and Cardiovascular Disease,* edited by S. L. Syme and L. G. Reeder, copyright 1967 and used with permission of *Milbank Memorial Fund Quarterly;* to A. Maslow, *Motivation and Personality,* copyright 1954 and used with permission of Harper and Row; to D. Mechanic, *Students Under Stress,* copyright 1962 and *Medical Sociology,* copyright 1968 and used with permission of The Free Press; to S. Schachter in *Psychobiological Approaches to Social Behavior,* edited by P. Leiderman and D. Shapiro, copyright 1964, reprinted with permission of the publishers, Stanford University Press; to H. Seyle, *The Stress of Life,* copyright 1956 and used with permission of McGraw-Hill Book Company; to E. Suchman, *Sociology and the Field of Public Health,* copyright 1963 and used with permission of Russell Sage Foundation; and to T. Shibutani in *Symbolic Interaction: A Reader in Social Psychology* edited by J. Manis and B. Meltzer, copyright 1967 by Allyn and Bacon, whose article originally appeared in the *American Journal of Sociology,* copyright 1955 by the University of Chicago Press and used with their permission.

This work was supported in part by Public Health Service Training Grant No. HS 00019, National Center for Health Services Research and Development.

G. E. M.

Contents

ILLNESS, IMMUNITY,
AND SOCIAL INTERACTION

CHAPTER I

Development of the Concept
of Biosocial Resonation

Industrialization seems to be accompanied by a waxing and waning of diseases in a particular sequence. The earliest consequences of industrialization and its accompanying urbanization have been the increase of infectious diseases. For example, in the United States and Great Britain there was a rise in tuberculosis rates, which reached a peak in 50 to 75 years and then declined. This occurred before the discovery of the tubercle bacillus and long before any organized antituberculosis program. Tuberculosis rates have declined at an even rate, despite discovery of new drugs for its treatment.

Tuberculosis as the major health problem was replaced by malnutrition syndromes, such as rickets in Britain and pellagra in the United States. These in turn were replaced by diseases of early childhood, which declined with improvements in sanitation and immunizations programs. These improvements do not entirely explain the decline. Childhood diseases were replaced by duodenal ulcer, especially in young men between the First and Second World Wars, and accompanied by a marked increase in the ratio of males to females having ulcers. For reasons still not understood, the rates of ulcers have declined and have been replaced by our current major health concerns, such as coronary heart disease, hypertension, cancer, arthritis, diabetes, and mental disorders. There is some

1

evidence that some of these, such as hypertensive heart disease, are already declining (Cassel, 1970).

> Despite intensive research, the explanations for the genesis of these changes in disease patterns has so far proved to be relatively unsatisfactory. Attention has been focused on the introduction of new pollutants and toxicants into the air and water and on the reduction of old ones, on the increasing amount of ionizing radiation, and on the hazards associated with pesticides and food additives. Changes in plant and animal life and the changing nature of the microorganisms with which man comes into contact, have also received considerable attention. The influence of certain aspects of behavior—exercise, diet, cigarette smoking, alcohol consumption—have been studied in some detail. None of these changes however, has afforded a very satisfactory explanation for the occurrence of the new disease nor for the decline of the old ones. One of the consequences of this dissatisfaction with the more orthodox explanations has been a reawakening of interest in the possible role of social and cultural "stress" factors as determinants of disease (Cassel, 1970, p. 190).

This renewed interest focuses on the awareness of the significance of changes in social relations, values, and attitudes accompanying industrialization. For Cassel (1970) the evidence indicating that social behavior influences health, especially through "stress," is still fragmentary and equivocal. We do not know which social activities are deleterious to human health, nor do we understand the intervening links between social processes and disturbed physiological states. In some cases the appropriate questions have not yet been asked.

Conceptualizations of the relationship between social and physiological processes and of social and psychological stress have been unsatisfactory for some time. Caudill in 1958, (p. 3) believed that "some broad conceptual sense of direction is needed" to orient stress research and to take into account social and cultural phenomena. Suchman in 1963 (pp. 56–57) found social epidemiological studies "deficient in the conceptualization of their social variables and in the development of a theory as to how and why the social factors become engaged in disease process." At a psychobiological symposium held in 1963, Leiderman and Shapiro (1964, p. 197) indicate that "better theories of social behavior on the biological as well as the social levels will be required" to solve problems facing psychobiological studies of social behavior. In a national workshop conference on socioenvironmental stress and cardiovascular disease held in 1966 (Syme and Reeder, 1967), Syme (1967, p. 175) suggested the need for more relevant questions that theoretically integrate ideas and hypotheses and for more appropriate methods. Upon reviewing findings that relate sociocultural incongruities and social change to cardiovascular disease T. Smith (1967, p. 35) concluded that a general framework providing a common language to encompass the range of social change and incongruity situations was needed. Levine and Scotch (1967, p. 169) expressed a need for new conceptualizations and theoretical frameworks in social stress. Similar complaints and suggestions were expressed at a conference on psychological stress held in 1965 (Appley and Trumbull, 1967).

Writing in 1967 Michaux et al. (1967, p. 361) declared that the literature on stress was at best potentially fertile and at worst theoretically unintegrated, and they decided that "a superordinate or strategic need is to develop a more effective theoretical and conceptual linkage between relevant somatic and psychosocial processes." Cassel in 1964 called for a conceptual scheme to indicate the social processes and cultural elements of potential relevance to health, and he seems to be still unsatisfied in 1970 (p. 199) when he expressed concern that advances in social stress would be limited "until the nature of those social processes influencing physiological responses (and thus, presumably, susceptibility to disease) can be more precisely defined and quantitated." Levine and Scotch in 1970 (1970c, p. 284) believe there is still a "crucial and overriding problem" of "linking and describing the dynamic interplay among the various components of stress." They think that although it is fairly well established that social factors are related to physical health, there is still surprisingly little solid research that demonstrates the processes connecting the two.

A major reason for the lack of progress in relating social and physiological processes is that the problem encompasses many disciplines and environments. It is difficult to find researchers capable of conceptualizing and measuring both social and biological properties. They are usually limited to perspectives and methods of their own discipline, and to studies of phenomena they can handle with their skills. Collaborative efforts are still relatively uncommon (Levine and Scotch, 1970).

The first task for scientists having some competence in both social and biological fields is to develop researchable and refutable conceptual frameworks. Without more effective conceptualization "quantification will be premature and lead to the danger of superficiality and sterility" (Cassel, 1970, pp. 200–201).

> While the translation of the concepts . . . into feasible research projects will be no easy task, and may indeed be beyond our current ingenuity, it seems important that the issues be raised and discussed as an essential prelude to further productive inquiry. Failing this, there appears to be the serious danger that future research will continue in the existing repetitive mold, documenting an association between certain social conditions and disease states without illuminating the processes involved or indicating further directions for research or improving our ability for informed intervention, either preventive or therapeutic (Cassel, 1970, p. 204).

The purpose of this work is to conceptualize some possible links between social behavior, physiological processes, and health.

The Roots of Biosocial Resonation in the Mind-Body Controversy

BASIC POSITIONS IN THE MIND-BODY CONTROVERSY

Swanson (1967, p. 41) believes that "Every problem of interest in social psychology requires that we make some judgements about the relations of mind to body and social organization." We are inclined to agree, however, with Pfaffmann (Glass, 1967, pp. ix, x) who believes that there has developed, if not an antibiological perspective, at least a nonbiological stance among students of social and cultural phenomena. Some use overly simplified biological theories, and others detach the study of behavior from biological underpinnings. Certainly considering the body and the mind and social organizations entities has a longer history and more devotees than seeing these elements as a whole. Flanders Dunbar (1948) in 1934 introduced the term psychosomatic to the English language to emphasize the inappropriateness of a dichotomy between the mind and body, and a distinctive perspective in medicine has grown around this concept and now flourishes. It has helped to hasten, at least in scientific circles, the abandonment of the artificial distinction between mind and body and has opened the way for the behavioral sciences to contribute to the field of medicine (Mechanic, 1962).

Krech (1969) lists three major scientific positions on mind-body interrelations. First, there is no relation between the mind and the body. Scientists holding this view believe that one can either ignore the brain and physiology when studying the mind or ignore the mind when studying the brain and physiology. Krech places most of the learning theorists (including the Watsonians and Skinnerians) in this category. Physicians often publicly claim to have rejected the mind-body distinction and yet privately operate in terms of such a distinction, often unwittingly (D. Graham, 1967). Second, Krech suggests a category of psycho-physical parallelism in which mental and physical activities are independent of each other but which fluctuate in harmony. They are correlated with each other, but there is no interraction between them. Krech feels that this was Titchener's position. The third position is called interactionist. Scientists holding this view insist that mental functions are brain functions. The two are simply aspects of the same biological phenomena. Krech endorses the interactionist position and attributes it to William James.

James is a towering figure in the study of mind and body. His ideas have been extremely fertile, and much of the more promising current work in this area is based upon or has grown from his findings. Perhaps because he was a physician he was better able to conceptualize physiological and psychological dimensions together. He suggested that we may assume that all experience and behavior are determined by neural (especially brain) activity and that experience produces some residual effects upon the brain (Krech, 1969, pp. 2–4). In his famous theory of emotions, he postulated that they were our feeling of bodily changes produced by the perception of the exciting situation (Schachter, 1964). The serious experimental study of emotions started with James (Bindra, 1970). He focused attention on discrimination, rather than association, as an important element in perception. He believed that discrimination could be improved with practice, that perceptual development was the gradual discrimination of distinctive properties through the experiencing of contrasts between different things of ever more similar properties. That is, one might first perceive only plants, but then one learns to tell trees from bushes, then pine trees from maple or oak, and finally one learns the different kinds of pines. Labels were used as an aid to identification when differentiation was clear and strong enough (E. Gibson, 1969). Our theoretical perspective of biosocial resonation owes much to James.

SOME HISTORICAL CONVERGENCES ON THE WHOLE MAN

The biosocial resonation perspective began to take form, like so many "modern" ideas, during the period of the Enlightenment in France. The Ideologues Cabanis—a physiologist and physician—and de Tracy brought the thought of de Condillac to a culmination in their study of the mind from the point of view of physiology rather than epistemology, empirically substantiating de Condillac's science of ideas.

De Condillac's science of ideas was based on two premises: first, that sensations are the primary data of cognition and second, that all ideas and all the faculties of human understanding, including perception, judgement, and memory, are compounds of sensations that can be resolved by analysis into their component elements. He thought that nothing was present in the mind that did not enter it through sense channels (Van Duzer, 1935, p. 16; Rosen, 1946, p. 331).

Cabanis thought that physiology, the analysis of ideas, and moral science were all branches of one science: the science of man. He became the father of physiological psychology through his work on the influence of sex, age, climate, diet, and disease on the quality of individual sensibility and, consequently, on the correctness of ideas (Rosen, 1946, p. 334; Chauchard, 1962, p. 8).

Destutt de Tracy, sometimes called the father of French materialism, declared Ideology a part of zoology, and with Cabanis rejected de Condillac's idea that above all there was a soul, spiritually autonomous, that did the "feeling," with the body organs as its agents. De Tracy thought that the "soul" or "feelings" were themselves sensations (Van Duzer, 1935). They declared all human behavior, including the mind, to be natural phenomena.

The Ideologues developed not only a physiological perspective on the mind-body relation but also a research methodology used effectively by Pinel—a contemporary and associate of the Ideologues—in his study of the mentally ill (Mackler and Bernstein, 1966; Lichtheim, 1967) that served as a basis for positivism (Zeitlin, 1968).

Although Bacon and Locke are accepted as the immediate forerunners of the Ideologues (Van Duzer, 1935), similar points of view were expressed by other Britishers, such as Hobbes, Berkeley, Hume, and the Mills. They all felt that knowledge arises from experience alone. In psychophysiology there is still concern over Berkeley's suggestion that sight perception depends on touch to perceive size, distance, and the like (E. Gibson, 1969). This point of view is sometimes called empiricist.

The opposing point of view was Scholasticism. It was based on the religious assumption that ultimate truth is stored as innate ideas in the mind, which is a part of the soul and thus is divine and beyond human comprehension. Consequently, Scholasticism encouraged the search for ultimate causes and emphasized the appropriateness of the methods of religion for research in science, denying the necessity of separate methods for religion and science (Van Duzer, 1935, p. 20). This point of view and those that developed from it are sometimes called "nativist." The debate over these two points of view is not yet over and is one of the great controversies of human history (E. Gibson, 1969).

Opposing medical philosophies emerged from each perspective. In eighteenth-century France more-conservative physicians believed that the body and soul are totally different, with few possibilities for mutual influence. They felt that the physician should study only the body and use only physical remedies. The more-liberal physicians followed the increasingly dominant trend, which closely connected the body and mind. They felt that cures dealing with the mind were connected with those for the body (Mackler and Bernstein, 1966, p. 704). Pinel and others believed that underlying most disease processes were disorders of the nervous system (Wolf and Goodell, 1968).

Through Pinel and Cabanis and the great influence of the Ideologues in Revolutionary France, especially in education and medicine, these ideas spread and, among other things, influenced the development of social medicine (Rosen, 1946). Unfortunately, Pasteur's nineteenth-century discovery of microorganisms or "germs" as causes of disease and the growing interest in microscopic study of cells eclipsed the refinement and development of this perspective. However, now that biological sciences are beginning to realize their limitations in explaining disease, interest is again turning to the influence of the nervous system and social behavior as contributors to the disease process.

The eighteenth-century focus on the nervous system was followed by a period of major development of the knowledge of the brain in the nineteenth century. The notion of the nerve cell and the application of the cellular conception to the nervous system were developed by Golgi (1873) and Ramon y Cajal (1894). Both actions opened the doors for in-depth study of brain functioning. The electrical nature of nervous impulses was demonstrated by discoveries of Galvani (1788), Matteucci (1842), and Du Bois-Reymond (1848). Elementary reflexes were examined by Pfluger; Broca (1861) contributed to the discovery of cerebral localizations for motor functions. Under the influence of Pavlov, brain study became objective at the beginning of the present century. Researchers limited themselves to the study of the mechanisms of behavior in the brain and shunned "recourse to the vocabulary of psychology" (Chauchard, 1962, pp. 8, 10). Currently research on the relations of the brain and behavior is moving beyond the "era of ablationists" in which various parts were destroyed or probed in search of the areas of the brain responsible for various behavior, to an "era of psychoneurobiochemists" in which researchers are more interested in what takes place in various areas of the brain (Krech, 1969, pp. 8–9).

What is most interesting is that development of the cellular and biochemical study of the nervous system has led neurophysiologists back to the problems of concern to the Ideologues and others, which were for a time in disfavor, that is, the relation between brain functioning and subjective experiences. As Chauchard points out:

> With Pavlov, neurophysiology had given up the oversimplified materialist dream of finding the mind or spirit in the brain. People no longer paid attention to anything but physiology (paths, reflexes, nervous impulses, excitations and inhibitions). Consciousness seemed to be eliminated from the physiologist's preoccupations. But the end result of this experimental effort has been, as it happens, the creation of a physiology of consciousness. We are beginning to understand how the cerebral mechanisms make consciousness and thought possible (1962, p. 79).

Psychoneurophysiology has progressed to the point that consciousness and subjectivity can no longer be ignored (Chauchard, 1962, p. 13). At the same time, psychology is returning to an awareness of the importance of the brain and physiology in studying behavior and psychological states.

Krech laments (1969, p. 5) the lost time in psychology resulting from the rejection of James' interactionist position in favor of the views of "psycho-physical parallelism" and nonrelation between mind and body. He thinks that Tolman, Hull, Spence, and Skinner engage in "mindless, brainless systems and learning theories and (if Skinner is to be taken at face value) learning non-theories."

> For this we now know and this James knew long ago, brain events and behavior events are not *two* sets of variables which can be theorized about independently. It is now, indeed, an *empirical* finding that they must be dealt with in interrelation. If our own 15 years of brain research at Berkeley have taught us anything at all, it is this: Brain chemistry and brain morphology determine behavior, but brain chemistry and brain morphology are just as clearly determined by the behavior they determine! (Krech, 1969, p. 6, emphasis his.)

The physiological-psychologists Gellhorn and Loofbourrow (1963, p. 163) hold similar views: "Behavior might be defined as the expression of the various chemical and physical processes going on in the organism." They insist there is "no evidence that a non-material mind causes physiological changes" (p. 187). "Mental" phenomenon are aspects of complex physiological processes peculiar to the brain. They go so far as to suggest that the term "psychological" be eliminated since the so-called "psychic events" are essentially physiological processes (pp. 142-143).

Engel (1962 p. 11) says:

> Processes within the body are usually considered to belong to the domain of physiology and those related to the external environment to the field of behavior, but clearly these are only convenient differences of perspective of the same process.

According to Engel it is an illusion to believe that we can solve psychological problems without regard to biology or by focusing entirely on physiology and ignoring subjective and behavioral dimensions. Both must be considered. The physiological-psychologists Leiderman and Shapiro (1964, p. 197) agree. Kaplan and Kaplan (1967) feel that there is a growing consensus among psychosomatic researchers that "psychic and physiological variables represent different aspects of the unitary phenomenon of affect (p. 1039)."

The modern Pavlovians, whose position Corson (1967) has labeled cerebrosocial psychiatry, feel that a cleavage between mind and body is no more possible than a separation of circulation from the cardiovascular system. They conceive of the brain-mind-social environment as a unit.

They see all illnesses as being influenced to varying degrees through higher nervous system activity, not just psychosomatic disease (Wittkower and Solyom, 1967). Hinkle (1961) also believes that the distinction between psychosomatic and other forms of disease is unwarranted, because all diseases are associated to some degree with the individual's responses to his environment. He has encouraged the abandoning of the "needless dichotomy of a 'physical' and a 'social' environment" view (Hinkle, 1968). Leiderman and Shapiro (1964, pp. 196–197) suggest that psychiatry needs to expand its conceptions of "mind-body" relations to include "the learning that can take place under varying social and group circumstances. Sociosomatic concepts must take their rightful place with psychosomatic concepts in psychiatric thinking." They call for more studies to clarify the relationships between subjective states of interacting people and bodily states, such as autonomic and endocrine functions. Mason and Brady (1964) agree that endocrine studies may prove fruitful in understanding social and subjective activities. These studies could include the study of the socialization of physiological responses and the possibility of developing classifications of social behavior based on behavioral-physiological relationships (Leiderman and Shapiro, 1964).

The conceptualization of social behavior and physiological processes as a whole holds much promise for fresh approaches to social and health problems, and may indeed provide a more realistic picture of man in his environment. However, for the picture to be complete it must encompass man's relationships with the environment, including among many factors such things as infrasound (Green and Dunn, 1968); ecology of plants and animals; and various rhythms, such as seasons, tides, days and nights.

The conceptualization of man in his environment and the influence of these relations upon his health has been called the "whole man" perspective. It comes to us from social medicine and can be traced to Cabanis and the Ideologues (Rosen, 1946), among others. The "whole man" idea has most often been used in emphasizing the importance of the social milieu for man's physical well being, especially in the hopes of influencing those in a position to improve matters, such as politicians (Rosen, 1947, 1958, 1963; Galdston, 1949).

BIOSOCIAL RESONATION

We have selected the term biosocial resonation to apply to our variation on the themes we have just discussed. Biosocial is preferred to emphasize the interrelationship of biological and social dimensions and the inappropriateness of the imagination of a "mind" or "psyche" intervening between the two. Resonation is preferred over similar words such as interaction because it is relatively free of connotations and meanings in sociology and psychophysiology. Gibson (1966) uses resonation to refer to the relations between perceptual systems and the environment, which is entirely compatible with our use of the term. Interaction already has a number of special uses and refers to particular perspectives (such as symbolic interactionism) in sociology, making it less desirable. In addition, resonation refers to a type of relationship that fits our conceptualization of the way biological and social variables reciprocally reinforce one another and thereby, in some cases, amplify each other.

This perspective is formulated in an effort to break away from arbitrary physical, psychological, and social distinctions, especially in stress research, in which efforts to apply the concept of stress to these three categories as though they existed somewhat independently may have some heuristic value but tend to distract us from the proper appreciation of the wholeness of man. It is also an effort to provide a way of looking at many of the ongoing processes involved at the same time and charting changes and interrelations between these processes that can be used in explanations and predictions.

The *cause-and-effect-approach* provides too-limited a view and tends to distort simultaneous relationships in an effort to locate the sequential chain. The time may have arrived when simple cause-and-effect thinking is no longer appropriate for the biological (S. Wolf, 1963) or social sciences (Buckley, 1968). Payne (1967) complains that there are so many multiple causes and causes of causes that one has difficulty logically answering the question, "What is a cause?" He suggests a new look at causation in disease in which

> by examining social factors, especially changing factors, quantifying them as best we can, and relating them to the accompanying changes, both favorable and unfavorable, in human well-being, we may be able to classify the latter in terms of the social factors which brought them about, rather than in terms of a so-called specific agent, infectious or other wise (Payne, 1967).

Caffrey (1967, p. 134) concluded that coronary heart disease results from the interaction of many factors operating over a long period of time and can hardly be envisioned as the result of a single cause. He thinks the omission of any of the involved factors may lead to "serious interpretative errors." Suchman described a model that reflects similar concerns.

> According to this model, social factors are analyzed as only one part of a complex causal nexus in which no single factor is a necessary and sufficient explanation of the occurrence of the disease. The acceptance of an open-system, naturalistic, multicausal model of illness and health as opposed to the closed-system, mechanistic, single-cause model of traditional medical and public

health research is of basic importance to social epidemiological research (1963).

Zetterberg (1965, p. 72) suggests the term interdependent relations to apply to those variable relations in which a small increment in one leads to a small increment in the other and vice versa. He believes that this type of relation is of special importance in sociology. However, this view is still not entirely satisfactory. In our resonation model, a change in a variable is accompanied by changes in many variables interrelated with it. These produce changes in other variables, some of which may, in turn, be influencing the original, all occurring in relatively short periods of time. The model is one of continuous variation, reaction, and response with no discernable beginning or end. Some of the variables persist, some appear periodically, others are transient. "Cause and effect" become analytical distinctions for those wishing to study in isolation some pair or small number of variables.

The researcher using the resonation model is interested in patterns of clustering variables that have some degree of continuity. He is concerned with how these pattern configurations fluctuate in relation to one another and how permanent changes proceed. Such knowledge permits a considerable amount of prediction on the basis of observed changes in a few central variables.

We have adopted the resonation model as a guiding orientation, and our concepts are framed as labels for configurations of dynamic, interdependent variables. Our concepts seek to call attention to configurations —singly and in constellations—relative degrees of dependency between variables, and relative ranges and limits of variability. In our biosocial resonation model we see physiological and social variables in resonation, suggesting constant interaction between them. We believe that no social variable can vary without an accompanying variation in human physiology, individual or collective.

Biosocial Resonation and Disease

BIOSOCIAL RESONATION AS A POSSIBLE BASIS FOR A NOSOLOGY OF DISEASE

It seems to us that the adoption of the biosocial-resonation perspective must in time require a recasting of our disease nosology. Our existing disease-classification schemes can themselves be classified in terms of whether they focus on the causes of disease or the states (effects) that constitute disease. Pinel in eighteenth-century France developed a nosology based on biological processes and systems involved in disease instead of just the symptomology, as then prevailed (Mackler and Bernstein, 1966; Rosen, 1946). With the discovery of germs we have added classification of diseases according to their causes, especially from microorganisms. As the scope of disease research has enlarged to include epidemiological components, the causes have been further elaborated in terms of vectors, such as water versus insect-borne diseases (S. Graham, 1970 b). Disease classification according to the systems involved (effect) and agents of disease (causes) continues in use, and we suspect that an informal, practical classification according to symptoms, especially when the manifestations are ambiguous, is still in use as well.

The suggestions for improving our disease nosologies still tend to focus on either causes or effects, rather than offering a fresh fundamental perspective. In the area of causes, for example, S. Graham (1970 b) suggests that in addition to existing categories we could classify disease according to the social situations in which they have been found epidemiologically to occur. These classifications include diseases more likely to be encountered by the poor or those in situations involving "familial instability," with each social category relating to many diseases. Cassel (1964) contends that we should abandon the anatomical and state-of-the-person classifications because they call attention to the condition of the physical or "mental" system and away from the reasons for that state. He prefers a new nosology based on etiology that would facilitate research on disease causation. Many diseases now classified according to various states would be designated differently if they were based on etiology. For example, he claims that the social properties of the schizophrenic have more in common with suicides and tuberculosis patients than with manic-depressives. The former three might be classified etiologically together.

One possible reason an etiological classification has not emerged is the difference in focus required in determining what causes a particular disease episode and what must be done to cure it. The physician, oriented toward cure, naturally is more concerned with nosologies that will assist him. He does not always need to know the specific cause to treat a problem satisfactorily, and how a particular malady was contracted is of less concern than what must be done to correct it. There are suggestions for perspectives on disease focusing on various states of the person or effects. The most frequently encountered example defines disease in terms of adaptation and homeostasis maintenance. Disease is seen as the over-straining of adaptive capacities, inappropriate adaptive responses, or both (see discussion in Cassel, 1967; Marks, 1967). Von Bertalanffy says (1968, p. 18), in the typical homeostatic-adaptive approach, "Disease is the life process regulating toward normalcy after disturbance, owing to the equifinality of biological systems and with the assistance of the physician." This makes disease a natural process for the maintenance of homeostasis (note also Selye's [1956 a] conceptualization of his general adaptation syndrome along similar lines).

Sociologists often view disease as a social definition. What is labeled as disease depends on a peoples' common experiences and their notions of what is normal. A people may consider many of their endemic physical malfunctions normal. Here, disease cannot be seen as a label for such malfunctioning, but as a form of deviance from a norm (see, for example, Parsons, 1958; Mechanic, 1968). Blackman and Goldstein (1968) have made a novel suggestion concerning mental health as a property of a community rather than just the individual. Health would apply to a particular state of several individuals together. Each of these suggestions, along with the existing nosologies, limits the scientist's perspective to the particular sets of causes or states with which the nosology deals, distracting attention from other relevant elements (Engel, 1962).

Disease definitions based on a biosocial resonation model would label particular configurations of resonating physical, social, and, eventually, environmental variables. There would no longer be physical and mental illnesses, but one classification of resonating configurations embracing physical and social-psychological processes and states in their social and environmental contexts. It would focus on neither causes nor effects but embrace both in a resonating pattern. The criteria used to decide whether a configuration is health or disease would be based in part on arbitrary decisions from social norms and in part on the nature and range of configurations observed in research. Such definitions must, however, wait until research has uncovered the nature of these biosocial resonating patterns. We cannot present a biosocial resonation disease nosology this early in the development of our theory, but we can in this book begin to move in that direction.

A more pressing need now is to develop a conceptual framework for categorizing relations between perceptions of the situation, physiological responses, and disease manifestations within a social context. For the time being it is necessary to use the disease definitions currently utilized in medical sciences. Suchman's (1963, pp. 53–54) suggestion seems appropriate for our work at this stage. He believes that sociology and medical science could be fruitfully wed by coupling social science definitions and measurements of etiological factors with medical science identifications and diagnoses of the disease state. We focus primarily on developing conceptual tools for identifying the situations most likely to evoke physiological and behavioral responses detrimental to the actor's health, limiting ourselves to physical illness and avoiding discussion of mental illness. Hinkle (1961, p. 292) sees this as a fruitful approach: "It is in helping us make rapid, working estimates of the 'probable meaning of the situation to the individual' that the social scientist can most aid the physician." Hinkle finds the techniques of psychiatry and psychoanalysis too cumbersome and time consuming to be of great value to the physician, and he warns against over emphasizing individual uniqueness.

Although no one has done what we have in mind, there have been similar efforts. Freidman and Rosenman (see Freidman and Rosenman, 1959; Rosenman et al., 1966) grouped people into categories according to the general configuration of their response to a variety of stimuli, such as tape recordings interrupted by irritating and irrelevant comments. Those people at the extremes of tension and agitated behavior were grouped as types *A* and *B* (the former high, the latter low). Subsequently type *A*'s were followed over time, and evidence relating this general response pattern to coronary heart disease was collected. The type *A* overt behavior pattern was found to be more effective than socioeconomic status, exercise, smoking habits, serum lipid values, blood coagulation parameters, and blood pressure in predicting those who would suffer coronary heart disease (Rosenman et. al., 1966).

GENERAL SUSCEPTIBILITY AS THE INITIAL RESEARCH
PERSPECTIVE ON DISEASE IN BIOSOCIAL RESONATION

The exact relations of social behavior and disease in biosocial resonation must emerge from research. But how do we begin to do research on such a broad conceptualization? It seems the sensible thing to do to start with an existing research frame of reference that is reasonably compatible with the new concept and does not distort it. The general susceptibility orientation seems adequate for our purposes. It gets us into the right places looking at the right things.

General susceptibility as an orientation has grown from dissatisfaction with specificity models (Thurlow, 1967). The specificity notion is usually associated with psychosomatic models. It seems to have originated with the assumption that since particular germs cause particular disease, then certain psychological states, attitudes, or experiences may also produce certain physical diseases. Stimulus specificity (Lazarus, 1966; see also Kaplan and Kaplan, 1967) has been suggested as a label for this idea. However, as psychosomatic and psychobiological research progressed, it became increasingly apparent that one could not satisfactorily predict syndromes or their occurrence on the basis of the psychological stimuli. A new perspective known as individual-response specificity (Lazarus, 1966; Kaplan and Kaplan, 1967) emerged in an effort to explain why the same psychological events and stimuli could produce different syndromes in different people. It suggested that the nature of the stimuli was not crucial, but the characteristics of the individual were, such as his past experiences, physiological peculiarities, and the meaning of events for him. These determined the nature and occurrence of physical syndromes. Thus one could predict syndromes only if one knew what a particular person's specific responses were for particular situations. However, additional problems remained that social studies might illuminate, such as why the same people responded differently to the same stimuli at different times and the influence of social processes on the occurrence and virulence of the stimuli. There is a contrasting perspective, sometimes called nonspecific (Kaplan and Kaplan, 1967), that suggests there are only a few physiological responses, such as sympathetic arousal or parasympathetic activation, which are produced in varying degrees of intensity and in various configurations for all psychological events and stimuli. Any resulting physical syndromes have little relation to the stimuli because many stimuli can produce the same syndromes. Thus a large number of stimuli and subjective interpretations can produce only a few physiological changes and influence much the same syndromes.

General susceptibility is a rather broad, loosely conceptualized (Thurlow, 1967) perspective on how to study disease in social contexts, and it is not limited to stress or psychosomatic relations as are the specificity and nonspecificity models. When this is applied to stress or psychosomatic relations it is similar to the nonspecificity approach. It suggests that susceptibility to a wide variety of illnesses is modified according to the meaning of the situation to the individual. Proponents of this perspective believe that the proper research approach is to look at disease as a whole rather than specific diseases and to examine those general risk factors common to all or many diseases. They warn us that we cannot be sure we have found specific causes for a disease until we examine other illnesses and make sure that what we have discovered is not a general risk factor.

This approach is not intended to replace more specifically oriented models or research entirely but rather to fill a large gap, thereby contributing to a more realistic picture of the disease process. So much of disease research begins with a particular illness and proceeds to search for the causes among the properties of those who have the disease compared with those who do not. The social-epidemiological researcher looks at people with a certain disease. Through location of social groups having higher incidence he gradually pins down some of the specific causes of the disease by noting the peculiarities of these groups. Percival Pott's discovery of soot as the cause of chimney sweeps' scrotal cancer is a classic example.

But if we are to correctly understand the specific causes we must first isolate those factors that are not specific for any disease but influence susceptibility to an array of illnesses. What remains, then, may be considered specific causes. Syme (1967) points out that many supposedly specific factors thought to be involved with particular diseases are in fact related to increased death rates for diseases in general. Cigarette smoking is associated with an excess of deaths from coronary heart disease, cerebrovascular disease, general arteriosclerosis, hypertensive disease, other circulatory diseases, and to a lesser degree with rheumatic heart disease, and also with cirrhosis of the liver, peptic ulcers, accidents, and murders. How can this be considered the specific cause of any particular disease? Married people, compared with those who are single or divorced, have lower age-adjusted death rates for coronary disease, cardiovascular disease, lung cancer, cancer of all sites, peptic ulcers, cerebrovascular disease, accidents, murder, cirrhosis of the liver, tuberculosis, appendicitis, hernia, nephritis, and others. Syme has found evidence that death rates from all causes may vary between groups. In one study he found Seventh-Day Adventists as a group had lower age specific death rates from all causes than the population in general living in the same area (Syme, 1970). This work suggests the possible importance of social properties of groups in disease susceptibility. As he says, "The study of disease in society may require a broader view of social and cultural forces which go beyond the sick person" (Syme, 1967, p. 178). Syme (1967; 1970) advocates the general susceptibility perspective and argues that the time has come for research to focus on disease in general instead of specific diseases as dependent variables.

Thurlow (1967) recently reviewed general susceptibility in illness, calling attention to Hinkle's work. Hinkle found that a quarter of the people he studied had over half of the illness episodes and accounted for two-thirds of the disability days. Another quarter had fewer than 10 percent of the illnesses. These illnesses sometimes occurred in clusters over a lifetime. In one study of 600 people, four-fifths of the people showed clusters of illness at some time in their life (Hinkle, 1961). What was most interesting about Hinkle's findings was the quantity and types of illnesses these various groups with high and low illness exhibited. The healthy and unhealthy differed only in the quantity and not the nature of illnesses. During clustering there were no special diseases occurring (Hinkle, 1961). Similarly, in a study of women Hinkle (summarized by Thurlow, 1967) found that those who had more episodes of illness also had a greater variety of illness, rather than many episodes of the same illness and had illnesses involving many organ systems. Other studies by Hinkle seem to have verified these general relations (Thurlow, 1967). If Hinkle's findings are verified, they have profound implications for our current approaches to the study and treatment of disease. Many of our current medical practices might turn out to be relatively uneconomical treatment of symptoms of individuals. Control and correction of the general suscepti-bility factors could reduce disease levels of all types for large numbers of people.

There have been some criticisms of Hinkle's methodology. Hinkle has worked primarily in industrial plants and corporations, judging illness episodes in terms of visits to the infirmary or absenteeism from work. The major criticism comes from Mechanic and Newton (1965) who point out that varying tendencies of workers to adopt the sick role have consid-erable influence on visits to medical facilities. Such visits, then, may not reflect the distribution of actual illnesses among the subjects. Thurlow admits that sick-role–seeking behavior may contaminate studies of minor illnesses in which medical facility visits are the main measure of illness, but he contends that sick-role behavior is not an issue in cases of serious illnesses in which there is little doubt of physical pathology. Thurlow says that Hinkle has found his findings hold for major as well as minor illnesses. Another dimension of the sick-role–seeking behavior could be suggested. If one assumes that physical and psychological prob-lems are not related—the separation of mind and body again—then ill-nesses and sick-role–seeking behavior are independent and should be measured separately. However, if one accepts the biosocial resonation ap-proach, then both illness and sick-role–seeking behavior may be the result of the same conditions and influence each other.

The general susceptibility orientation still leaves us with many unan-swered questions as to how susceptibility is changed by social-psychologi-cal experiences. The research on emotions offers some important answers.

Emotions in Biosocial Resonation

If we are to understand the links between social behavior and disease we must understand the relations between subjective social-psychological ex-periences and physiological responses. Much of the hard research in this area has been carried out by students of emotion. Even if one concedes that emotions or feelings are all part of the body's functioning and have nothing to do with spirits or minds manipulating or finding expression through the body, there are still unanswered questions; the most impor-tant is the relationship between emotions, perception, and physiological responses. Are emotions the intervening link between perception and physiological responses? Are emotions and physiological responses sepa-rate responses to perception? Or are emotions simply the perception of physiological responses? Is the concept of emotions even really necessary for our purposes? The historical debate over these issues provides some valuable insights into these questions.

HISTORICAL DEVELOPMENT OF THEORIES ON THE PHYSIOLOGY OF EMOTION

Until the nineteenth century most of the medical world believed emotions circulated in the vascular system (Pribram, 1967). With William James, serious experimental study began (Bindra, 1970). The *James-Lange theory,* which has been and is still one of the most influential theories of emotion, proposed that bodily changes follow the perception of an exciting situation. The visceral and somatic changes are, in turn, perceived, and these perceptions of physical changes as they occur are emotional feeling. Emotions were seen as the result and not the cause of visceral and somatic responses. This equating of bodily changes and feelings of emotion led researchers to expect that different emotions could be explained by locating different visceral and somatic changes, with each emotion having a distinct configuration of physical change. However, psychophysiological research does not support this idea of unique visceral and somatic configurations for each emotion (Pribam, 1967; Gellhorn and Loofbourrow, 1963; Schachter, 1964).

The *Cannon-Bard theory* grew in part from Cannon's criticisms of James' theory. Cannon's work showed only two broad visceral patterns of response, the sympathetic and the parasympathetic dimensions of the autonomic response. He argued that visceral reactions were too diffuse to provide the distinctive physiological patterns of emotion apparently required by James' theory (Bindra, 1970). Cannon felt that emotions were determined in the thalamus (a brain structure, see H. Gray, 1959, p. 874) when the thalamus was released from cerebral cortical inhibition. Unless this release occurred, the thalamus relayed to the cortex only simple impulses. However, when released from cortical inhibition it added to perception the peculiar qualities that distinguish various emotions (Gellhorn and Loofbourrow, 1963). Consequently, visceral and somatic emotional responses were seen as the result of emotional thalamic processes rather than as being the cause of emotional feeling, as in the James-Lange theory (Gellhorn and Loofbourrow, 1963; Bindra, 1970). Modern lesion work has indicated that emotional behavior could be produced by other parts of the brain besides the thalamus and that the idea of emotions as the result of the release of the thalamus from inhibition is questionable. The hypothalamus subsequently has emerged as more central to emotion than the thalamus (Gellhorn and Loofbourrow, 1963; Pribram, 1967).

The *Papez-MacLean theory* of emotions, proposed by Papez and elaborated by MacLean, was based on electrical brain stimulation studies. A portion of the cerebral cortex called the limbic system was conceived as a "visceral brain" in which experience is interpreted in terms of feelings rather than "intellectualized" symbols. Other portions of the brain, such as the hypothalamus, were accepted as important, but the limbic system was seen as the cap of the hierarchy of control over visceral and autonomic functions. Again, electrode and lesion studies indicate that emotional behavior can be elicited through other parts of the brain, and indeed lesions in the limbic area in man leads to loss of specific memories or their deficiency, although emotional changes are difficult to ascertain (Pribram, 1967; Gellhorn and Loofbourrow, 1963).

Arousal and Activation Approaches. Much of the current work on the physiology of emotions is loosely conceptualized and is oriented toward measuring correlations between various neurological and physiological conditions, such as correlating the amounts of hormones and neural excitation with the amount of subjective emotional arousal or observed emotional behavior (Gellhorn and Loofbourrow, 1963; Lazarus, 1966). Such work is generally concerned with the degree of arousal or activation and can be divided into those studies based on peripheral measurements, such as galvanic skin response, and more direct studies of internal processes, utilizing measures such as hormone levels in the blood (Pribram, 1967). These studies have indicated a number of autonomic and physiological similarities between the processes we call stress, emotion, motivation, and arousal and tend to question such conceptual distinctions as they relate to psychophysiological processes (Pribram, 1967).

Pribram (1967) suggests a unique model of emotion. He suggests that activation is not an increase in neuronal excitation but the sudden materialization of different states of neural organization or disorganization. In sharp contrast to the models discussed previously, Pribram minimizes the contribution of visceral and somatic processes to emotion and emphasizes perceptual processes. He rejects concepts of emotions as particular physiological configurations or resulting from drives. In his model emotions are the experiencing of an appraisal of incongruity between the input and one's memories and expectations or neural programs and plans. He postulates two mechanisms for handling the incongruity through modification and regulation of the input. One mechanism, which he calls preparatory, is selective perception that shuts out information which might produce an incongruity. The other mechanism he calls participation. It involves paying attention to the information input and reorganizing neural representations to mesh with the input. Pribram feels that emotion and its expression should be separated. He feels that the James-

Lange and Cannon-Bard theories confuse the two. For Pribram, emotion does not include visceral physiological response, physical action, or motivation. These are different responses to emotion. His model portrays emotion in terms of reflective aspects of information processing rather than as behavior.

Pribram has been criticized for the overemphasis of novelty and mismatch per se as sources of emotion, for equating orienting and cognitive processes and mismatch with emotion, for separating emotion and motion, and for not adequately accounting for the autonomic system functions in emotions (Melzack, 1967; Flynn, 1967). However, Bovard has mentioned that through electrode stimulation of the human brain mood changes can be obtained without any relation to autonomic changes (Lazarus, 1967, p. 176). Brady (1967) seems to suggest a similar dichotomy in which emotions are activity and feelings are reflective. We are inclined to agree with Pribram that incongruities between the expected and experienced are very central to changes in subjective feelings and appraisals. His preparatory and participation notions offer some insight into the neurological changes accompanying some fundamental approaches to information. However, we agree with his critics that he does not adequately account for the autonomic and other physiological aspects of emotion. Although the role of incongruities in emotion may not yet be clear, the central part that discrepancies between the expected and experienced may play in relations between social behavior, physiological processes, and physical health will emerge as our presentation unfolds.

Of the models of emotion in current use, the one we find most compatible with our perspective is that of Schachter (1962 a, b; 1964; 1967) who successfully combines both the subjective and physiological elements and is widely cited.

Schachter's theory (1964) suggests that William James' theory, properly modified, is still the better perspective. The nature of these modifications are clearly seen in his discussion of Cannon's five-point critique of the James-Lange theory:

> 1. The total separation of the viscera from the central nervous system does not alter emotional behavior.
> 2. The same visceral changes occur in very different emotional states and in nonemotional states.
> 3. The viscera are relatively insensitive structures.
> 4. Visceral changes are too slow to be a source of emotional feeling.
> 5. The artificial induction of visceral changes that are typical of strong emotions does not produce emotions (Schachter, 1964, pp. 138–139).

Schachter feels that his new position answers Cannon's objections and clarifies James' position. In Schachter's model the states of physiological arousal for many emotions are the same, and cognitive elements are crucial to identification of the emotion. In contrast to Pribram, Schachter contends that both physiological arousal and appropriate cognitive elements are necessary for emotions to occur. He offers the following propositions. First, a given state of physiological arousal for which an individual has no immediate explanation is labeled and described by him in terms of the cognitions available, especially in terms of the situation in which he finds himself. The same physiological state might be labeled joy, fury, or any number of emotions. Second, if the person has a completely appropriate explanation for a given state of physiological arousal "no evaluative needs will arise and the individual is unlikely to label his feelings in terms of the alternative cognitions available" (p. 142). Third, "given the same cognitive circumstances, the individual will react emotionally or describe his feelings as emotions only to the extent that he experiences a state of physiological arousal" (p. 142). In a situation in which there is no physiological arousal because of surgery, trauma, or the use of drugs, but which formerly had been emotion-inducing, a feeling of "as if" or "cold emotion" is experienced. One goes through the behavioral motions for that emotion which one has learned is appropriate in the situation, but one "feels" nothing. Schachter claims that the emphasis on emotion as visceral activity in interaction with cognitive or situational factors is clearly modified Jamesian.

Schachter thinks that Cannon's critique of James was the most lucid and influential attack on the visceral view of emotion. He reconsiders Cannon's objections mentioned previously in light of his own model. He believes that Cannon's fifth objection, concerning the inability of artificial induction of visceral changes typical of emotion to produce emotion, is exactly what should be expected since the cognitive elements are as essential as the visceral changes. Physiological change alone is not enough to produce them. Cannon's second objection, that the same visceral changes are found in varying emotional and nonemotional states, seems to be essentially correct. The evidence may not be as "damning" as in Cannon's day, but such differences in physiological states as occur between emotions must be very subtle, according to Schachter. Cannon's third criticism, that viscera are relatively insensitive, Schachter considers irrelevant as long as there is some sensation from the viscera. Cannon's first and fourth objections were based largely on lesion studies and make the same point, that there are "conditions in which there are apparently emotions unaccompanied by visceral activity" (Schachter, 1964, p. 163), James' defenders, including Schachter, have answered this criticism by demonstrating that emotional behavior is well learned and persists despite sympathectomy, trauma, or other damage.

Schachter (1964) points out an underlying assumption of his model, that people feel a need or pressure to evaluate ambiguous and novel bodily states, "to decide what is felt . . . how these feelings are to be labeled, and, perhaps to decide whether these feelings are pleasant or unpleasant ones (p. 167)." These evaluations of bodily states and their labeling are dependent on social relations. He cites Becker's *Outsiders,* in which social contact was important in learning to recognize the effects of marijuana in the novice user. He also cites evidence (Schachter, 1964; 1967) that so basic a physiological state as hunger may not be labeled accurately without social interaction to assist the child to discriminate between physiological states such as sympathetic arousal and those which indicate the need for food. A mother who is unable to differentiate between hunger and distress in her child may feed the baby at every sign of distress. Raised by such a mother a person may be unable to discriminate between fear, anger, anxiety, and hunger, and he may become chronically obese.

Schachter warns against assuming a one-to-one relationship between a specific biochemical change or a physiological process and a specific behavior. It seems to be more the rule that various physiological processes may be associated with various behavioral and subjective experiences. He says:

> If we are eventually to make sense of this area, I believe we will be forced to adopt a set of concepts with which most physiologically inclined scientists feel somewhat uncomfortable and ill-at-ease, for they are concepts which are, at present, difficult to physiologize about or to reify. We will be forced to examine a subject's perception of his bodily state and his interpretation of it in terms of his immediate situation and his past experience. We will be forced to deal with concepts about perception, about cognition, about learning, and about the social situation (Schachter, 1967, p. 119).

Although realizing that many of these information-processing activities have physiological correlates, he emphasizes that "we can and must use nonphysiologically anchored concepts if we are to make headway in understanding the relations of complex behavioral patterns to physiological and biochemical processes" (Schachter, 1967, p. 119). Thus, like Cassell, Chauchard, Krech, and others we have mentioned, Schachter is calling for interdisciplinary work and conceptualization to focus on the social-subjective and physiological aspects, despite the large and real difficulties and pitfalls involved.

Stein (1967, p. 154) agrees with Schachter in the importance of terminating the search for the cause of emotions and directing, instead, "our energies toward a complete description of the organism in its environment, and the nature and the process involved in behavior." Pfaffmann summarizes:

Counter to the strategy of the searching for some fixed autonomic-endocrine response that 'is the emotion' or that defines different emotional states, more recent studies show that the subtle interaction between social factors and perceptions of the emotion-producing situation are so much a part of emotion that, in fact, they change the emotion. Such studies reiterate more clearly than ever the theme that explanation of behavior cannot be made by a one-way analysis of physiological mechanisms. The proper study of behavior includes both the study of physiological process and the interactions of physiology with environmental or situational determinants (Glass, 1967, pp. x, xi).

All of this, especially Stein's comment, fit our biosocial resonation concept very well.

Bindra (1970, p. 14) after discussing the current state of evidence and theory in emotion research rejects existing models of emotion and suggests it is time for an approach "which seeks to explain emotional phenomena of all types without reference to 'emotion' as a theoretical concept."

A working assumption, being increasingly accepted by psychologists, is that there exist a few key processes which play a part in all behavioral phenomena. Thus, the processes that produce phenomena described as 'emotional' are considered to be no different from those that produce behavior described as 'motivational' or 'perceptual'.

We might add that they are no different from phenomena labeled stress.

Emotion no longer need be considered the necessary intervening link between social experience and physiological processes. The focus has expanded to the relation between social and environmental situations, subjective interpretations, and physiological processes, setting aside old labels of emotion, stress, and the like to permit exploration of fresh conceptualization. We find Schachter's model acceptable when one feels the need to explain emotions. More interesting is the possibility suggested by Schachter's work, and compatible with the general susceptibility perspective, that there are a few general physiological responses, such as autonomic processes, that accompany a wide variety of subjective interpretations of social and environmental situations.

Summary

In this chapter we have presented a number of issues and historical trends in the conceptualization of the relations between social behavior, physiological processes, and illness. These issues illustrate that despite the ambiguities and discontinuities in the existing picture, there is a convergence in the themes of many theoretical and research areas toward a similar view of the links between social and physiological processes. We have presented a concept that we believe embraces the key properties of these links as far as we now understand them. We have suggested the name "biosocial resonation" for this concept.

Brain and psychophysiological research indicates that there is no dichotomy between the mind and the body and that socialpsychological and physiological processes are simply two aspects of the same thing. Our concept of biosocial resonation emphasizes this dynamic wholeness of physiological and social activities. Our concept calls attention to the relations between the social and physiological and away from concepts that seem no longer useful for this purpose, such as emotion, stress, and motivation, which distract us by calling attention to themselves as intervening variables.

Biosocial resonation also points out the limitations of cause-and-effect notions and replaces them with a focus on a given situation and the relations and configurations of clustering variables at that time. In research, one would focus on a given situation and what is taking place within rather than on particular properties and their modification over time. The research implications, especially for prospective studies in medicine, are discussed in a later chapter. We have suggested a suitable research orientation for beginning biosocial resonation research is that of general susceptibility, as illustrated in Hinkle's work, which suggests that social experiences modify one's susceptibility to illness in general.

We believe that a new, unifying nosology of disease might conceivably be developed some day, based on biosocial resonation in which disease refers to particular configurations of resonating social and physiological variables, eliminating the distinction between physical and mental disease.

Biosocial resonation serves as the basic reference point for the rest of this work and is developed throughout.

CHAPTER II

Evaluation of Stress Models

Stress research has been applied to practically every aspect of human existence from social systems to physiological processes. Some models deal only with one area, such as large organizations, mental health, or physical responses to organic agents, conceptualizing stress in terms of processes and properties peculiar to each of the areas and taking little of the other areas into account. Other models attempt to locate isomorphisms in the areas covered by stress research in a search for some general theory that is correct for all cases of stress. Some have insisted that the term stress applies only to physiological conditions and cannot be applied to social and psychological phenomena (Levine and Scotch, 1970; Mechanic, 1962). It seems fitting that we should look here for some clues to the broad relations between socioenvironmental factors, physiological processes, and health to further develop our concept of biosocial resonation. We have selected here those stress models that have had the greatest influence on our thinking for discussion.

Stress as Physiological Responses to Physical, Chemical, and Organic Agents

HANS SELYE'S MODEL OF STRESS

Although there have been many observations and studies through the centuries that can be categorized under stress, it is Selye's work that is most responsible for crystallizing the concept and ushering it into the scientific vocabulary. His theory and findings still seem to be the most profound and exciting of the theories of stress and must stand as one of the outstanding scientific achievements of our time. It has stimulated an enormous amount of research not only in biology but in the behavioral sciences was well.

Selye is an M.D. and an endocrinologist, and his work is best understood from this perspective. His work on the adrenal glands and their relation with the pituitary and other organs and physiological processes is alone a major contribution. Because his model comes to grips most effectively with the physiological and health aspects of adrenal functioning and because the adrenals are central to our own model, it is worthwhile to discuss Selye in some detail.

We will use as our sources several works that came out in 1956, a year when the concept seemed finally to distill down to its essential elements (Selye, 1956 a, b, c, d). Although there have been advancements in endocrinology since then, the essential framework has not changed, and many of the relations have been clarified and supported rather than refuted. *The Stress of Life* was the major work to appear in 1956 and has become a classic, still widely read.

Selye defines stress as "the state manifested by a specific syndrome which consists of all the nonspecifically induced changes within a biologic system" (Selye, 1956 a, p. 54; see also b, p. 26; and c). This emphasizes that stress is a state *manifested* by a specific syndrome, not the syndrome itself. Specific and nonspecific are also key phrases. The syndrome is a *specific* configuration of physiological processes and states called the General Adaptation Syndrome (G.A.S.) that occurs in essentially the same general configuration in response to a wide variety of stimuli in practically everyone. This is what is meant by *"nonspecifically* induced changes." The syndrome is elicited by no one or two particular stimuli, but by many.

All agents of disease, whether organic, physical, or chemical, have certain effects on the body by which the physician diagnoses the disease and locates the specific agents. These specific effects are distinctive syndromes or configurations of physiological processes peculiar to the particular agents. All these agents also produce another particular syndrome that is the same no matter which agent is involved. This syndrome has been observed through the years but was largely ignored by physicians in Selye's student days because it gave no useful clues to the nature of the particular disease. This syndrome is the manifestation of stress. Selye has focused on the nature and health consequences of this nonspecifically induced syndrome. In doing so he has not forgotten that there are nearly always specifically induced effects occurring simultaneously with these nonspecifically induced effects, but he chooses not to consider them (1956 a).

The various stimuli or agents that produce the G.A.S. are called stressors and are defined simply as "that which produces stress" (Selye, 1956 a, p. 64). Although we are aware of its occurrence, we cannot really explain what stress is. Selye has referred to it as "essentially the rate of all the wear and tear caused by life" (1956 a, p. viii) and as "the outcome of a struggle for the self-preservation (the homeostasis) of parts within a whole" (1956 a, p. 253; see also 1956 b, p. 37). If there is no resistance or struggle for health there is no disease and presumably no G.A.S., thus, presumably, no stress is occurring (1956 a, p. 11). Although this is of some help, it still leaves us somewhat mystified. Nevertheless, the concept is still very useful.

The G.A.S. is the central element of Selye's stress. He says, "Stress is defined as the state which manifests itself by the G. A. S." (1956 a, p. 47). The G.A.S. was observed in rats that had been subjected to cold or various injections or whose movement had been temporarily restricted by fastening the legs down. These animals were sacrificed and opened. Three visible modifications of the internal organs formed a triad characterizing stress: considerable enlargement of the cortex of the adrenal gland; the atrophy or shrinkage of the thymus, spleen, lymph nodes, and other lymphatic structures including the almost complete disappearance of eosinophil cells (a type of white blood cell, as are lymphocytes); and bleeding ulcers in the lining of the stomach and duodenum (Selye 1956 a, pp. 20–21).

As work progressed, various physiological processes were also observed to characterize the G.A.S. In broad outline (Selye 1956 a, pp. 110–117; Selye 1956 b, pp. 32–37) the G. A. S. revolves around the secreting of adrenocorticotropic hormone (ACTH) by the pituitary. ACTH is carried in the blood stream and stimulates the adrenal cortex, even though the G.A.S. can sometimes occur in part without the adrenal cortex. The adrenal cortex secretes two general groups of hormones (Selye 1956 a, pp. 92-93; White et al., 1959): (1) glucocorticoids—so called because one of their properties is to raise blood sugar levels—include the hormones cortisone and cortisol. These two, especially cortisol, inhibit inflamation and thus are also called anti-inflammatory corticoids by Selye; (2) mineralcorticoids—so called because they increase retention of sodium and chloride in the body and decrease potassium—include the hormones deoxycorticosterone and aldosterone. Selye calls this group pro-inflammatory corticoids because they promote inflammation.

Included in the overall outline of the G.A.S. is the kidney, which is essential to homeostasis maintenance. It regulates the chemical composition and water content of the blood and tissues by eliminating various substances. The kidney can be damaged and blood pressure raised by large amounts of corticoids. The pro-inflammatory corticoids are capable of producing kidney disease and changing artery walls producing arteriosclerosis. The thyroid gland is often affected by stress to stimulate intensely metabolism in the tissues. The liver is a source of sugars, and it regulates sugar, proteins, and other tissue foods. It can check excesses of corticoid hormones, but the feedback mechanisms that normally control the levels of corticoids in the blood stream seem to be bypassed in stress, permitting higher levels of concentration in the blood (Selye, 1956 a, p. 199). The white blood cells, which regulate "serologic immune reactions and allergic hypersensitivity responses to foreign substances" (Selye, 1956 a, p. 112) are reduced or influenced in their functions. An increase in the level of adrenalin occurs mainly from the adrenal medulla but also from certain nerve endings. All of these are interrelated with the adrenal cortical and pituitary secretions.

Inflammation plays an important role in Selye's model. One of the most important functions of the cortical hormones relates to inflammation. "Inflammation has been defined as 'a local reaction to injury' " and is characterized by the familiar components of swelling, reddening, heat, and pain (Selye, 1956 a, p. 99). It can be caused by a wide variety of agents from microorganisms, dust, x-rays, insect bites, and plant pollens, to an excess of waste products in muscles being exerted. Muscle soreness following such exertion is the result of inflammation of the muscles. Whereas all these varying agents can produce inflammation in virtually every part of the body, the cellular changes are always essentially the same (1956 a, pp. 100, 120).

> The reddening and heat are due to a dilation of the blood vessels in the inflamed area. The swelling is caused, partly, by the leakage of fluids and cells from the dilated blood vessels into the surrounding solid tissues, and, partly, by an intense proliferation of the fibrous connective tissue, whose cells rapidly multiply in response to irritation. The pain is due to an irritation of the sensory nerve-endings which are caught in and invaded by this inflammatory process (Selye, 1956 a, p. 101).

This inflammation tends to wall in the attacking agent and prevent it from spreading to other parts of the body. It permits the destruction of invading organisms by the antibodies, white blood cells, enzymes, and other defenses of the body and prevents food sources from reaching the invaders. This local inflammation response is apparently the main element in Selye's Local Adaptation Syndrome (L.A.S.). The attacking agent or stressor produces the L.A.S. and in some unknown way helps trigger the G.A.S. The G.A.S. reacts in turn on the L.A.S., especially in influencing the course of the inflammation through the adrenal cortical hormones.

Inflammation is strongly influenced by the two above-mentioned groups of adrenal cortical hormones (pro- and anti-inflammatory). The adaptive reaction to a stressor requires a balanced or selective application of these two groups to promote inflammation when it would be beneficial. Inflammation is appropriate when only one or a few areas are attacked and the potential damage done by the inflammation is less than that of an attacker allowed to spread unchecked. It should be remembered that inflammation itself damages the body, independent of the damage done by the attacking agent. It involves the destruction of cells in the immediate area and may leave scar tissue. Inflammation is inappropriate if the attacker is capable of doing less damage than the inflammation would do, for example, hay fever reactions to innocuous pollen; or if the attack is so massive that the level of inflammation required to contain it would cause very serious damage to the body and would deplete the body's energy resources, diverting the limited energy from essential survival processes (see Selye, 1956 a, chapters 12 and 13).

The G.A.S. over time passes through three phases: alarm, resistance, and exhaustion. This sequence reflects the body's adaptation to the stressor. Selye says that "an essential feature of adaptation is the delimitation of stress to the smallest area capable of meeting the requirements of a situation" (1956 a, p. 120). Stress is more than a response; it is a process that maximizes the body's ability to resist the stressor by enhancing the functioning of the organ system best able to handle it. The alarm response involves large territories of the body with no specific organ system coping with the stressor. Adrenal cortical secretions rise sharply during this phase. During the resistance phase, the adrenal cortical secretions drop somewhat below normal, and adaptation is obtained as a result of the "optimum development of the most appropriate specific channel of defense" (Selye 1956 a, p. 121). This "channel of defense" may be an organ system or physiological process. Thus in the resistance phase only a limited number of organ systems and bodily processes, the ones best suited to handle the problem at hand, are involved, in contrast with the more general processes of the alarm phase. Although resistance to the particular stressor being handled is high during this phase, resistance to disease in general may fall somewhat below normal. The exhaustion phase occurs when the particular organ system handling the stressor is exhausted and breaks down. Here again adrenal cortical secretion rises, and there is a shift away from the specific organ system that has been carrying the burden to the nonspecific bodily response similar to the alarm phase.

This process does not always lead to pathology, nor should stress be equated with damage. Selye sees it as the body's way of shifting work from one organ system to another to prevent overexertion. In the exhaustion phase of one organ system, a new system is selected or developed to handle the burden. This process goes on until the stressor is controlled or the body is no longer able to make adaptations. There are two broad types of adaptation the body can make. One is developmental or homotrophic adaptation, which is the enlargement and multiplication of preexisting cell elements without qualitative change, such as muscle enlargement during continued heavy work. The other is redevelopment or heterotrophic adaptation in which "a tissue, organized for one type of action, is forced to readjust itself completely to an entirely different kind of activity" (Selye, 1956 a, p. 228). For example, in inflammation bacteria or the debris of dying cells in contact with a muscle cell causes the cell first to lose its acquired characteristics, become "de-differentiated," and then transform into a cell for engulfing (phagocytosis) and destroying the materials. Stress is very powerful in promoting de-differentiation and rejuvenation of cells. The many reports, especially historical, in which various sources of stress have benefited the patient, such as fever, blood letting, chemical and electrical shocks, and bewitchment, may be the result of this process of getting the body "out of a rut," so to speak, and shifting the work to different organ systems and developing fresh cells to handle the problem (Selye, 1956 a).

The adaptation process as it occurs or if it is not successful or breaks down may contribute to the occurrence of many diseases. These are loosely called diseases of adaptation, but there is no disease that is solely caused by adaptation (Selye, 1956 a). The diseases of adaptation are just ordinary diseases to which the G.A.S. or the failure of adaptation contribute. They are not peculiar or unique illnesses occurring only as a result of stress.

Among the diseases of adaptation Selye discusses are high blood pressure, kidney diseases, cardiovascular diseases, eclampsia (convulsions in pregnant women), rheumatic and rheumatoid arthritis, skin and eye inflammatory diseases, infections, allergic and hypersensitivity diseases, nervous and mental diseases, sexual derangements, digestive diseases, metabolic diseases, cancer, and diseases of resistance in general. The influence of the G.A.S. on these diseases is seen as the result of adrenal and pituitary hormones and especially of the inflammation processes (Selye, 1956, pp. 120–121). In a great many infectious diseases, we are constantly in contact with the microorganism involved, but they do us no damage unless our resistance is lowered. The hormones of the pituitary and adrenals help to maintain this resistance, but under stress these defenses are disrupted, and the microbe may gain entry. Tuberculosis bacilli are quite common and may be present in the lungs encapsulated by the fibrous barricades of inflammation. When stress occurs, the blood level of the anti-inflammatory hormones of the adrenal cortex rises, which removes the barricades, prevents inflammation from blocking the entry of additional bacilli, and permits the infection to spread. Thus encounters with various microbes during stress periods are more dangerous because inflammation is less able to do its protective work (Selye, 1956 a, pp. 166–168). "Addison's disease is due to a destruction of the adrenals, and one of its most outstanding consequences is an almost total breakdown of resistance" (Selye, 1956 a, p. 188). This breakdown includes hypersensitivity to infection, intoxication, exposure to cold, nervous tension, or fatigue, all of which can put the person in a state of shock unless adrenal cortical hormones are administered.

The increase of cortisol levels during stress episodes may inhibit growth. Cortisol selectively injected can even retard the growth of one area such as a paw or an ear of a rat. The increased levels of adrenal cortical hormones may also influence mental activity. It can produce a sort of mild drunkenness and may even produce anesthesia if high enough. Cortisol and cortisone (anti-inflammatory hormones) may produce an extraordinary sense of well-being and excitement, but with insomnia, and may improve skill performance to a point (Selye, 1956 a). On the other hand, the pro-inflammatory hormone deoxycorticosterone can in certain conditions produce brain lesions similar to those often found in old people and can produce temporary paralysis.

Throughout his work Selye calls attention to the importance of the larger context of conditioning influences within which stress occurs, such as inherited properties, and diet. He emphasizes that the interrelationship between germs, other conditions, and our bodily reactions, all are causes of disease, not just the germ.

In addition to his model of stress discussed above, Selye also suggests a unifying theory of biology and psychology that is worth mentioning here because it is in the same vein as our biosocial resonation model. This theory is based on the notion of "reactons," which are the smallest unit of living organisms that can react selectively to stimuli. Reactons may be processes or substances, but they are definitely smaller than cells and are not necessarily anatomic structures. Selye conceives of this theory as a *gestalt* of biological and psychological dimensions:

One may therefore conceive of physiologic, biologic, or psychologic events as occurring, not through the mere summation of distinct elements, but through the functioning of the *Gestalt* (shape) as a single unit (Selye, 1956 a, p. 219, emphasis his).

He adds that "the shape of each disease functions as a single unit, although it is made up of innumerable simple reacton-responses (p. 219–220)."

Critique of Selye's Model. There are a number of problems concerning the usefulness of Selye's model to us in linking social behavior to physiological processes and disease. Selye has focused on the influence on the body of various physical, chemical, and biological agents. He has not considered systemically the pathways or links between social and psychological processes and the physiological processes he calls the G.A.S. Also, as he points out, physical, chemical, and biological agents all produce *specific* as well as *nonspecific* responses in the body. However, there is considerable question as to whether there are both specific and nonspecific physiological responses to subjective interpretations of experiences and social encounters. There is no doubt that there is a general nonspecific response, in the sense that many stimuli produce the same response, to social-psychological events. The dimensions of this response revolve around the sympathetic and parasympathetic autonomic responses and the associated hypothalamus-pituitary-adrenal gland axis. (See Gellhorn and Loofbourrow, 1963; Schachter and Singer, 1962; and the discussion in Chapter 4). Thus the first inadequacy of Selye's model for our purposes is that there are no specific physiological responses to social-psychological events comparable to the specific events accompanying the contact with the body of various physical, chemical, or organic agents.

Selye's model refers to only one nonspecific response, which essentially is the same in all cases, the G.A.S. However, there are two separate general configurations of physiological activity in response to social-psychological events, one involving sympathetic arousal and adrenal cortex secretions and the other involving parasympathetic activity.

In addition, in social situations the only things coming into or invading the body, after excluding the physical, chemical, or organic materials encountered as a result, is information through the senses. This information pickup is part of the normal functioning of the sense organs and body. The physical aspects of the information cannot be considered to be physiological stressors unless they are excessive enough to become physical trauma.

Selye's model also deals with the body's direct efforts to handle an attacking agent or stressor through inflammation. It is doubtful that the physiological responses to social-psychological events are significant in handling such events.

Thus Selye's *model* of stress is not applicable directly to our problem. It would require us to make at least four unacceptable assumptions about the relations of physiological responses to subjective interpretation of information and social experience: (1) a clear-cut specific response to the particular social-psychological event, (2) a single, nonspecific response configuration, (3) an invasion or imposition on the body of something materially foreign or incompatible with the body's normal functioning, and (4) the physiological response to social-psychological events as a major or direct effort to handle the situation.

The portion of Selye's work still highly useful to us shows the enormous importance of the pituitary gland and the adrenal cortex and their secretions for health. He has shown how many diseases can be encouraged nonspecifically by high levels of adrenal corticoids. It is reasonably well established (see Chapter 4) that emotional upset and distress are likely to be accompanied by increased levels of these hormones, even though the means by which they are triggered in their secretion involves different pathways initially than in Selye's stress. The role of these hormones in inflammation, as described by Selye, helps explain the accompaniment of emotional upset by greater susceptibility to all kinds of infectious diseases.

Selye's model deals with stress as the body's response to natural substances. Several models deal with stress as the body's response to symbolic experiences, to social and psychological events. One of the most prominent of these latter models is that of Harold G. Wolff (1953).

Stress as Physiological Responses to Social-Psychological Stimuli

HAROLD G. WOLFF'S MODEL OF STRESS

Stewart Wolf and Helen Goodell completed Wolff's revision of *Stress and Disease,* disrupted by Wolff's death in 1962, submitting it under the same title in 1968. Although this revision levels some of the emphases of Wolff's 1953 edition and focuses more on how social and psychological processes can produce physical pathologies, we have chosen to cite primarily the 1953 edition because of the distinctiveness of the arguments Wolff presented there and their widespread currency in stress research. Wolff's findings are drawn primarily from laboratory and clinical observations.

Wolff defines stress as "the internal or resisting force brought into action in part by external forces or loads" (1953, p. v). "*Stress* becomes the *interaction* between external environment and organism, with the past experience of the organism as a major factor" (1953, p. v; emphasis

Wolff's). The capacity of the organism to withstand the strains and loads determines whether homeostasis is reestablished or disruption and death occur. However, man's interactive responses to these external forces are not always appropriate in terms of effectiveness in handling the force or load. As he says, "man, confronted by threats, especially as they involve values and goals, initiates responses inappropriate in kind as well as magnitude" (1953, p. vi). These inappropriate responses are the mobilization of *physiological* defenses, sometimes called protective reaction patterns, normally used against physical, chemical, or organic agents in response to *symbolic* (social and psychological) sources of threat. These physiological defense responses are occasionally symbolic of what the person might like to do about the threat. However, they are of no practical use against social-psychological sources of threat and may do damage to the body, especially if the threat is chronic.

Wolff does not conceptualize affect or emotions and bodily changes as causally related but rather as separate manifestations of responses to stimuli. This conceptualization eliminates the necessity of considering the content of emotion in order to predict the configuration of physiological response. Instead, the nature of the person's attitudes and desires concerning a particular social situation are the crucial determinant of physiological response. Which reaction patterns are associated with which situations depends on the individual's past experiences and current definitions and attitudes toward the situation. Similar definitions and attitudes in different people may be accompanied by similar reaction patterns. For example, desire for aggressive self-expression was associated with hyperfunction of the stomach, with the stomach prepared for eating, which may itself be symbolic of the desired action. A number of gastrointestinal patterns involving ejection, such as diarrhea, vomiting, or ulcerative colitis, were associated with fear, panic, and feelings of being confronted with more than can be managed. Large bowel constipation was associated with feelings of holding back and involved "sadness, dejection or cheerless striving." "It is as though the individual, unable to face and grapple with the threat, were nevertheless firmly 'holding on' or tensely awaiting an attack which is indefinitely delayed" (Wolff, 1953, p. 88).

Wolff emphasizes that all the organ systems can be involved in this type of response to threats. In overall mobilization of protective reactions there is an increased heart rate that remains high and a tightening of the diaphragm that reduces the ability to draw a full breath, both leading to fluctuations in circulation and ventilatory efficiency. Perhaps in time such a reaction may lead to cardiovascular disease. He suggests that severe and prolonged emotional disturbance may be harder on the heart than everyday physical exertion. There are nasal disorders, such as hyperemia and swelling of nasal structures accompanied by hypersecretion and obstruction, and also tears, sneezing, coughing, and spasms of the diaphragm and intercostal muscles (connecting the ribs), all normally used to shut out or wash away noxious natural substances. The mucosa membranes of the body can react in stress and emotional conflicts with engorgement, ischemia, hemorrhage, edema, erosion, modification in secretion, ulceration, altered reaction to chemical agents, modification of cellular components, inflammation, and the lowering of the pain threshold, and all may lead to irreversible tissue damage.

Wolff considers other organ systems and protective reaction patterns, but these serve to illustrate the nature of his approach. His work is generally considered reasonably sound empirically and methodologically and free of esoteric conceptual notions. He has made a valuable contribution in calling our attention to the fact that many organ systems can be directly influenced by social participation to the point that susceptibility to disease is increased and even to the point of producing irreversible damage through hyperactivity or other changes in the body functions.

We find Wolff's emphasis on individual social-psychological properties in determining which situations produce physiological changes acceptable. However, Wolff goes beyond the scope of our perspective. We are interested only in prediction of changes in general susceptibility to disease and not the prediction of organ systems involved or which illness will result for particular people as the result of particular attitudes or desires. The protective reaction pattern framework is a special framework that is too limited to provide the broad scope needed to handle the problem of this work. As Mechanic (1968, p. 316) notes, "Wolff is no doubt correct that physiological adaptive responses can be generalized to symbolic threats, but the true extent of this process and its role in a wide variety of disease states are unknown."

BASOWITZ, PERSKY, KORCHIN AND GRINKER'S MODEL OF STRESS

Basowitz et al. in *Anxiety and Stress* (1955) presented an interdisciplinary study utilizing physiological and psychological measures. They studied Army paratroopers in training. They placed anxiety at the center of their model.

Anxiety is defined as the "conscious and reportable experience of intense dread and foreboding, conceptualized as internally derived and unrelated to external threat" (Basowitz et al., 1955: p. 3). The existance of real danger cannot be distinguished from imagined danger by means of anxiety. Fear is seen as related more to internal psychological problems.

Stress is defined in the following terms:

. . . any stimulus may in principle arouse an anxiety response because of the particular meaning of threat it may have acquired for the particular individual. However, we distinguish a class of stimuli which are *more likely* to produce disturbance in most individuals. The term *stress* has been applied to this class of conditions (Basowitz et al., 1955, p. 7, emphasis theirs).

"Stress is the threat to the fulfillment of basic needs, the maintenance of regulated (homeostatic) functioning, and to growth and development" (Basowitz et al., 1955, pp. 7–8). They conceive of situations on a continua from those that evoke anxiety in everyone (stress) to those that are only meaningful to individuals. They emphasize the importance of considering stress stimuli in terms of the life situation and its subjective meaning. Although they do not think that physiological responses can be predicted on the basis of objective stimuli evaluation, they do believe some prediction could be made concerning anxiety response from the nature of the stimuli if it falls in the stress category (Basowitz et al. 1955, p. 289). Stress comprises stimuli that produce anxiety in most individuals, resulting in a number of physiological, psychological, and behavioral changes, possibly pathological but also possibly leading to higher levels of functioning and new forms of adjustment. Basowitz et al. primarily studied situations that "evoked anxiety and its physiological concomitants" (Basowitz et al. 1955, p. 289).

Urine hippuric acid, plasma amino acid, and blood eosinophil levels were measured in relation to anxiety. Blood eosinophil and plasma amino acid levels dropped, and urine hippuric acid levels increased in those reporting anxiety. Basowitz et al. postulated that hippuric acid (benzoyl glycine) production was mediated through the release of adrenocorticotrophic hormone (ACTH) from the pituitary gland, triggering the release of adrenocortical hormones. These hormones in turn depleted the tissue glutathione resulting in increased hippuric acid levels. The plasma amino acid levels also dropped in response to adrenal cortical hormones, particularly glycine, a precursor of hippuric acid. These findings suggest that anxiety is capable of initiating ACTH release from the pituitary. This work supports Selye's emphasis on the pituitary-adrenal cortex axis being central to stress research and contributes important evidence that subjective states of anxiety are capable of activating the pituitary and adrenal glands as well.

Using the Bender-Gestalt test, which measures the capacity to perceive and properly reproduce simple geometric forms, they also found evidence that anxiety can cause disturbances of perception.

Their concept of anxiety could be called many other things, but their emphasis on the subjective meaning of situations is compatible with our model. From our point of view their most important contribution is the evidence that pituitary and adrenal secretions can be triggered by subjective interpretations of situations. Basowitz et al. (1955) admit that there is little correlation between subjective states of anxiety and the various physiological measures, making anxiety a poor predictor of particular physiological states. However, anxiety might be useful in predicting the direction of physiological changes in general among large populations. The lack of social dimensions and conceptualizations in the study also limits its use for our purposes.

ON PSYCHOSOMATIC-PSYCHOANALYTIC MODELS

A number of psychosomatic models from a psychoanalytic perspective have been suggested for the relations between social-psychological and physiological variables (Scott and Howard, 1970). Among these are Grinker and Spiegel's 1945 study of combat bomber crews and Janis' 1958 study of surgical patients.

A prominent example is that of Franz Alexander (1950), which emphasizes the centrality of emotional factors (Mechanic, 1962; Weiss and English, 1957). Illness may occur when there are preexisting physical vulnerabilities and certain emotions in relation with particular psychodynamic configurations (elements of what used to be called the personality). Certain symptoms appear as relief from emotional tension when no adequate symbolic expression can be found. This may produce organ neurosis, and, perhaps, permanent damage (Alexander, 1950; Mechanic, 1962; Kaplan and Kaplan, 1967). Stress can manifest itself through various linked open systems, and tensions not handled on one level may find expression in another (Mechanic, 1962; Scott and Howard, 1970). Weiss and English (1957) suggested the notion of "organ language" in which the tensions and anxieties not finding symbolic expression may be expressed through the organs.

Among the shortcomings of these and other psychoanalytic models is their emphasis on early childhood experiences as an explanation of later psychosomatic disorders, such as explaining specific organs involved in terms of stresses experienced during childhood (see, for example, Weiss and English, 1957). Although in some cases this may be so, without an autopsy it is difficult to know which organs have been damaged by past stressful experiences creating preexisting physical vulnerabilities, thus limiting predictive capacities of such models. It is "impossible to demonstrate empirically that an individual's early life experiences are in fact responsible for the physiological changes that occur in later life" (Mechanic, 1962, p. 197). In addition to the emphasis on childhood and adolescent periods, psychoanalysis' major efforts have been in the dynamics of unconscious processes such as motives, defenses, and conflicts (Janis, 1958). Such an emphasis tends to distract us from social to intrapsychic processes.

Alexander has been criticized for starting out with his psychosomatic work to bring mind and body together but ending up by eliminating physiological measures and limiting research to psychological measures instead of developing a true conceptual and research union of both. Psychoanalysts rarely utilize physiological measures in conjunction with their concepts (Corson, 1967). The notion of organ language has been criticized as a simplistic interpretation of mind-organ interaction (Corson, 1967; Wittkower and Solyom, 1967).

These limitations, along with the lack of efforts to specify psychoanalytic concepts so they can be submitted to empirical tests and possible disconfirmation (Engel, 1962; Corson, 1967; Mechanic, 1968) and the difficulties of relating psychoanalytic theories to other theories without distortion, make this perspective inadequate for our problem.

CAUDILL'S SUGGESTION

Caudill (1958) was one of the first to suggest that social and cultural considerations should be part of a stress model. Like Wolff, he defined stress as the interplay between stimuli and the defenses of the person (or system) erected against it. However, he called attention especially to the need to understand the organization of the social sources of stress, defenses against it, and adaptation to it. As a general orientation he suggested physiology, personality, relatively meaningful small groups, and other social structures be considered as linked-open systems, each attempting to maintain equilibrium or steady states in the face of impinging conditions. The strain on one system could be transmitted to others so that several of the linked-open systems could become involved in stress and the defense against or adaptation to it. He recognized societies' capacity for self-change, giving the linked-open systems considerable flexibility in adaptation.

Caudill's article (1958) is more of a suggestion than a presentation of a model of stress. It points out the need for broader scope and more effective conceptualization of social and cultural aspects of stress. However, his conceptualizations are too general for translation into research projects. There is considerable doubt as to what concretely to call stress in the various portions of the linked-open system, for example. However, as Caudill suggests, we must take the whole man and his biological, psychological, and sociological dimensions into account if we are to properly understand both the sources and effects of stress.

Thus far we have considered models in which physiological processes are influenced by natural agents and models in which physiological processes are influenced by social-psychological situations. Now we will see if we might learn something from some models of social-psychological situations influencing psychological processes.

Stress as Behavioral Responses to Social-Psychological Stimuli

DOHRENWEND'S MODEL OF PSYCHOLOGICAL STRESS

Dohrenwend (1961; Dohrenwend and Dohrenwend, 1970) has attempted to take Selye's model for physiological stress and apply it to psychological stress. He sees Selye's stress as "a state of the organism that underlies both its adaptive and maladaptive reactions" (1970, p. 114). Dohrenwend's paradigm of Selye's model contains four elements: (1) an antecedent *stressor,* which is an agent that produces stress; (2) antecedent mediating factors, which increase or decrease the effect of the stressor, such as climate or diet; (3) the *adaptation syndrome* "indicating an intervening state of stress in the organism," such as nonspecific chemical changes; and (4) consequent *adaptive,* "or, when there has been 'derailment' of the mechanisms underlying the adaptive syndrome, *maladaptive* responses," such as high blood pressure and heart or kidney disease (1961; 1970, p. 114). In translating these elements into a social-psychological model he conceives of stress as the response to internal or external processes reaching some threshold level beyond which psychological and physiological integrative capacities break down (1961).

Dohrenwend's concept of stressor is based on Koos' formulation of trouble (*Families In Trouble,* 1946, p. 9). Troubles are "situations outside the normal pattern of life . . . situations which block the usual patterns of activity and call for new ones" (1970, p. 115). Dohrenwend's stressors are primarily social in nature, such as economic disasters or broken homes, and "major social stressors" are "objective events that disrupt or threaten to disrupt the individual's usual activities" (1970, p. 115). These stressors are not necessarily negative, nor do they necessarily involve a subjective crisis. Whether a stressor induces crisis depends on the individual's characteristics. However, in a manner similar to Basowitz et al. (1955), upon whom he draws heavily, he limits the term stressor to objective events that are likely to disrupt the customary activities of all or most normal people experiencing them (1970, p. 115).

The second element of the paradigm, mediating factors, is a very important one in Dohrenwend's model. These factors help determine whether stressors will produce maladaptive behavior. They are conditions generally beyond the person's control, such as social status, business cycles, and internalized norms. The product of stressors and mediating factors are internal and external constraints. Internal constraints are the result of primarily internalized rules or self-prescriptions, and external constraints are the result of external social conditions beyond one's control.

"Constraint is here considered to be the psychological force exerted consciously or unconsciously by the individuals to inhibit a course of action called for by events" (Dohrenwend, 1961, p. 296).

> When force is exerted by the individual to suppress action demanded by inner events in favor of action demanded by outer events, the individual may be said to experience external constraint. When, in contrast, he attempts to inhibit action demanded by outer events in favor of action demanded by inner events, the individual may be said to experience inner constraint (1961, p. 296).

In general, the stronger the external events, the stronger the force required in internal events to oppose them and the greater the feelings of external constraint experienced by the person. Dohrenwend's discussion focuses on the conflicts between inner and outer constraints and their relative strength.

The adaptation syndrome is the third element of the paradigm. In translating Selye's G.A.S. into psychological terms, Dohrenwend finds some question as to whether there is a "general" adaptation syndrome in social-psychological phenomena. He feels that research must be undertaken to explore this possibility. He refers, instead, simply to an adaptation syndrome. This syndrome represents efforts by individuals to reduce constraint, and this is a central assumption of Dohrnewend's model (1961, p. 299). He sees the adaptation syndrome as a manifestation of efforts to adapt to constraint, composed of three factors: (1) affective: emotional aspects; (2) conative (sic): changes in social activities as a result of constraint; and (3) cognitive: primarily changes in one's self-prescriptions and other personal orientations.

> There is no ready answer to the question of how these various affective, conative, and cognitive facets of adaptation combine to form one or more baseline syndromes that serve as relatively neutral standards against which adaptive vs. maladaptive departures can be assessed (Dohrenwend 1961, p. 300).

He is clearly aware of the difficulties of evaluating adaptation on the psychological level and with establishing as normal some affective, conative, and cognitive behavior in certain circumstances.

The fourth element of the paradigm is adaptive and maladaptive responses. Given the difficulty of establishing a baseline for evaluating adaptation or maladaptation, Dohrenwend suggests that an appropriate alternative is letting the social definitions of maladaptive behavior that develop from actions of health, law, educational, and other social institutions serve as the definition of maladaptation. He recognizes that these definitions change and may even be conflicting at times. He says, "In this approach, the focus is on mental disorder within a wider framework of social deviance" (Dohrenwend, 1961, p. 301). He offers eight propositions relating these four dimensions.

Dohrenwend's model demonstrates the difficulties of trying to build social-psychological models based on biological adaptation models. The tendency to define social-psychological adaptation in terms of social deviance, which seems to be inherent in this type of model, could not be avoided by Dohrenwend. There is too much dependency on arbitrary and changable judgements required for this type of model to ever be of any practical utility in linking social behavior and physical health, in our opinion.

In addition, we think that his conceptualizations are frequently too vague. What are we to look at to determine the strength of external events or to measure the amount of force required by internal events to oppose them? These may be measurable, but Dohrenwend gives us few clues as to how we should operationally conceptualize them. His model is also not adequately thorough. Although he handles conflicts between inner constraints of two or more people as a form of external constraint, he does not discuss the conflicts between two or more inner constraints in the same person, or two or more outer constraints occurring competitively, both of which might conceivably produce subjective reports of feeling constrained.

For the task of this work, Dohrenwend's model offers little of practical value. It does not, as it was not designed to, provide clues linking social behavior and physiological changes. It does not provide us with a workable conceptualization of social or social-psychological phenomena that might be utilized in building a larger model, including physiological processes. Dohrenwend exhibits considerable ingenuity and insight, nonetheless.

LAZARUS' MODEL OF PSYCHOLOGICAL STRESS

Richard Lazarus in *Psychological Stress and the Coping Process* (1966) and a later article (1967) has developed a model of stress in which cognitive processes are paramount, with threat and appraisal his two central concepts.

"Threat implies a state in which the individual anticipates a confrontation with a harmful condition of some sort" (1966, p. 25). Harm is the subjective evaluation of motive-thwarting stimuli. Stimuli must have been previously connected with harm if an appraisal of threat is to occur (1966, p. 85). Threat has two main properties: (1) "it is anticipatory, involving expectations of future harm"; and (2) "it is dependent on cognitions" (1966, p. 83).

Stimuli as cues of some future condition are "evaluated by the cognitive process of *appraisal*" (1966, p. 25, emphasis his). Appraisal relies on two classes of antecedent conditions: (1) factors in the stimulus configuration, such as the comparative power of the harm-producing condition and the individual's counterharm resources; the imminence of the harmful confrontation; and degree of ambiguity in the significance of the stimulus cue (1966, p. 25), though ambiguity does not necessarily lead to threat unless it occurs in the context where threat is appraised (1966, p. 119); and (2) "factors within the psychological structure of the individual, including motive strength and pattern, general beliefs about transactions with the environment, intellectual resources, education, and knowledge" (1966, p. 25). Much of Lazarus' work elaborates on these antecedent conditions and their influence on appraisal of threat.

A major emphasis of Lazarus' model is the necessity of separating appraisals of threat from coping processes. "The mere fact that the individual anticipates harm and is therefore threatened or anxious does not, by itself, permit us to predict the nature of the reaction" (1967, p. 153).

Once a threat is appraised, "processes whose function it is to reduce or eliminate the anticipated harm are set in motion" (Lazarus, 1966, p. 25). These are the coping processes. The coping process also depends on cognitive appraisal, which Lazarus labels secondary appraisal to distinguish it from appraisals determining threat. There are three classes of factors in this secondary appraisal: (1) "degree of threat"; (2) "factors in the stimulus configuration, such as the locatability and character of the agent of harm, the viability of alternative available routes or actions to prevent the harm, and the situational constraints which limit or encourage the action that may be taken"; and (3) within the psychological structure processes including the evaluation of the price of coping alternatives, ego resources, defensive disposition, and general beliefs about the environment and one's resources for dealing with it (1966, p. 25). Whenever Lazarus uses the term coping he is referring to strategies for dealing with threat (1966, p. 151).

Secondary appraisals determine the form of the coping process. He says:

we are reasonably sure that it is the combination of interaction of stimulus and dispositional properties that determines much of the reaction. And when we say that an individual appraises a situation in choosing a form of coping process, we are opening the way to seeing the effects as caused by a transaction with a particular environment by an individual with a particular psychological structure. In effect, we're asking what the individual needs to know or believe about the situation for him to react one way or another. . . . The individual appraises the personal and social consequences of his act, his belief of his resources and about the environment, the degree of threat involved, location of the agent of harm (can he?), the social constraints, and then selects a coping process from the alternatives (1967, p. 162).

Lazarus handles the apparent overemphasis on rational and reflective evaluation by emphasizing that cognition and appraisal do not imply awareness, good reality testing, or adaptiveness, but only that thought is involved. It need not even be reportable. He points out that "beliefs, expectations, perceptions, and their motivations underlie how a threat stimulus is reacted to" (1967, p. 168).

In his critique of Magda Arnold (1966, pp. 52–55; 1967, p. 161), Lazarus makes it clear that his appraisal processes are more than instantaneous, vague, sensory responses. Arnold suggests a model for emotions in which "intuitive appraisal of the situation initiates an action tendency that is felt as emotion . . ." (1967, p. 161). She emphasizes the instantaneous and indeliberate qualities of the process as compared with more abstract and reflective thought (1966). Lazarus accepts her point, that appraisal can be rapid, but rejects her emphasis on sensory and nonabstract elements. He claims that appraisal is a process of considerable complexity and abstractness, even though it may be rapid, and involves a considerable amount of learned information.

One of the most crucial points of Lazarus' model is that the observable aspects of threat appraisal are the reflection of the coping process selected. The form of the coping process is observed in affective states, motor activity, alterations of adaptive function, and physiological reaction patterns. There are specific, observable patterns for various coping processes, and those processes being used can be determined on the basis of these specific, observable patterns. Emotions are viewed as a part of the expression of the coping process rather than a motivating element in coping. "It is the cognitive processes leading to emotion that organize behavior, not the emotions themselves" (1967, p. 152). He maintains that each negatively toned affect informs us of some different coping process, with the strength of the affect or response indicating the degree of threat.

In regard to physiological responses he says ". . . to understand and predict the physiological pattern of stress reaction we must know the nature of coping; conversely, the coping processes can be inferred from the pattern of reaction" (1967, p. 160). These patterns of physiological reaction, although having features in common with each other, "will also diverge in important details as a function of different types of coping processes" (1967, p. 160). Different emotional states are accompanied by different physiological reaction patterns, although these patterns do not always involve arousal (1966, pp. 320, 363, 368–369). Physiological excitement or arousal does not necessarily occur whenever or only when one is threatened. Lazarus is not interested in physiological arousal per se, but rather in the observable aspects of threat (1966, p. 368).

Lazarus does not go into detail about the kinds of responses produced by various coping processes, but he does offer a very general classification of coping-reaction patterns and the general kinds of appraisals involved. For example, coping-reaction patterns are classified as (1) direct actions, including *attack patterns,* which vary with anger, without anger, or anger without attack expression, and also including *avoidance patterns,* which vary with avoidance with fear, without fear, or fear without avoidance expression; (2) defense appraisals; and (3) anxiety-reaction patterns. He discusses the appraisals for each, including threat appraised, location and evaluation of agent of threat, evaluation of coping capacities and alternatives; social situation constraints, and individual internalized constraints (1966, p. 312–318). He applies the terms threat reaction to the "self-reported affective disturbances and behavioral evidence of threat"; physiological stress reactions or just stress reactions to physiological responses to threat; and structural strain reactions to social level responses to threat (1966, p. 28).

Lazarus' model is stimulating, and there is much that we find useful, especially his emphasis on the centrality of appraisals in determining which situations produce stress. However, we cannot entirely accept his suggestion that physiological responses in stress are not the result of appraisals of the situation but rather of the coping process utilized. He emphasizes that the coping processes are expressed as particular physiological, affective, and behavioral configurations, with emotions having distinctive physiological processes. This perspective takes us back to William James, whose work produced the sterile search for the physiological manifestations of every emotion. Followed to its logical conclusion, research on Lazarus' model would lead us to search for particular physiological, behavioral, and affective configurations. We doubt that we would find physiological variations of great enough magnitude to greatly influence the susceptibility to illness in such a search, even if such distinctive configurations do exist and could be measured.

Lazarus' model focuses on the physiological and other responses involved in threat, whereas we are interested in physiological processes aroused or produced by social-psychological events of sufficient magnitude to influence health. As he notes, there are many cases of physiological arousal and modification in situations other than those appraised as threatening; some of them may even involve positive affect. Consequently, Lazarus' threat model is not adequate for our purposes, although his elaboration of threat may prove useful in understanding a good many physiological changes and states of arousal.

There is also some doubt about the utility of his distinction between appraisal of an event and coping for our model, which emphasizes resonation. It is conceivable that coping is going on at the same time as appraising in terms of the handling of the information. What will we call selective perception, a predisposed coping process or an aspect of appraisal? Given Lazarus' belief that perception and appraisal can take place without awareness by the person and his emphasis on the rapid time sequence in appraisal, he would probably say that selective perception is a defense appraisal, a coping with a perception of which one is not aware. In our model we will not distinguish between appraisal and coping in any rigorous way, although we may speak of the interpretation and handling of the situation.

EDWARD GROSS' APPLICATION OF LAZARUS

One of the few efforts to make some moves toward a model of psychological stress incorporating social processes utilizes Lazarus' model in part. Edward Gross (1970) in looking at the work milieu defines stress as "the failure of routine methods for managing threats" (p. 55), and defines threat as "an imagined possible future deprivation of something one values" (p. 57). By limiting stress to threat he tries to avoid making stress equivalent to problem-solving, which he feels is too broad a definition. He notes that Lazarus' classification of coping techniques apply only to "what the individual may do *in those situations in which he must act alone or on his own resources*" (p. 59, emphasis his). He feels that the means of managing human stress (threat, in his case) would include individual techniques such as those described by Lazarus, but also collective behavior and organized or regularized methods based on organizational forms, cultural traits, and the like.

DAVID MECHANIC'S MODEL OF SOCIAL-PSYCHOLOGICAL STRESS

One of the very few studies of psychological stress in a social milieu by a sociologist is David Mechanic's *Students Under Stress* (1962). It is a study of graduate students preparing for and experiencing Ph.D. examinations in a department of a large university. He subsequently elaborated his views on stress (1968).

He says that stress "refers to the difficulties experienced by individuals as a result of perceived challenges" (1962, p. 2). In his study of Ph.D. students he defines stress as "the discomforting responses of persons in particular situations" (1962, p. 7). He defined stress as a discomforting response because he felt that it permitted focusing on a person's definitions and perceptions of situations and the factors influencing these perceptions (1962, p. 8). He says:

> It is the contention of the author that whether or not a person experiences stress will depend on the means, largely learned, that he has available to deal with his life situation. Thus, the degree to which a person is able to avoid discomfort will depend on his abilities and capacities, the skills and limitations provided by group traditions and practices, the means made available to him by his social environment through learning experiences, and the norms which define when and how he may utilize these means. Thus, stress is likely to become evident when the individual perceives these means as lacking or insufficient, or when they actually do become so (1962, p. 8).

Stress is characterized as "a discrepancy between the demands impinging on a person . . . and the individual's potential responses to these demands" (1968, p. 301). Although fear, anxiety, and depression do not correlate well with biochemical and endocrinological states, he believes that most researchers would agree that these affective states are stress responses. "The decision was made, therefore, to attempt to measure stress by taking into account all recognizable, discomforting responses (anxiety, depression, fear, and so on)" (1962, p. 166).

Mechanic sees his model as one of adaptation. He defines adaptation as the "way in which a person deals with his situation and his feelings aroused by the situation" (1962, pp. 2, 210). Adaptation as he defines it has two components: (1) coping: dealing with the situation, and (2) defense: dealing with one's feelings about the situation.

> Coping . . . refers to the instrumental behavior and problem-solving capacities of persons in meeting life demands and goals. It involves the applications of skills, techniques, and knowledge that a person has acquired. The extent to which a person experiences discomfort in the first place is often the product of the inadequacy of such skill repertoires (1968, p. 302).

Defense in Mechanic's terms:

> refers to the manner in which a person manages his emotional and affective states when discomfort is aroused or anticipated. Thus defense involves in large part the inner techniques through which persons deal with their feelings of anxiety, discomfort, or threat (1968, p. 303).

Mechanic feels that the ability to control one's emotions is beneficial to the coping process. Whether these defenses "restrict, distort, or falsify reality has no important meaning in and of itself" as long as it facilitates coping. However, the defenses cannot be so out of line with social conventions that they bring negative social reactions and loss of social support. Defenses are part of the coping process, and those divorced from or hindering the coping process are usually viewed as emotional disturbances (1968, p. 308).

Most situations are not experienced as threatening because they do not tax one's capacities. Mechanic contends that "the central and most important process in adaptation to stress involves practice, experience, and familiarity with modes of dealing with a situation" (1968, p. 305). His student study showed those who felt unprepared experienced strong feelings of discomfort, even though they may have had adequate skills. When one does not have an opportunity to practice or demonstrate his capacities he may feel uncertain (1968, p. 306). Thus preparation inadequacy is a major determinant of stress.

He refers to the ability to actively master the situation and one's feelings aroused by it as reversibility (1962, p. 10). This term applies to the personal, social, and cultural means for adapting to the situation and their adequacy. It is essential to consider not only personal capacities but also the manner in which these capacities are shaped and supported by the social structure of the community. In examining the social dimensions of adaptation in his later work (1968) he adds the person's motivation or involvement in the situation to coping and defenses as major components of adaptation, and he suggests that these three components of adaptation correspond to three societal institutions: (1) preparatory institutions, which "are various organizations and practices designed to develop skills and competence" including schools, apprenticeships, and informal avenues; (2) "incentive systems," which are "values and systems of reward and punishment within organizations and communities that influence activities in particular directions"; and (3) "evaluative institutions," which provide the "approval and support of disapproval and disparagement resulting from following particular courses of activity" (1968, p. 308).

Societies usually provide the means for adapting, but the individual must learn how and must develop the capacity to use them. "On the societal level a stress situation is one in which most people either have insufficient means to deal with the situation, or if sufficient means are available, lack the capacity to manipulate them effectively" (1962, p. 210).

An adequate culture and tradition teach the young how to deal with environmental exigencies, and an adequate person learns effectively to do this. The magnitude of stress is dependent upon the extent of imbalance between the group's environment and the patterns available for dealing with the environment. When imbalances exist between environmental problems and cultural and social resources, we have what we might call 'stress situations' inherent within the cultural and social systems (1962, p. 220).

Thus the extent to which one experiences stress depends upon the kind of society in which he finds himself, its requirements and goals, preparation offered, and so forth (1968, pp. 306–307).

Mechanic's model is based on a conceptualization of man as "an active agent molding and effecting to some extent the conditions to which he will be exposed" (1968, p. 302). He believes that our "conceptual vocabulary is phrased in terms of the intrapsychic reactions to environmental stress, and our language is relatively impoverished in its coverage of the areas of active striving and social adaptations" (1968, p. 302). He likes W. I. Thomas' concept of crisis in which there is no situation as long as life runs smoothly and habits are working. But when habits do not work or are disrupted, new stimuli demand attention, and a crisis may occur. The difference between crisis and progress depends on the preparation of the individual and his ability to revise his notions on the basis of past experience (1962, pp. 203–4; 1968). Mechanic is trying to encourage examining stress as a cross-sectional picture of the situation rather than in terms of the developmental-historical approaches most frequently—and often fruitfully, he adds—used by stress researchers. He sees a person as attempting "to maintain cognitive integration by controlling the information that enters the cognitive system and by making it congruent with his views and needs" (1962, p. 117; he took this from Festinger). He focuses on symbolic behavior, such as definitions of the situation, communication, and symbolic defense, in his study of students, and he emphasizes that no matter what stress response we look at, we must take these into account.

Of all the models we have discussed, Mechanic's contains more of the elements we see as crucial to the conceptualization of the social dimensions of the relations between social behavior and health. We like his position that information processing, definitions of the situation, and their interrelation with social systems are crucial in stress responses. His emphasis on preparation, on stress as a consequence of the failure of preparations and formerly productive habits, and on society's adequacy in providing preparation and resources is excellent. We agree with his view of man as active and involved in mastering his environment. We approve of the shifting of the research emphasis from a historical-developmental one to a situational cross section.

Still, there are reasons why this model cannot be used to solve the problem under study. Mechanic's definition of stress as discomforting responses is inadequate because, as he noted, there is poor correlation between subjective states such as anxiety, discomfort, fear, and physiological processes. We are most interested in relating social and subjective processes to these physiological processes. He has made no effort to conceptualize the links between social and physiological processes and physical health. His distinctions between coping and defense seem unnecessary. As far as we are concerned, his defense is a type of coping—that of coping with one's own feelings—which frequently may require external behavior and the obtaining of help such as counselling. Nevertheless, Mechanic's work is an oasis on the way to a workable model of social behavior and health interrelations.

SCOTT AND HOWARD'S GENERAL MODEL OF STRESS

Scott and Howard (1970; Howard and Scott: 1965) have developed what they hope is a general integrative model of stress into which stress models on organic, psychological, and social levels can be translated without distortion. For individuals they assume that "each human organism tends to develop a characteristic level of activity and stimulation at which it most comfortably functions" (1970, p. 270). These characteristic levels vary between individuals and are determined by both genetic and behavioral factors. They cast their model in problem-solving terms, with the problem defined as "a stimulus or condition that produces demands on the human organism that require it to exceed its ordinary level of functioning, or that restrict activity levels below usual levels of functioning" (1970, p. 270). They classify problems into four types according to the sources of the stimuli or conditions: (1) internal physical environment; (2) external physical environment; (3) one's own psychological environment; and (4) the sociocultural milieu. They also distinguish between efforts to solve the problem and actual solution of the problem.

They have labeled the initial response to provocative stimuli indicating a problem as tension. If the problem is successfully solved, the customary level of activity is regained, and tension is dissipated. If the problem is not solved, tensions persist. Stress is a result of this condition:

> In effect, failure in mastery requires the organism to use an excess of energy and resources in maintenance activities over what would have been required had mastery been achieved, and the necessity of excessive maintenance activity involves the organism in a state of continuous mobilization or tension. To the extent that excess maintenance tension exists, the organism can be said to be experiencing stress. In effect, stress is regarded as a state that results from the excess tensions produced by a failure of the organism to master threats from one or more of its environments (1970, p. 273).

In this model, one does not experience stress until one fails to solve a problem. Solution of the problem improves the organism's capacity to handle similar problems in the future. Failure to solve the problem is accompanied by persistent tensions until some means is found to cope with them. The person experiencing undissipated tension can either simply live with it, which may lead to total exhaustion if the resources for handling tension over time are too high, or he may "temporarily dissipate some of the accumulated tensions through a variety of physical, psychological, and social mechanisms of tension release" (1970, p. 273).

There are five factors determining whether the threat or problem will be solved or mastered. The first is the person's energy potential, including his overall capacities, amounts of energy available for the particular problem, and in part, his customary levels of activity. Resources are second, and these are "anything that contributes to the resolution of problem situations" (1970, p. 271) whether they are general resources, such as intelligence and health, or specific resources, such as skills, tools, materials, or knowledge. The third factor is the solvability of the problem. The problem must be solvable in principle. There are three situations in which it may not be: (1) the capacities to solve the problem are lacking in a particular person; (2) the problem is not solvable; (3) the solution precludes solution of some other problems, thus making contradictory demands. The fourth factor is the person's definition of the problem and his physiological and psychological "set" at the time. The fifth factor is the general type of response selected. It may be an assertive or aggressive attempt to solve the problem; or it may be divergent, diverting energy and resources from confronting the problem; or it may be inert, failing to mobilize energy with regards to the problem.

Scott and Howard emphasize the importance of the availability and distribution of knowledge, skills, and tools as crucial in determining whether a situation is stressful for a particular person. They note that one can have generalized anxiety because of a general feeling of inadequacy, or they can have anxiety considering a particular circumstance that threatens mastery.

This model is a bold effort to find something in common in the various models of stress without distorting the findings in the several areas. Scott and Howard are aware of the limitations of their model, particularly the need for theories of the middle range to fill the gaps between their theory and particular substantive research problems. They do feel their model helps put apparently conflicting models in new perspective to show their compatibility and complementarity. However, in focusing on those properties in common between stress models dealing variously with physiological or psychological states or the two together, they have of necessity, as they are well aware, been required to work at a level of generality that makes the practical application of the model difficult. The researcher is on his own in translating their general concepts and relations into the particular parameters of the area he is studying. This factor also makes research tests for refutability difficult, because one is not sure what is being refuted, Scott and Howard's theory or one's interpretations of it.

The definition of tension does not indicate whether this is to be understood as a psychological state, physiological state, or a particular combination of both. Their definition of stress is inoperable unless some criteria is established for measuring or at least conceptualizing customary levels of activity for the particular person, and even worse is the thought of having to determine for each subject of a study what constitutes excessive maintenance activity. They seem to imply that this refers to a combination of physiological and social-psychological properties, but they are not explicit. They have not considered the possible incompatibility between physiological and social-psychological customary levels of functioning or activity. It is conceivable that what is customary on one level may not be conducive to health and well-being on another. Besides, they give us no clues as to how and why one's activity is customarily maintained at one level or another, and, more important, why it should continue to be maintained at that level and not some other level. They do not indicate what things might influence fluctuations in this customary level without producing tensions and stress. Yet their model seems to imply that customary levels of activity are desirable and good. We would insist 'that whether they are or not must be evaluated from a number of viewpoints, and the reasons considered for that level obtaining in that person.

Scott and Howard's model points out neither isomorphisms between social, psychological, and physiological processes that might conceivably be developed into a general model of stress in all environments, nor a singular model of relations between all environments in stress into which all others may be translated or fitted, nor is it a thorough model of social-psychological processes and physiological states in stress. It seems to fluctuate between the three, never certain of its identity. Their model, we think, should not be presented as a general integrative model, but should be more precisely conceptualized and presented as a particular social-psychological model considering physiological processes. As such, it could have considerable merit. We find nothing to recommend it as the proper language into which all other models should be translated. We would resist such a translation on the grounds that the more viewpoints on a problem as yet unsolved, the greater the probability we will be able to observe all of the properties of the phenomena at hand.

Some Contributions of Stress Research

ON THE ADEQUACY OF THE CONCEPT OF STRESS

We have reviewed a number of the more prominent and fruitful models of stress, and we have found none of them adequate for the purposes of this study. There are, of course, many other models that might have been included, and new ones are appearing even now. Of those of which we are aware, the ones mentioned are among the more representative and successful. Each of these models has made some contribution, some lasting ones, in the development of theory of social behavior and physiological processes and health. We have utilized some of their findings and ideas in our own perspective, as noted throughout this discussion. None has adequately embraced the whole spectrum from social to physiological. We now turn to some general criticisms of stress models and research and look at some of the general conclusions from stress research important to the conceptualization of a model of social behavior, physiological processes, and health. We briefly examine the concept of stress itself to determine if it is to our advantage to use it in our work. It is not our purpose to provide a lengthy and thorough critique of the stress literature here, but simply to discover what, if anything, stress as a concept may offer us.

Stress as a concept has been used in many disciplines and in tens of thousands of articles since its introduction by Selye in 1936 and its popularization in the 1950s. If every discipline used it in the same way, it could provide a basis for interdisciplinary cooperation. However, this has not been the case, and the multitude of definitions has led to confusion rather than a common understanding (Appley and Trumbull, 1967 b). For the most part it remains ambiguous and vague when viewed through the literature and seems to perpetually elude a sound defining (Mechanic, 1968; Levine and Scotch, 1970).

A major reason for the conceptual confusion surrounding stress is the number of assumptions about the nature of stress in common use that current evidence indicates are not tenable. Some of these assumptions seem logical enough if one has fallen into the common trap of trying to apply Selye's model of physiological stress to social-psychological or psychosomatic conceptualizations of stress. Selye conceptualizes the physiological stress response as, in general, elicited by a wide variety of natural substances and phenomena, common to all members of a species, and invariant in its individual configuration. Consequently, it is common to find social-psychological stress models which assume that any and all unpleasant situations are stressful, that situations stressful for one person are inevitably stressful for others, and that a situation stressful for a person at one time will be stressful to him at any other time as well (Appley and Trumbull, 1967 b; Scott and Howard, 1970; Levine and Scotch, 1970). These assumptions have led to equally common methodological errors of assuming that what the reasearcher thinks is unpleasant *is* unpleasant for the subjects and stressful to all of them (Appley and Trumbull, 1967 b; Marks, 1967).

An even more common erroneous assumption is that stressful events must lead to disruptive and pathological states and must invariably impair performance (Appley and Trumbull, 1967 b; Levine and Scotch, 1967; Michaux et al., 1967). This is not even true in Selye's model. Despite Selye's emphasis that the G.A.S. is an adaptive process often having positive consequences, the literature on social-psychological stress rarely considers the possibility of positive consequences of stress (Croog, 1970). It seems hard to avoid the conclusion that stress as it is used in much of the literature is an evaluative term meaning something bad, just as disease does (note the use of anxiety, threat, discomfort, problems, and the like in social-psychological definitions of stress in the models discussed).

Still another untenable assumption is that all the internal effects and behavioral responses in stress are correlated. The idea that subjective affect, emotional behavior, physiological responses, and coping activities are all so interrelated that measurement of one is an adequate indicator of the others is not supported by the evidence (Appley and Trumbull, 1967 b). Research based on this assumption commonly errs by measuring one indicant of the stress response, such as galvanic skin response, heart rate, or subjective reports, and assumes all the other indicants have changed in the same direction, leading researchers to use single measures as adequate evidence of the existence of stress (Appley and Trumbull, 1967 b; Trumbull and Appley, 1967). A more tenable position seems to be to measure several physiological processes at the same time, noting their interrelations and configurations in particular people, not between people, and to correlate these processes with various subjective states and behavior measured separately (Lazarus, 1966; Ruff and Korchin, 1967; Appley and Trumbull, 1967 b).

The imprecision of all available measures of stress must be kept in mind, although this is no reason to abandon research in the area. There is still considerable imprecision and lack of agreement in physiological measurement, and there is even greater confusion in the area of mental health, in which experienced psychiatrists have been known to disagree on 80% of the diagnoses. There frequently is a lack of agreement on disease diagnoses, for example, in rheumatoid arthritis and hypertension (Levine and Scotch, 1970 b). Researchers may also confuse the processes producing illness with those that influence recovery from illness, which may not be the same. Sometimes differences between people already sick are taken as evidence of how the disease was produced when they may be nothing of the kind (Cassel, 1970).

Conceptual confusion concerning stress derives in part from many preexisting definitions, connotations, and popular notions about stress. Stress was and is a term with popular meanings. It has been used in various ways before and since Selye to mean something particular in various disciplines, especially in engineering and physics. Moreover, it is consistently used in an ambiguous way by many researchers (Levine and Scotch, 1970).

Stress research and models still have the tendency to focus on only one or two dimensions at a time. Social scientists frequently fail to take physiological states into account, and physiologists and physiological-psychologists are just beginning to appreciate the importance of the social context in understanding and predicting physiological processes (Appley and Trumbull, 1967 b). Payne (1967) warns of the contradictions in findings and the problems that can arise when researchers study only a part without regard to its place in a whole, then try to fit these fragmentary observations together. Stress studies are still too limited to particular disciplines and their areas of analysis and frequently are incomplete in their treatment of relevant variables at even these restricted levels. Stress researchers have been prone to deal with events of a highly traumatic nature, overlooking the more mundane sources of stress and their prolonged effects (Scott and Howard, 1970), and they have been too quick to explain their observations in terms of stress instead of examining alternative possible explanations (Croog, 1970).

Phenomena are often labeled stress for what appears to be purely arbitrary reasons. If one ignores the labels and looks only at what is being studied, this confusion is considerably reduced and the nonessentiality of the term stress in understanding the phenomena becomes apparent. These labels can be divided into two main groups in terms of their referents, those that deal with situations or stimuli as stress and those that deal with responses as stress.

Among the stimuli and situations labeled as stress are "situations characterized as new, intense, rapidly changing, sudden or unexpected" and "stimulus deficit, absence of expected stimulation, and fatigue-producing and boredom-producing settings" and "stimuli calling for conflicting responses" (Appley and Trumbull, 1967 b, p. 5). Stress stimuli include all sorts of mechanical and chemical stimuli, including electric shock, adrenalin injections, and physical restraint. They also include "battle conditions, impending surgery, rapid cultural change, intense competition, life crises (such as the loss of a loved one or job demotion), natural disasters (floods, tornadoes, or earthquakes), acute illness or injury, frustration and failure, isolation and so on" (Mechanic, 1968, p. 297).

The responses labeled and characterized as stress fall into three general categories: (1) physiological responses; (2) behavioral responses, including the common practice of inference of emotions from behavioral responses; and (3) subjective states, generally self-reported. The physiological responses to indicate stress include "change in blood eosinophils, an increase in 17-ketosteroids in the urine, and increase in ACTH-content or glucocorticoid concentration in the blood, or changes in heart rate, galvanic skin response, change in critical flicker fusion threshold, inspiration: expiration . . . ratio, and so on" (Appley and Trumbull, 1967, p. 5). Among the behavioral responses used as operational definitions or indexes of the occurrence of stress are "such performance shifts as perseverative behaviors, increased reaction time, erratic performance rates, malcoordination, error increase, and fatigue" (Appley and Trumbull, 1967 b, p. 5). Some of the behavioral responses mentioned as inferences of emotional states and consequently stress are "tremors, stuttering, exaggerated speech characteristics, and loss of sphincter control" (Appley and Trumbull, 1967, b, p. 5). Emotional activity is sometimes used post facto to indicate that stress occurred. The subjective states to indicate stress include reports of threat, anxiety, troubles, unsolved problems, reported somatic symptoms, and depression.

Although most researchers try to utilize both a situation that presumably produces stress and an independent measure that stress has occurred, there are some researchers who have difficulty keeping independent and dependent variables separated. Studies using subjective reports run the danger of circularity in which the subjective response is "taken as evidence both that the situation is stressful and that stressful situations produce undesirable symptoms" (Cassel, 1967, p. 45).

This brief discussion illustrates how little consensus there is on what stress is and how to measure it. There is not much more consensus on whether the term should be modified, abandoned, or used as it is. Appley and Trumbull (1967 b) think that the future usefulness of the stress concept in psychology depends on the adequacy of the conceptual differentiation between the stimulus, organism, and response in the stress situation. Mechanic (see Pepitone, 1967, p. 199) believes that trying to identify the sources of stress is an endless process and wonders if it is worthwhile. We agree with Syme (1967) that we should abandon the concept of stress in the study of the relations between social, psychological, and physiological phenomena and look instead at these phenomena with an eye for fresh concepts. Like emotions, rejected as a meaningful research concept in the last chapter, stress has served its purpose in guiding research in a very large and amorphous area, and the research has now outgrown the concept. We now need fresh conceptualizations of the themes emerging from stress research. These conceptualizations would help distinguish the dimensions of the various themes, consolidate the advances of research that uncovered them, and encourage the study of interrelations between them. However, like emotions, stress still has considerable subjective meaning and will undoubtedly remain a familiar part of our common vocabulary.

We use the term stress in this study only when it is needed to prevent distortion of cited authors' intentions.

SOME GENERAL CONCLUSIONS RESULTING FROM
STRESS RESEARCH

The evidence in stress literature relating social behavior and physiology comes from a number of general sources including: (1) impressions of clinicians, which mostly are scientifically inadequate because they use very small numbers, lack controls, depend on retrospective reports, and lean toward personality traits as explanations; (2) laboratory studies, animal and human, which have measured physiological processes accompanying stress (portable devices may soon measure physiological changes in normal living outside of the laboratory); (3) disaster studies; (4) variations in prevalence and epidemiological studies, dealing with correlations between demographic variables and various diseases, which for the most part have yet to search for and test possible relations between stress and various diseases; (5) logic and common sense (Levine and Scotch, 1970).

The general conclusions of such research, especially the psychophysiological studies, which are central to our model, have been admirably summarized by Appley and Trumbull:

If one tries to gain some overall perspective on what stress studies have so far revealed, and especially on their relation to studies of frustration, conflict, and anxiety, one is led to these kinds of general observations.
1. Stress is probably best conceived as a state of the total organism under extenuating circumstances rather than as an event in the environment.
2. A great variety of different environmental conditions is capable of producing a stress state.

3. Different individuals respond to the same conditions in different ways. Some enter rapidly into a stress state, others show increased alertness and apparently improved performance, and still others appear to be "immune" to the stress-producing qualities of the environmental conditions.

4. The same individual may enter into a stress state in response to one presumably stressful condition and not another.

5. Consistent *intra*-individual but varied *inter*-individual psycho-biological response patterns occur in stress situations. The notion of a *common* stress reaction needs to be reassessed.

6. The behaviors resulting from operations intended to induce stress may be the same or different, depending on the context of the situation of its induction.

7. The intensity and the extent of the stress state, and the associated behaviors, may not be readily predicted from a knowledge of the stimulus conditions alone, but require an analysis of underlying motivational patterns and of the context in which the stressor is applied.

8. Temporal factors may determine the significance of a given stressor and thus the intensity and extent of the stress state and the optimum measurement of effect (1967 b, p. 11).

From these and other conclusions there are two conditions of extreme importance to our model that seem reasonably well established. First, physiological response patterns vary between individuals and in response to various situations. The proportions and patterns of physiological manifestations in given individuals and situations cannot be assumed to be known beforehand; they must be measured by examining a number of physiological processes and states of arousal during the event. Yet in given individuals these physiological patterns may be fairly consistent over time (Trumbull and Appley, 1967). Second, subjective interpretations determine which situations produce physiological responses. On this point there seems to be considerable agreement (Appley and Trumbull, 1967; Trumbull and Appley, 1967; Basowitz et al., 1955; Lazarus, 1966; Hinkle, 1961; Engel, 1968; Wolff, 1953). Situations cannot as a rule be assumed beforehand to produce physiological responses in anyone encountering them. The meaning of that situation to the person resulting from past experiences, socialization, emergent properties of the event, and the like must first be understood in order to predict responses.

SOME ELEMENTS OF A THEORY LINKING SOCIAL AND
PHYSIOLOGICAL PROCESSES SUGGESTED BY STRESS RESEARCH

From the stress literature, a number of limitations on a successful theory linking social behavior, physiological processes, and health emerge. It must not be limited to one disciplinary focus but must involve conceptualization of the interrelations between social, psychological, and biological properties. It must be able to explain, at least in principle, the general findings mentioned in the preceding section, in particular the individual variations in responses to situations. There should be a minimum of conflict between the general conceptualizations of the theory and concrete observable events. These general concepts should permit prediction of individual cases (which may be changes in groups, not necessarily in a particular person) and should be able to show the nature of the connection between particular qualities and particular events (see Zajonc, 1968). The abstraction of a general model or theory need not divorce it from particular events.

There seem to be four major categories of elements in a particular encounter to be considered:

1. Past personal history, including physiological properties inherited and resulting from experiences, socialization, repertoire of situations experienced and mastered, repertoire of customary responses, and group memberships.

2. Subjective perception and interpretation of a situation within a sociophysiological context.

3. The "fit" between the subjectively perceived situation and the person's past history, including his capacities and available resources both "real" and believed.

4. The resonating configurations of which the situation and individual are a part at the time and the emergent properties of these, including social patterns and physiological changes detrimental to health (for similar sets of suggestions see Levine and Scotch, 1967, 1970 b; Appley and Trumbull, 1967 b; Marks, 1967; Cassel, 1967).

In our model these four are divisible only analytically and in a particular situation are blended together in a particular biosocial resonation configuration. For example, subjective interpretation may be seen as an active process with the subjective meaning in part a result of past history, in part emerging from the situation as activity progresses, and in part influencing the form the situation subsequently takes. In the full picture physiological and social elements must also be considered.

Summary

In this chapter we have examined several models of stress and have learned much from them although finding none of them adequate for the purposes of thus study. Contributions of the several models of stress have been discussed. We have found the concept of stress to be unsatisfactory for our purposes and have decided not to use it in our model. Two central ideas in the stress models and research findings that serve as central concerns of our model are (1) the subjective interpretation of the situation determines which situations produce physiological changes; and (2) physiological responses to subjective definitions of situations follow fairly consistent patterns within individuals, but vary between individuals. Among the physiological processes stress research indicates are important are those involving the pituitary and adrenal glands and the autonomic nervous system.

CHAPTER III

The Central Nervous System
and Perception
in Biosocial Resonation

Information processing is central to the concept of biosocial resonation. In this model we have excluded consideration of physical, chemical, and organic agents of disease, except as susceptibility to them is increased.

We focus only on the changes in susceptibility to illness and in physiological processes resulting from resonation with the environment, primarily the social milieu. Essentially the only thing received from the social milieu in this case is information. Consequently, it is important that we have some understanding of the physiological processes involved in perception and recording of information. In this chapter we look at some of the relevant central nervous system processes involved and examine some of the current thinking on perception.

The activities and condition of the central nervous system have consequences for the physiological activity of the body and its vitality and health. Hinkle says:

> It has become evident over the years that the central nervous system exerts a high degree of control over all of the endocrine glands. Through them, and through its neural connections, it influences almost every metabolic process of the human organism. By a combination of the effects of endocrine and neural influences, and by the effects of the gross behavior of the person, any disease, whether it be infectious, parasitic, traumatic, metabolic, degenerative, or neo-plastic, may be influenced to some extent, by the interactions of man with his society and other men (1968, p. 80).

Wolf agrees:

> There is a very large body of data to indicate that stimuli reaching the highest integrative levels of the central nervous system may lead to widespread and often disabling bodily changes, including damage to tissue and even death (1963, p. 110).

In coronary heart disease the central nervous system stimulation has been found to produce changes such as necrosis and atherosclerosis in cardiac tissues and elevations in serum cholesterol. Cholesterol and lipid concentration in blood seems to be governed by mechanisms responsive to "impulses arising in the interpretative areas of the brain" (Caffrey, 1967, p. 122). The autonomic nervous system, especially the sympathetic system, is linked with atherosclerotic pathology. "Whatever is being searched for in the social system, its pathogenic impact on the cardiovascular system is most probably channeled through the central nervous system" (Jenkins, 1967, p. 144).

Some General Properties of Information Processing of the Central Nervous System

The central nervous system (CNS) is composed of the brain, spinal cord, and autonomic nervous system. This chapter focuses on the brain and sense organs, reserving the discussion of the autonomic nervous system for Chapter IV.

The central nervous system functioning in man is related to the nature of the world he lives in. Our world is composed of energy, either in the usual sense or in that manifestation of energy we call matter. Matter exists as solids, liquids, or gases. The kinds of information the central nervous system in man must deal with involves all three forms of matter; where as a fish, for example, deals primarily with solids and liquids. Gravity provides for man an orienting constant and is a continuing source of information, both because of organs of equilibrium in the inner ear and because of the pressure of the earth against his feet or body. The geometric permanences of places and constancy of shapes and sizes of solids provides him with additional information.

SOME NOTES ON HOW NERVES AND THE BRAIN WORK

As we have frequently been told, man's only claim to fame in the animal kingdom is his brain. He is otherwise unspecialized, having the dentation of an omnivore and the limbs of a plantigrade. Although man's brain is not the largest or heaviest or even proportionately the heaviest in the animal world, it does have the largest number of nerve cells and interconnections, four times those of a chimpanzee. Even so, some parts of his brain are smaller, such as the hypothalamus, which in "lower" animals contributes to instinctive behavior (Chauchard, 1962). Thus with the greater capacity of the brain comes a greater dependency on the information it can acquire to guide behavior (Chauchard, 1962). The brain does not make man human in the social sense but merely provides the possibility of being human. His body has the capacity to learn speech, but the brain provides no language. To learn a language, to develop human behavior characteristics, and to refine information processing "it is neccessary that man learn socially and culturally how to use his brain, a task that will never be finished" (Chauchard, 1962, p. 42).

The brain is composed of living cells and is not dormant between stimulations. The nerve cell is not simply a passive conductor of impulses like a copper wire but varies in sensitivity itself and thus influences which impulses are carried and which are not. Excitation and inhibition are terms applied to variations in this sensitivity; they are poles at either end of a continua of sensitivity. There are three distinctive stages of the continua: (1) excitation—the increased sensitivity to stimuli capable of initiating a response in the cell; (2) repose—the cell is not excited, just living; and (3) inhibition—a state of "super-rest," or active "braking" in which excitability is diminished (Chauchard, 1962, pp. 61–63).

These changes are simply variations in concentrations of sodium, potassium, and chloride ions between the inside and outside of the cell. The propagation of the nervous impulse also involves changes in concentrations of these ions. The chloride ion has a negative electrical charge, and the sodium and potassium ions a positive one. The chloride ion is larger than the other two, so that when these ions contact the semipermeable cell membrane of the neuron, the positive ions can pass through more readily than the chloride ions. Thus the changes in ion concentrations on either side of the cell membrane is due primarily to movement of the sodium and potassium ions. Potassium moves across the membrane more easily than sodium in the resting cell. The resting nerve cell tends to transport sodium outside itself, where as potassium is retained but still able to move across the membrane. Thus we have a high sodium concentration outside the membrane, with some potassium producing a slight positive charge on the outside of the cell membrane and a slight negative charge on the inside of the cell membrane because of the passage of some of the potassium to the outside. This difference of charge is called the membrane potential.

Excitation is a depolarization of this membrane potential, which means the difference in charges between the inside and outside caused by the larger concentration of positive ions on the outside is decreased, thus making it easier for the neuron to pass the electrochemical impulse of a stimulation. Inhibition is a polarization or increase of the differences in charges across the membrane by increasing the positive charge on the outside and negative charge on the inside by transporting potassium to the outside as well as sodium. This change makes it much more difficult to pass the stimulation impulse.

The reason excitation encourages and inhibition discourages passage of the stimulus impulse is easily understood when we examine the nature of the passage of a nervous impulse. The resting nerve cell membrane is more permeable to potassium than sodium, but when an impulse passes along the neuron's membrane, it does so because of a momentary change in the permeability of the cell membrane so that it becomes more permeable to sodium than potassium ions, allowing sodium to move into the cell but retaining potassium. When an impulse passes like a wave, the cell membrane potential momentarily drops to zero or reverses so that there is a negative charge on the outside and a positive charge on the inside of the membrane as a result of the influx of sodium ions. This passage of a nervous impulse along the cell itself modifies the state of the cell and its capacity to carry another impulse. The neuron undergoes fluctuations of excitability and inhibition immediately before and after the impulse, with a short refractory period following the impulse passage when the neuron is unexcitable (Chauchard, 1962; Guyton, 1961). An excited neuron that is partially depolarized, then, requires less energy to reduce or reverse the membrane potential and can conduct rapid and numerous impulses. The superpolarized or inhibited neuron requires much more energy to reduce or reverse the membrane potential so that it conducts few impulses, and these are slow and tend to disappear (Chauchard, 1962).

Thus the unceasing electrical activity in the central nervous system has two aspects: (1) the modifications and fluctuations of the neuronic polarization, which is the index of the state of excitation and inhibition; and (2) the electrical pulsations, which are the waves of propagated nervous impulses involved in the neural handling of information.

Ensembles of neurons are submitted to waves of excitation or inhibition, including or excluding them from the immediate participation in impulse propagation and information processing. Says Chauchard:

It would thus be possible to draw up a color chart at any given moment showing all the neurons, with different shades graduated for all the levels between extreme excitation and extreme inhibition. Everything of the same color would be in the same state, making up an ensemble functioning together at the same rhythm. We can therefore have several circuits in the brain functioning simultaneously but independently, thanks to this physiological barrier of the level of excitation. . . . A message will be received or emitted by the brain only if the inhibition barrier does not stand in the way (1962, p. 62).

Physical laws govern the propagation of nervous impulses so that nerve cells matched at the same levels of excitation are best capable of resonance, with propagation increasing with excitation. A great many things can upset and prevent the match or harmony between neural elements, such as deficiency or excesses in hormones.

There are a multitude of impulses being passed throughout the brain at any time. They do not follow a single chain but irradiate in a "network of multiple links including backtracking" (Chauchard, 1962, p. 86). These multiple passages of impulses make it very difficult to destroy memory and thought with lesions, because the same idea evidently can be represented by several combinations of neurons, and the impulses simply bypass a damaged neuron (Eccles, 1966). It is these multiple impulses in a brain over which changing patterns of excitation and inhibition are passing that is primarily responsible for subjectivity.

DEVELOPMENT OF THE BRAIN

The electroencephalograph (EEG) patterns of the adult are not observed in the newborn infant. The usual signs of awareness, such as reactions to light and sound and accompanying sleeping and waking, are absent (Berelson and Steiner, 1964). Although the nerve cells in the brain are at their complete complement for life at birth, the development of an anatomically complete nervous network is not finished until about the age of seven (Chauchard, 1962). The adult cortical EEG patterns appear only gradually, usually being complete around the age of eighteen (Gellhorn and Loofbourrow, 1963; Chauchard, 1962).

Social stimulation is essential for the development of the brain. As the brain matures, the appropriate social and physical environment is required for the full realization of potential. For example, if the language centers are not used they do not develop at the appropriate period, and the person is permanently less capable of articulation (Chauchard, 1962). Studies on rats are suggestive. Rats given an enriched environment with considerable opportunities for stimulation showed a heavier, thicker cerebal cortex with a better blood supply to the brain, larger brain cells, and greater activity of enzymes (such as acetylcholinesterase) than their littermates who had the same physical activity levels but had been raised in a deprived environment. These enriched rats showed superiority in problem-solving and learning. However, if the enriched and deprived rats' environments were exchanged, the enriched rats backslid and lost some of their earlier advantage, and the deprived rats made some substantial gains (Krech, 1968; Bennett et al., 1964; French, 1968; Bennett and Howenzweig, 1968).

A number of scientists (Chauchard, 1962; Engel, 1962; Harlow, 1969, who also cites William James) have suggested that accompanying the maturation of the central nervous system, certain spontaneous forms of behavior occur in interaction with the environment. Study of these spontaneous forms of behavior has been dampened by the blistering attacks on instincts in man. These spontaneous behavioral patterns may be recognized because they are manifest at the appropriate stages of development in the appropriate situations by all members of the species and they do not require either instructions or rewards or punishments to appear (Engel, 1962, pp. 15–16). Many of these spontaneous activities have considerable importance for social development of the person, such as the imitation of sounds; standing, crawling, toddling; exploration and perception seeking; and play (from William James, see Harlow, 1969).

> It is cerebral maturation that makes a baby babble in its cradle, but if the sounds do not become socially interesting as communication . . . the development of the language centers will be impeded (Chauchard, 1962, p. 51).

This does not necessarily suggest that human development should be considered in stages. Bijou (1969) suggests that we look afresh and if there are stages, let them emerge from the research. He believes that the existing sequential models, such as those of Gesell, Piaget, Freud, or Erickson, have a tendency to be developed from shaky and sometimes negative evidence.

MEMORY

Information retention or memory is still somewhat of a mystery, although there are plenty of ideas, and computer technology has provided some working analogies. Lashley's life work illustrates the direction memory theories have moved. His search for structural representations or memory traces in particular places, "engrams," was abandoned for the other extreme in which memories are more diffusely distributed and not limited to a small group of interconnected neurons in a particular part of the brain (his law of equipotentiality). He seems to have concluded that:

> . . . the learning process must consist of the attunement of the elements of a complex system in such a way that a particular combination of pattern of cells responds more readily than before the experience (Gibson, 1966, p. 276).

Eccles agrees:

> . . . memory of any particular event is dependent on a specific reorganization of neuronal associations . . . in a vast system of neurons widely spread over the cerebral cortex (1966, p. 338).

The terms engram or schemata are still sometimes used to refer to this more-expanded notion of neural patterns. Why the cells should respond more readily after an experience is the focus of much of the current neurophysiological research on memory and learning. The major competing theories are the synaptic change model and the molecular model. In the more widely accepted synaptic change model, information is retained as the result of changes in the synapses between a collection of neurons. (A synapse is the juncture between the axon of one and the dendrites of the other of two or more neurons; they do not actually touch but stimulate one another across the space by chemical means.) This change is postulated to be a microgrowth of the synapse or of the neurons across the space separating them, which makes it easier for the impulse to follow that particular pattern. The encountering of similar situations strengthens the pattern, contributing to continued microgrowth.

The second perspective is the molecular model. Here information retention is the result of deoxyribonucleic acid (DNA) production of a specific ribonucleic acid (RNA, responsible for constructing substances according to the code on the DNA), which produces a transmitter substance. Memory is conceived of as the resonance-like reaction in which the transmitter production is increased as a result of encounters with similar situations (Eccles, 1966). Both theories recognize the positive effect of RNA on learning and memory, but they explain it in different ways, one in terms of enhancing microgrowths and the other in producing more transmitter substances.

It should be noted that memory is not simply branded onto the brain but goes through phases of permanence. Apparently, recent experiences are more labile in their neural representations, with memories only gradually becoming more stabilized and permanent. Blows on the head, electroshock, and electrode stimulation of the hippocampus (a part of the brain) can prevent fixation of memories of recent events. Stimulants such as caffeine and amphetamine taken immediately after an experience increase the period of lability (Chauchard, 1962; John, 1967). The labile phase seems to be mediated by a continued reverberatory activity in the neural networks, where as the long-term phase seems to be related to ribonucleic acid and protein syntheses (John, 1967).

AWARENESS

Another area on which there is still considerable controversy is awareness. At one extreme are those who maintain that there are a conscious and an unconscious, with differing properties, and at the other extreme are those who believe there is a continuum of awareness fading off into unreportable vagueness. Some believe there is subliminal preception, which is the picking up of information without being consciously aware that the information is there. Others maintain there is no "unconscious consciousness," and the difference is between reportable and unreportable preceptions (see Hilgard, 1969; Schaefer, 1966; Chauchard, 1962; Gellhorn and Loofbourrow, 1963; Berelson and Steiner, 1964).

Gellhorn and Loofbourrow (1963) believe that the evidence indicates the reactivity to stimuli, acuity of perception, and precision of performance follow a bell-shaped curve of arousal. Acuity declines as one moves in either direction from the alert stage: from alert to relaxed to asleep, or from alert to excited to panic. Being awake is not enough; one must also pay attention (Chauchard, 1962). Attention seems to influence the excitation-inhibition patterns of the brain and consequently what is picked up. For example, electrographically, clicking noises can be measured in the cochlear nucleus (in the brain) of a cat. But when a mouse is placed in the cat's visual range, even though the clicks continue, they are not recorded electrographically. The cat not only is not paying attention to the clicks; they apparently are not even being noted in the brain (C. P. Deutsch, 1967). Attention may be more important to learning than association, specific qualities of particular external events, or rewards (Bakan, 1969). William James, so full of insight, suggested that the central problem of will was "the strain of keeping the attention focused" (see May, 1969, p. 79).

In general in this work, we accept James' notion, endorsed by Hilgard and others, that there is a physiological unconscious in which there are biological processes going on of which we are unaware, but that there is no unconscious and that awareness fades off into unreportable vagueness, although not unrecorded altogether (Hilgard, 1969). This unreportability may be as much because of the limitations of language as the lack of clarity of information, so that we may be able to know and feel many things we cannot express symbolically. Meanwhile, the battles rage, and we will be interested to see what the physiological psychologists finally decide (see Naylor and Lowshe, 1958; Chun and Sabin, 1968; Silverman and Spiro, 1967; Shevrin et al., 1969, 1970).

THE CNS AND INFORMATION OBTAINING

The distinctions between memory, learning, perception, and expectations are hazy and of little practical value for our purposes. It is exceedingly difficult, if not impossible, to distinguish them physiologically because they involve much the same processes (Gibson, 1966; Berelson and Steiner, 1964).

All the information a man obtains from the environment must come to the central nervous system through the senses (Berelson and Steiner, 1964; Gibson, 1966; Chauchard, 1962). There are innumerable sensory receptors spread over the body, in the skin, muscles, and tendons, or located in special sense organs such as the retina of the eye, the cochlea of the ear, the taste buds of the tongue, the olfactory zone of the nose, and the semicircular canals in the ear (Chauchard, 1962; Gray, 1959).

Although thought and memory may utilize vast areas of the cortex, there are specialized areas in the brain that receive sensations and control motor activity. The sensory localization area of the cerebral cortex is behind and parallel to the central fissure in the parietal lobe. (Imagine a watermelon with a line around the middle where you are about to cut it in half; that is roughly the location of the central fissure in the brain. The parietal lobe is just behind the fissure.) The motor localization area is just in front of the central fissure in what is called the frontal lobe. In both areas the body is disproportionately represented, with greater representation for the hands, thumbs, face, tongue and other phonatory organs, upper limbs, and feet but with less for the trunk and lower limbs. The special sense organs each have their special areas, with vision localized in the occipital lobe (the very back—posterior—end of the watermelon), auditory localization in the temporal lobe (along the lower sides of the watermelon), and olfactory sensations received directly into a primitive olfactory brain composed of the hippocampus and limbic system (roughly in the anterior-ventral or bottom front portion of the watermelon). The cellular structure of the brain in sensory and motor areas is different under the microscope. Large pyramidal cells characterize the motor areas, and smaller granular cells dominate the sensory areas (Peele, 1961; Gray, 1959; Chauchard, 1962). These sensory localizations are not always complete, with little sensation from the internal organs except in pain, hunger, thirst, and the like, and sometimes messages for two different senses arriving at the same neuron. Some cutaneous zones may receive small amounts of information from visceral areas (Chauchard, 1962).

Adjacent to these areas of sensory localization in the cerebral cortex are neural areas, which coordinate sense messages so that we can recognize objects and our body and its movements. These areas are called gnosias. Our image of our body as distinct from other objects depends on the parietal gnosia behind the sensory localizations for the body (Chauchard, 1962, pp. 107–109). The sensorial brain coordinating localized zones and utilizing all the senses includes essentially all the lateral and posterior neocortex, especially the parietal, occipital, and temporal lobes and their connections with basal center (Chauchard, 1962, p. 110).

Agnosia is the inability to recognize familiar objects or symbols through one sense or another (Chusid and McDonald, 1962, pp. 183, 108). Verbal blindness in which one can see letters but not give them a meaning as words and verbal deafness in which one hears vocalizations but cannot give them meaning as words are examples of agnosia (Chauchard, 1962).

Similar functions for the motor activities are performed by praxias located in front of the motor area, and there are apraxias involving inability to carry out motor requests. Apraxias include the inability to vocalize symbols. One may still be able to "talk to oneself" using symbols, but he may not be able to articulate the words (anarthria or motor aphasia) or to write (agraphia) (Chusid and McDonald, 1962). Unless it is a reflex, cerebral images of the motor activity are necessary before movement; thus physical training in skills involves cerebral training (Chauchard, 1962).

ON THINKING

Thinking is one of man's most subjective experiences and depends for the most part on the cerebral cortex. The cerebral network of interconnections acts as a unit, integrating all neural elements and permitting comparison and abstraction, which provides the basis for objectivity from ongoing events. Few other animals, the chimpanzee being one exception, can pay attention to anything but the immediately unfolding experience (Hebb and Thompson, 1968). Human perceptual and thought development seems to move from a dependency on the presence of stimuli and the manipulating of objects to solve problems to independence from concrete stimuli with an ability to manipulate symbols and images in order to produce solutions (M. Deutsch, 1967).

Physiological variability, which contributes to emotional experiences, is tied into the cerebral cortex in many ways, including, notably, connections between the frontal lobe and thalamus and thence to the autonomic nervous system. Stimulation of the frontal lobe produces widespread autonomic effects, including changes in circulation, respiration, pupillary reaction, and other visceral changes (Gray, 1959). Increased muscle tone characteristically accompanies, and may facilitate, thinking. The tensed muscles need not be related to thought content, since leg muscles tense with almost any mental activity. This tensing of motor muscles may assist learning and thinking (Berelson and Steiner, 1964; Chauchard, 1962).

Apparently, when attentively using our brain we do not engage in several lines of thought simultaneously but attend to different things alternately so that it appears simultaneous (Hilgard, 1969). Work on daydreaming while performing a task indicates that the:

> individual clearly has greater potential "channel space" than he ordinarily uses and, under pressure, can manage the task of detecting signals accurately at an amazingly rapid rate without giving up his prerogative of engaging in fleeting fantasies or other manifestations of the stream of thought.
>
> It is as if the individual, in effect, makes some rapid estimates of the degree of attention demand the environment will make of him in the course of performing some task, and he allows himself an appropriate margin of time or channel space to indulge in fantasies, interpretive glosses, or some other form of self-stimulation (Singer, 1969, p. 68).

There are limits for each person in the amounts of varying kinds of information he can handle at a time. If the volume of information he must deal with becomes too great, he begins to abstract, to take short cuts, and finally the quality and quantity of his information handling and motor performances decline (Schroeder et al., 1967).

The development of an idea may involve a logical reflective approach, but often one forms and uses concepts without being articulately aware of the properties upon which the category is based or the step-by-step process by which conceptualization was accomplished. Most people are capable of skills they cannot explain but they can perform. They know when things "feel right." This applies to symbol and image manipulation as well as motor skills (Gibson, 1966; Berelson and Steiner, 1964). Editors may have a clear sense of what kinds of articles are right for their magazines without being able to write out in words what exactly satisfies them (Gunther, 1968). In everyday language we sometimes refer to these feelings as intuition.

The development of an intuitive insight may come suddenly in a flash of understanding, sometimes called the "a-ha" or "eureka" experience, or it may unfold gradually. It may be a mild sense of "getting it," or it may involve a rather intense and sudden physiological response akin to the startle response. It may turn out that the physiological response in this case may be a developmental differentiation of the surprise or startle responses of infants. Once these insights are attained they seem to be rather stable and do not seem to degenerate gradually, as conditioned responses do (Berelson and Steiner, 1964). The common psychophysiological model for such insights is one of the association of neural representations not previously associated. The occurrence of these associations and the production of the intuitive insight or flash of understanding do not seem to be under our decisive control, although we can improve their probability by focusing our attention on relevant information.

LANGUAGE

The greater complexity of the human brain provides the sensory and motor precision required to make sounds, write letters, and discriminate and relate those sounds and visual stimuli comprising symbols. This capacity involves representations in the brain of the auditory stimuli of the word's sound, the visual structure of the word read, the motor and sensory image of the position of the phonatory muscles saying the word, and the motor and sensory image of writing the word (Chauchard, 1962). The capacity to think in terms of symbols, to talk to oneself, both seem to be a distinctively human capacity. Men seem to carry on a sort of running silent commentary on what is going on, and disturbances in this capacity to carry on inner conversation sometimes affects problem-solving adversely (Hilgard, 1969; M. Deutsch, 1962). The disruption of the ability to think in terms of language, like thought in general, can only be disturbed with extensive lesions of the brain. An example is Wernicke's aphasia, "in which the patient can articulate but can no longer find his words" (Chauchard, 1962, p. 120, 180).

Even though animals do not, as far as we know, use symbols, they may communicate with signs and may "think" by association of images and thereby solve problems. Although a child who has learned a language quickly surpasses the monkey, "it is not only the possibilities of speech that are involved here, but also the sheer cerebral maturation that makes this speech possible. A man who has not learned how to speak still has a way of thinking by means of images that is very superior to an animal's way of thinking by means of images" (Chauchard, 1962, p. 121; see also M. Deutsch, 1967). Images cannot be communicated, but if one has symbols he can discuss the images he subjectively experiences.

The degree to which language determines or distorts what is perceived is still not clear. At one extreme are those that believe that thought and perceptions are determined by the structure and content of the language, for example Whorf. At the other extreme are those who believe that language need not distort one's perceptions and that the perceptual process can expose language inadequacies (for example, Gibson, 1966). In the middle are those like Vygotsky, who suggest that thought is a "shadow" lacking refinement and development until language becomes part of thought (M. Deutsch, 1967; Gibson, 1966).

There seem to be at least two dimensions of attentive thinking. One is the degree to which one is thinking in terms of symbols or in terms of images of a nonsymbolic nature. The other dimension is a continuum from uncritical awareness to sharply focused attention. At one extreme are the free-association and stream-of-consciousness experiences in which one pays attention to images and symbols but in a very open, uncritical, relaxed, and usually nonmanipulative way. At the other extreme is sharply focused attention in which images and symbols are carefully related in a logical or rational way.

This brief introductory discussion of neurophysiology and neuroanatomy has been included in the hope that it makes our model more comprehensible, particularly our conceptualization of subjective. In our model subjectivity is defined as the experience of being a functioning organism. It is a property of organisms in resonation with the environment. Objective observations of neurological functioning inform us of subjectivity only to the degree that the person observed tells us what he is experiencing at the same time.

Let us now look at two broad models of perception for clues to the nature of the information exchange between the environment and the resonating person and for an answer to the question of what information is.

Models of Information Perception and Learning

The acceptance of the idea that all information comes to us through the senses rather than from some supernatural source has not meant that a complete consensus has been reached on how man obtains information from his environment. We now examine two models of perception and learning, neither of which is entirely adequate, but each contributes to our understanding of major aspects of perception and learning. There seem to be two major categories of learning that can be separated analytically but which occur together in living situations: (1) the learning of information and (2) the learning of behavior. These two distinguish between acquiring information about the environment and learning responses to the information. The first of the two models we discuss is subsumed under the general label of the sensation model.

THE SENSATION MODEL

There are two basic assumptions underlying the sensation model: (1) the senses are the only source of knowledge about the environment, and (2) each sensory organ provides unique qualities (sensations) of experience. The first assumption was formulated in 1690 by John Locke in his doctrine of the *tabula rasa* or "blank tablet" of the mind at birth. It was pursued in both England and France during the eighteenth and nineteenth centuries and is now widely accepted in science. The second assumption came from Johannes Muller's doctrine of the specific qualities of nerves in 1826, strengthened by Sherrington's position in 1906, that there had to be special receptors for each of the senses (Gibson, 1966).

The five senses stated by Aristotle and still widely taught are inadequate. They do not include other kinds of experiences, such as what is now called proprioception (awareness of position and location of body parts, especially the limbs). Efforts to inventory the sensations have all failed, with distinct sensations fading off into vague unreportable feelings. The list of sensory modalites or senses in textbooks vary from 6 to 12, with no acceptable list yet produced. Boring in 1942 in *Sensation and Perception in the History of Experimental Psychology* reviewed these efforts (Gibson, 1966).

Chauchard defines sensation as an:

> elementary state of consciousness informing us of the stimulation of an organ of the senses; their co-ordination produces perception. Sensation is judged by behavior or, in man, by what he says about it. Sensation is the awareness of a cerebral pattern which is the reflection of sensorial excitation. The existance of a pattern of sensation therefore does not depend on awareness (1962, p. 187).

C.P. Deutsch defines sensations or sensory data as the "uninterpreted product of the stimulation of end organs, or receptors . . ." (1967, p. 152). Sensation is fundamentally a matter of energy change or differentiation. A certain amount of differentiation and contrast in sensory stimuli is necessary for normal orientation, contrast being "one of the most attention-compelling attributes of a stimulus" (Berelson and Steiner, 1964, p. 100).

Man is constantly being stimulated by a vast array of input, and usually he can respond to only a small fraction of it at a time. Each sense organ is stimulated only by particular physical phenomena and can reproduce only an incomplete picture of the situation. The image of the event is not transferred unchanged and whole like a picture to the brain, as Johannes Muller thought. There are difficulties with transposing different phenomena into a single electrical code, which is further deformed in the course of its ascent through various relays to the brain, then transformed from electrical code into a mosaic of excitations and inhibitions and neural configurations in the brain (Chauchard, 1962; C. P. Deutsch, 1967).

Sensations can be related into a single synthetic image only if earlier sensations have been retained to be combined with the later ones. Thus it is necessary to conceive that every sensation and synthesis of sensations lays down a trace in the brain of some sort. These traces accumulate and are capable of presenting again the original information. Usually these traces are conceived of in terms of changes in neural structure, as discussed earlier (microgrowth of synapses and so forth). These accumulated traces provide "meaning" for later sensation input. The sensations have no meaning until they are related to past associations and syntheses of similar sensations, when they take on meaning (Gibson, 1966). Symbols are thought to be learned by conditioning or by association with sensation syntheses. The symbols, once learned, provide meaning for the sensation syntheses they label (Chauchard, 1962).

Perception is generally defined as "the process of organizing and interpreting sensory data by combining them with the results of previous experiences" (C. P. Deutsch, 1967, p. 152). Followers of this perspective generally argue that perception cannot occur without memory. There is no perception without previous experience, just the experiencing of sensations (C. P. Deutsch, 1967; Gibson, 1966). Man does not educate his sensitivity or ability to pick up sensation, but rather he learns to interpret the cerebral sensory image better, distinguishing details and assigning meaning. The elementary sensations and the capacity to synthesize and integrate them is innate. The actual production of syntheses, however, is the result of the association of sensations that repeatedly occur together, and it is enhanced by acquired skill and training. One is perceiving when he is paying attention to the synthetic image of a collection of sensations and is less aware of the sensations themselves (Chauchard, 1962; C. P. Deutsch, 1967).

The sensation-model learning theories that predominate are those dealing with the observation of changes in behavior. The emphasis is on the role of reinforcement in the modification of behavioral responses to environmental stimuli. The reinforcement can come from other people or from adaptive usefulness of the behavior. Learning is generally defined as a relatively permanent change in behavior resulting from reinforced training or practice, usually expressed in terms of the increased probability of a behavior taking place, with learning inferred from the observation of performances (Bachrach, 1967). There are two major classifications of conditioning learning: classical and instrumental.

Classical conditioning is dominated by Pavlov. He originally called it conditional reflex, which is a reflex occuring under certain conditions. This term has been mistranslated to conditioned reflex or conditioned response, and these mistranslations are now part of our vocabulary (Bachrach, 1967). The stimulus that normally produces a response, such as food, is the unconditioned stimulus, and the normal response to that stimulus, such as salivation, is the unconditioned response. The conditioned stimulus is one that is not normally able to produce the unconditioned response that through training it becomes able to do. This combination of the conditioned stimulus and unconditioned response is the conditioned response (Bachrach, 1967). Conditioned stimuli are referred to as positive or negative depending on whether they are associated with a stimuli that the animal finds pleasant or unpleasant.

If the conditioned stimulus is repeatedly presented without also presenting the reinforcing unconditioned stimulus, the conditioned stimulus becomes less and less likely to produce the unconditioned response; this is called extinction of the conditioned response. Neither conditioning nor extinction requires conscious attention or awareness of the stimulus (Berelson and Steiner, 1964). The conditioning can sometimes be observed in brain responses. For example, the visual cortical area (occipital lobe) records no noticeable effect when sound is the stimulus, but if the sound is conditioned to a light, then that sound alone can produce neural activity in the visual cortex (Berelson and Steiner, 1964).

Once the conditioned response is established, there is an automatic generalizing to stimuli similar to the conditioned stimuli. That is, the more similar the stimuli to the one that the animal is conditioned to, the more likely that stimuli is to produce the same response, as though the animal were conditioned to it also. This reaction continues unless the animal is taught by reinforcement to discriminate between the similar stimuli and to respond only to one.

The extrapolation of work in classical conditioning on stimulus generalization to social behavior offers some intriguing possibilities for explanation. Whole classes of social phenomena can become conditioned stimuli through stimulus generalization. For example, hatred for one's father could become hatred for all males or all authority figures, with no discrimination between the male authority figure who was the father and other males or authority figures. A collection of rather innocent stimuli can also become associated with a negative stimuli. For example, one may respond with fear to a color associated with the garments of the hated father (Berelson and Steiner, 1964).

Conditioning-learning theories offer one plausible, probably the most popular, explanation for the way language is learned. The spoken sound, which is a "word," becomes associated with an object, such as a bottle, and the sound is capable of producing images of the bottle. Then the conditioned stimulus, the spoken word "bottle," becomes a reinforcement to establish a conditioned response to the written word "bottle." The spoken and written words "bottle" can be used as reinforcements to learn foreign language equivalents. This is called second-order conditioning (Berelson and Steiner, 1964).

Instrumental or operant conditioning is generally associated with Skinner. Essentially, instrumental conditioning involves a freely moving animal with certain behaviors being reinforced by pleasant stimuli or by the avoidance of unpleasant stimuli. New tasks can be learned or taught by reinforcing each successively more effective approximation of the desired new act. When the response is followed by a reward or other reinforcement, the probability of the recurrence of that response increases. When the reinforcement no longer occurs, the response rate tends to return to preconditioning levels. This process is called extinction. Punishment or negative stimuli that has been conditioned to an animal's freely emitted behavior reduces the probability of the recurrence of the response but does not seem to extinguish it. When punishment or a negative stimulus is withdrawn, the previous response rate is reestablished. A stimuli that becomes associated with a wide variety of reinforced behavior can itself become a powerful generalized reinforcer, effective under a variety of conditions and extremely difficult to extinguish. Instrumental, like classical, conditioning can occur without awareness, even in the case of language as reinforcers (Berelson and Steiner, 1964).

The manner in which the reinforcements are applied has some interesting consequences on the way behavior is learned and maintained. One can reinforce every correct performance, which is the quickest way to establish new behavior. It is also the quickest to be extinguished when reinforcement stops, presumably because the fact that the behavior is no longer going to be rewarded is immediately apparent. One may partially reinforce the behavior by either rewarding every *n*th correct performance or the first correct performance after a given time lapse. This manner takes longer to establish the new behavior, but it also takes longer for the learned behavior to be extinguished, presumably because the animal takes longer to be sure that the behavior is not going to be rewarded since he has become accustomed to unrewarded performance. One may be rewarded for correct performance at various inconsistent periods of time or rates or completely at random. Behavior learned through such reinforcement seems to be the most stable of all once learned. Gambling and superstitious behavior might be learned and then persist as a result of such reinforcements. These reinforcement relations hold generally for negative reinforcement or punishment as well as positive reinforcement. There seems to be evidence that a goal is more attractive if it takes more responses or work to attain it, and the frequency of response may decline with the increase in the frequency of reinforcement (Berelson and Steiner, 1964; Homans, 1961).

The findings on transfer of training also are of interest. If the stimuli of the new task is similar to that of the old and the new response is similar to the old, there is high transfer; if the new stimuli are dissimilar and the new response similar to old ones, there is slight transfer; if the stimuli are dissimilar and the response is also dissimilar, there is no effect; but if the stimuli is similar and the response dissimilar, there is a negative transfer effect. Thus if one is faced with similar stimuli, such as words, but different responses, such as having to learn to put the fingers in different places on a rearranged keyboard, one may find learning the new task is very difficult, and even if successful the old responses are likely to reappear under the worst possible circumstances, as in times of crises (Berelson and Steiner, 1964, p. 161). Conflicts in new responses required for old stimuli, then, should bear special attention in a study of social requirements and their influence on physiological responses of participants.

Most conditioning studies are on animals, a few on humans, but all are limited to rather narrow forms of behavior, usually in a laboratory. The principles have been freely extrapolated to interpretation of human behavior and do seem promising. However, as Bijou (1969) and Harlow (1969) warn, primate social behavior cannot be explained in terms of learning alone. Learning should be considered an element in a whole. Learning by conditioning cannot explain social behavior; it cannot even explain all forms of information learning.

There is too much information learned about the environment and exchanged through verbal communication that is not explained by the conditioning learning theories. An advocate of the sensation model might argue that such information processes and insights not explained by conditioning theory could be explained in terms of association of neural traces in the brain. This may be true, but if association is not the same as conditioning by reinforcement, then the theoretical explanation of the processes by which associations develop and interrelate seems to be more at the level of conjecture than of empirical findings.

The conditioning models of perception and learning are useful in many ways, but it is difficult to see how one would apply them to sociological research. The discovery of which phenomena one has been conditioned to in social experiences, permitting predictions of behavioral and physiological responses to social situations, would require of each person arduous and time-consuming examinations in a laboratory. Even then a crucial conditioned stimulus might be missed. Consequently, this perspective hardly seems satisfactory for developing conceptualizations of the relations between social behavior and physiological processes that could assist physicians and medical workers in making rapid assessments or predictions.

The following model is discussed at some length because it is compatible with our model of man as an active agent in the environment resonating with the information it contains. It builds upon the sensation model and tries to overcome some of its shortcomings.

SENSES AS PERCEPTUAL SYSTEMS MODEL

This model is the work of James J. Gibson (1966) and his wife Eleanor J. Gibson (1969). It is built upon the same kind of hard, empirical evidence and even much of the same evidence as the sensation model, but it offers a fresh way of conceiving of information obtaining and processing in humans. One of the essential differences is that the sensation model views sensory impulses as meaningless, with meaning or information properties being the result of association and synthesis of sensations in the brain in conjunction with the memory of past experiences. The perceptual systems model views sensory data as that already containing information. The information is always present in the environment, and the sensory equipment and brain simply pick it up and apprehend it. Memory of past experiences is not requisite for this to occur. Gibson believes:

> the available stimulation surrounding an organism has structure, both simultaneous and successive, and . . . this structure depends on sources in the outer environment. If the invariants of this structure can be registered by a perceptual system, the constants of neural input will correspond to the constants of stimulus energy, although the one will not copy the other (Gibson, 1966, p. 267).

Gibson distinguishes between sources of stimulation (such as objects and events) and stimuli. The stimuli are "patterns and transformation of energy at receptors," which may specify the source but is emphatically not the same thing as its source (Gibson: 1966, p. 28). In the case of the eyes, "the retina jerks about . . . it has a rapid tremor . . . it even has a gap in it (the blind spot) . . . it is a scintillation, not an image" (Gibson, 1966, pp. 262–263). But even so, the neurophysiological correspondance to the stimuli from a source is such that:

> meaningful information can be said to exist inside the nervous system as well as outside. The brain is relieved of the necessity of constructing such information by *any* process—innate rational powers (theoretical nativism), the storehouse of memory (empiricism), or form-fields (Gestalt theory). The brain can be treated as the highest of several centers of the nervous system governing

the perceptual systems. Instead of postulating that the brain constructs information from the input of a sensory nerve, we can suppose that the centers of
the nervous system, including the brain, resonate to information (Gibson,
1966, p. 267).

The brain and the sense receptors are seen as ways of actively seeking
and extracting information from the "flowing array of ambient energy"
in the environment rather than as initiators of signals to be carried as
messages to the brain, which organizes and processes them. For Gibson,
to sense is to detect something rather than to have a sensation. It is not
necessary for sensations to be paid attention to for the stimuli information to be perceived. One does not have to pay attention to sweet, sour,
heat, and so forth to perceive barbequed spare ribs.

Gibson criticizes existing work on sense organs for telling us a good
deal about sensations but little about how sense perception is actually accomplished. The measurement of physical properties of stimuli, such as
intensity, duration, and the like, has little to do with information, which
may vary along innumerable dimensions not measurable by physical in-
struments. In addition, most of the sensation studies focus on passively
stimulated animals.

Gibson uses receptor to refer to the immobile part of the input system
and organ for the mobile parts. Receptors—cells and units of cells—may
respond to mechanical energy, chemical energy, or radiation energy, such
as light and heat. Mechanoreceptors are distributed throughout the
body: in the skin, tissue, muscles, and skeletal joints. The nerve endings are of considerable variety, such as branches, sprays, baskets, and
encapsulated. Chemoreceptors are mostly in the nose and mouth of mammals, which respond to volatile and soluble substances. The photo-
receptive cells in man are the rods (for dim light) and the cones (for
color and bright light) in the retina of the eye. Receptors are usually
grouped into units connected to a single ingoing nerve fiber called the
primary afferent neuron.

A receptive unit may set off a train of impulses in its fiber but more often it
modulates an already existing train of impulses when energy is applied to it.
An "off" unit, for example, stops its spontaneous firing when excited. "On-
off" units fire bursts of impulses at the beginning and end of excitation.
Moreover, there are units of visual reception that fire only when a sharp border of the retina image falls on them, and others that fire only when a *moving* border occurs, and still others that respond to the *inclination* of a border,
or its *curvature* (Gibson, 1966, p. 40, emphasis his).

Receptors seem to modify their input as a function of changes of energy,
which provide information about sequential order, and relations of en-

ergy, which inform one of adjacent order, and not simply as a result of application of energy (Gibson, 1966, p. 41).

Organs of sensitivity contain many receptors and receptive units capable of muscular adjustment to modify the input. They must have both afferent (to the nervous system) and efferent (from the central nervous system) nerve fibers, which may be collected in a single bundle or nerve or distributed in many bundles (Gibson, 1966).

THE PERCEPTUAL SYSTEMS

Animals are by nature active information seekers with two forms of information pick-up: (1) passive, in which the stimuli are not sought, and (2) actively sought, which is the main source of information in the natural living situation of animals. The involvement of physical movement and many senses together as perceptual systems produces much richer sources of information than does the passive condition. The usual visual illusions of psychological research, such as distorted rooms, are quickly discovered if the person is allowed to move about instead of being held in one place and allowed, in most cases, to use only one eye (Gibson, 1966). The term perceptual system refers to these collections of sensory and motor elements engaged in searching out particular kinds of information. There are five perceptual systems, or modes of external attention:

1. The *basic orienting system's* main organs are the vestibular organs (semicircular canals of the inner ear) along with organs of touch. These mechanoreceptors pick up stimuli from gravity and acceleration of the head. The information they yield includes the direction of gravity and its relation to the surface on which the person is placed, the passive movement of the body, and the beginnings and endings of body movements. This system provides a frame of reference for the other systems.

2. The *auditory system's* organs are the mechanoreceptors in the cochlear organs of the inner ear that with the aid of the middle ear and auricle yield information on the nature and location of sounds by movement of the head, until the slight differences in intensity and sequence of arrival of the sound in the two ears is eliminated. By using head and body movements one can search for the sources of sound.

3. The *haptic system's* organs are mechanical and, possibly, thermoreceptors found in the skin, joints, ligaments, muscles, and tendons. Its primary mode of attention is touching. The stimuli include deformation of tissues, stretching of muscle fibers, and configurations of joints. It provides a vast amount of information including object shapes, material states, and solidity or viscosity. The receptors in the joints are of major

importance because they provide information about the relative position of limbs and parts; in the case of the hand they provide information about the shape of the object being held in terms of the configuration of the joints of the fingers, as in holding a ball (Gibson, 1966, p. 50). Both skin and joints are projected to the somesthetic area of the cortex. Skin and joint information seem to be combined into one system to register "one kind of invariant stimulus information" (Gibson, 1966, p. 114).

Gibson (1966, p. 109) suggests that painful touch is still a puzzle. The free nerve endings in the tissue cannot be exclusively concerned with pain because they seem to participate in several other kinds of haptic experience. Presumably, some unknown pattern of excitation of a combination of nerve endings specifies the onset of injury, and the event is said to hurt.

> Pain has always had a doubtful status in psychology. It is sometimes considered as one of the senses because it yields a sensation like color or taste, but it is more often considered a motive or emotion like hunger or sex because it impels to action. It depends on nervous input, for it can be eliminated by blocking nerves, but no specific receptors have been identified. . . . Internal pains do not carry much information about their causes or locations. . . . Even the correlation between pain and injury is imperfect (Gibson, 1966, p. 131).

4. The *taste-smell system's* organs are the nose and mouth. Although they may be considered as distinct organs, they act in combination to make a superordinate system that tests the "volatility, solubility, chemical composition, and physical consistency" (Gibson, 1966, p. 53) of the food. Although one can sniff food, taste requires receptors in the mouth and nose together. Eating involves feeling food as well, and this is part of the haptic system. This system has two modes of attention: (1) smelling, with chemoreceptors in the nasal cavity providing information on the nature of volatile substances; (2) tasting, with chemo- and mechanoreceptors in the oral cavity, providing information on the soluble properties of a substance and its texture (Gibson, 1966, p. 50).

Sweet, sour, salt, and bitter have been distinguished as sensation in taste, but no such distinct list of primary sensation in smell has been discovered, although some have tried (for example, Henning). It seems better to treat taste and smell as a unit seeking meaningful information rather than sensation (Gibson, 1966, p. 137).

5. The *visual system's* mode of attention is looking. Its organ is the eye with photoreceptors in the retina, and it includes ocular mechanisms such as the intrinsic eye muscles controlling the pupil dilation and ex-

trinsic muscles that control eye movement and their relation to the head and body as a whole. It picks up information from the ambient light (diffusely reflected light from objects). Although this is the most studied system, it still is not clear how the eyes pick up information. It is useful for picking up information concerning the layout of the surroundings, detecting changes, and detecting and controlling locomotion and movement (Gibson, 1966, p. 50).

In actual practice these five perceptual systems overlap, reaffirm, and complement one another in the information they obtain.

> Consider the fire . . . It is a source of four kinds of stimulation, since it gives off sound, odor, heat, and light. It crackles, smokes, radiates in the infrared band, and radiates or reflects in the visible band. Accordingly, it provides information for the ears, the nose, the skin, and the eyes. The crackling sound, the smokey odor, the projected heat, and projected dance of the colored flames all specify the same event, and each alone specifies the event (Gibson, 1966, p. 54).

Gibson further refines his model of perception with classifications along the dimension of perception-proprioception and of imposed (passive) obtained (active): (1) *imposed perception,* in which the sense organs are passive, which is the main emphasis of experimentally oriented psychologists; (2) *imposed proprioception,* the result of passive movement in which the muscles are not used, such as the passive movement of members of the body recorded by receptors in the joints; (3) *obtained perception* arising from the sense organs as they are used to explore the environment through adjustments of the body, which is Gibson's main emphasis; (4) *obtained proprioception,* occuring whenever the person moves as the result of voluntary action or reflexes, including the guiding of behavior through feedback loops (Gibson, 1966, pp. 44–46).

Gibson finds the common distinctions of receptor and effector or sensory and motor unsatisfactory because the distinctions actually are not sharp or simple. He prefers classifications that embrace both as they occur in actual behavior. Thus he has classified the acquiring or perception of information or afferent impulses in terms of obtained-imposed, perception-proprioception, as we noted previously. He suggests classifying the efferent impulses as (1) exploratory activity of the perceptual systems and (2) performatory activity of the executive systems (Gibson, 1966, pp. 44–46). In manipulations and locomotion he sees the visual system dominating the action sensitivity of muscular and articular systems. (Gibson, 1966, p. 36).

Information. Information is in the structure of the stimulus, not in the sensations experienced (E. Gibson, 1969, p. 13). "Stimulus energy, unless it has structure conveys no information" (Gibson, 1966, p. 245). The various forms of energy, (mechanical, chemical, radiation) are reflected, modified, transmitted, or produced by components of the environment. These various forms of energy, which are perceived as sights, sounds, smells, and the like, carry information about their sources in a "wholly objective way" (Gibson, 1966, pp. 14–18).

Information is obtained by perception of invariants and inhomogeneities, of same and different. Contrast is a primary requirement for this detection. It is not the uniform but the differential stimuli that provide information. A uniform visual field, such as in a white-out, provides no information. One of the techniques of sensory deprivations is to provide homogeneous sensory environments (Cohen, 1967). Contrasts or inhomogeneities provide two kinds of information about order: (1) *adjacent order,* in which the stimuli have borders and patterns and (2) *successive order,* in which the stimuli occupy time, at the very least having a beginning and an end (Gibson, 1966, p. 40).

One may examine an object he encounters with his perceptual systems from many perspectives. He may touch it, pick it up if it is small enough, walk around it, smell it, taste it, kick it, and see what happens. It may just sit there, run or fly or swim away, fall apart, bite him, make a loud noise, get a dent, drop a coconut on his head, taste good, or otherwise provide essentially objective information about itself. "The exploratory perceptual systems typically produce transformations so that the invariants can be isolated" (Gibson, 1966, p. 271). Stimuli can invariably (relatively) be experienced together in a particular configuration and be perceived through one or a series of encounters as a unique structure.

Events are perceived as invariants of continuous transformation in time, such as the properties of a fluid being poured, the melody in a symphony, or the social system in human relations. For a unitary event to be perceived, one must detect a higher-order invariant property of a sequence (E. Gibson, 1969).

Men and animals find perception of information satisfying in and of itself and do not require reinforcement from the environment in terms of rewards or practical adaptive usefulness. Successful perception is highly subjective and cannot be readily observed by an onlooker. The perceptual systems seem to hunt or tune in or resonate to information, with clarity and reduction of uncertainty themselves as rewards. The pickup and registering of information seem to reinforce the neural activity and organ adjustments that brought it about. When information is inadequate, men seem to search for more information and for clarity and to retain that which reduces uncertainty (Gibson, 1966; E. Gibson, 1969).

Perception of information, then, is the differentiation of the qualitative dimensions of the phenomena and the detection of the invariant combination of these qualities. This can be done without either previous encounters with a similar experience or dependence on memory. What past experience provides is the refinement of attention and capacity to differentiate and recognize invariants. Attention is extremely important in the development of perception. In time one can accomplish a maximum of "knowing" about the situation with a minimum of distractions by selectively perceiving, which the Gibsons call economical perception. Economical perception permits the recognition of the invariants or at least the salient ones necessary for understanding of the situation. Thus one learns the diagnostic features of the situation, the minimum information required to identify something (Gibson, 1966; E. Gibson, 1969).

Gibson (1966, p. 272) believes that much of classical conditioning can be explained alternatively by using the perceptual systems model of information pickup. The learning of Pavlov's dog to salivate at the sound of a bell that had formerly been rung when food had been presented may also be interpreted as the dog's detection of the bell-food invariant in that given situation and its response to that information. Once the animal detects that this invariant relation has terminated, we could expect his behavior to change as well. The various lengths of time required for response extinction seem to be related to the requirements for assuring that the invariant has indeed changed. In the case of instrumental learning Gibson feels that his model also applies, but that in this case behavior must precede perception. At any rate Gibson believes that classical, instrumental or other models of association of stimulus-response learning do not adequately account for the pickup of information.

Expectations and memory are both treated in the same framework by Gibson in terms of the continued perception of information. One perceives both adjacent and successive information about an object or event over time. The successive order may be perceived over varying time spans and may involve both continuity or discontinuity of contact. Past, present, and future are analytical and subjective concepts, not descriptions of successive order perception. Information does not exist as an event distinguished from the past or future. "Now" is the subjective attention to one's body at the moment and is self-consciousness rather than perception of successive order. Physical events may conform to the relation of before and after but not to past and future. Over time one perceives different aspects of the same thing or process as continued encounters clarify the invariants. One is engaging in one long, drawn-out perception in which the invariants are constantly becoming clearer.

Memory, then, is not so much an accumulation of neural traces as a state of resonance between the perceptual systems and information, with information not limited to the present as it is subjectively experienced. Panoramic views, for example, are actually looked at sequentially, but the relations are not seen as sequences but as an invariant. This is successive sampling and simultaneous grasping. A baseball player adjusts his movements as he observes the trajectory of the ball, and he moves to intercept it. This action is the result, through practice, of perception of the invariants of the ball trajectory, and it does not require conscious expectation recalled from memories. Gibson believes that one can recognize without recalling and that one can learn or perceive without remembering. He feels that there is some kind of memory in some new sense that permits man's contemplation of his past history, but learning and perception do not require it.

Gibson's treatment of memory may seem odd unless one realizes that he is reacting to the emphasis by sensation model advocates that memory is necessary for learning and perception. He is trying to clarify his own unique perceptual model in which information obtaining is a process of resonation with the environment rather than the matching of sensations against previously acquired templates or memory.

Perceptual error—misperception or illusions—may be the result of the inadequacy of available information in the environment and/or deficiencies of the perceptual process in the person. One way in which available environmental information may be inadequate might be because of a lack of minimal energy to excite receptors:

> When perception is conceived as the detection of information, the weakness of physical stimulation may cause it to be piecemeal, partial, and dependent on personal motivation. But this does not imply subthreshold perception or subception; it only suggests that a perceptual system may be sensitized to one level of information and not another (Gibson, 1966, p. 291).

Environmental information may also be inadequate because of blurring (for example, fog or haze), masking of structure (for example, sounds masked by noise or visual camouflage of many animals), conflicting or contradictory information such as when perceptual systems expected to correlate together do not (for example, a pilot flying by "the seat of his pants" may feel right side up but looking at the ground may find himself at an angle or even upside down), or as the result of various manmade distorting devices (for example, prisms or lenses).

The perceptual process may be deficient because the information is available but not picked up, such as in the failure of organ adjustment at high intensity (for example, dazzle of too much light in the eyes) or due to physiological after-effects (for example, the after-sensation of the complementary color spots). The conflict between two kinds of attention (for example, seeing railroad tracks as coming together in the distance versus perceiving that they are parallel and never join) is another instance. Selective, economical perception may have progressed to the point that exceptions or changes are not recognized. In such cases one may subjectively believe his own senses tell him the world is a way it is not (Gibson, 1966).

Perceptual learning is the increased ability to extract information from the environment. Although the newborn infant is fully equipped with perceptual systems that immediately begin to pick up information, it appears that there are some things a child cannot perceive until his body matures to a certain point. Gibson (1966, pp. 267–269) says the child "is not simply an adult without experience, or a sentient soul without memory. . . . The ability to select and abstract information about the world grows as he does." Gradually, the child learns to orient the perceptual systems more precisely and to pay attention and to respond more selectively and precisely. His growth and learning is the learning to use perceptual systems more skillfully, with his attention becoming "educated to the subtleties of stimulus information" (Gibson, 1966, p. 5; see also E. Gibson, 1969). Thus where sensation model learning theories emphasize enrichment of the meaningless sensory data through attaching new responses to old stimuli or new stimuli to old responses, the perceptual systems model shifts the emphasis to "the discovery of new stimulus invariants, new properties of the world, to which the child's repertory of responses can be applied" (Gibson, 1966, p. 6).

The education of attention in conjunction with maturation is required for perceptual development. As the child matures physically and learns, his attention becomes less captive by the stimuli and more exploratory, the exploratory search becomes more systematic and less random, and attention becomes selective and exclusive (E. Gibson, 1969, p. 456). For example, in the development of visual perception, the infant pays attention in an almost compulsory manner to high-contrast spots, edges, and corners. Differentiation of the face features begins with the eyes, then the mouth, especially when moving and widening; after the first six months unique faces and facial expressions can be discriminated. As the child grows and gains more bodily control, exploration is more effective, and slowly the child begins to discriminate separate dimensions from the "blooming, buzzing confusion" as James put it. Space perception begins as the perception of objects in terms of their edges and surfaces in relation to other objects and to the observer, not as an abstraction of dimensions such as used in drawing. Gradually from the exploration the invariant properties are detected. The perception of sameness seems to be part of the early capacities of the infant, with discrimination then developing (E. Gibson, 1969).

The effects of early deprivation are still not established. Evidence suggests a lack of perceptual curiosity and inability to sift out distinctive features from situations may develop, that is, poorly developed selective attention. There is little doubt, however, that instruction and practice can improve one's accuracy in discriminative judgements and identification.

Positive examples (what a thing is) are more useful than negative examples in learning. Being exposed to contrasts along a dimension in graduated amounts is effective in teaching continuous relational properties. Discrimination accuracy is greater if the contrasts are great enough to permit the isolation of the relative properties or dimensions. Being exposed to properties on a continuum is not so effective. Contrasts and relational and directional differences must be detected for abstraction of the invariant dimensions to be perceived.

Self-reinforcement through the feedback from one's own performance seems to be very important in perceptual learning. Language naming and production of copies facilitate perceptual learning by providing information for monitoring one's performance, as well as calling attention to distinctive features and higher-order relations (E. Gibson, 1969).

What is learned in perceptual development, then, is not content so much as skills and capacities for perceiving and for responding in a discriminating way to information not responded to previously (E. Gibson, 1969).

Representations such as pictures, maps, diagrams, and models supplement our language and provide information about invariant relations. The more the representation approximates the real experience, such as a photograph, realistic painting, or recording, the less associative learning is required (Gibson, 1966).

Language. Gibson (1966, p. 244) suggests that there are two kinds of meaning for man: verbal and perceptual. Utilizing in part Ogden and Richards (*The Meaning of Meaning,* 1930), Gibson represents these two types in the following way:

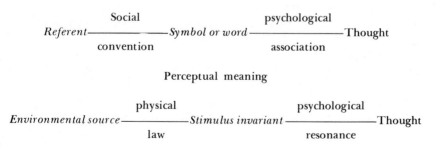

Verbal meaning

$$\text{Referent} \underset{\text{convention}}{\overset{\text{Social}}{\text{———————}}} \textit{Symbol or word} \underset{\text{association}}{\overset{\text{psychological}}{\text{———————}}} \text{Thought}$$

Perceptual meaning

$$\text{Environmental source} \underset{\text{law}}{\overset{\text{physical}}{\text{———————}}} \textit{Stimulus invariant} \underset{\text{resonance}}{\overset{\text{psychological}}{\text{———————}}} \text{Thought}$$

A very important point to be made is that according to Gibson it is possible to have considerable information about the environment without dependence upon a language. Let us look more closely at the role language plays in Gibson's model.

Gibson sees language as labels for invariants, as a means of secondary experience, and as a means by which one person can focus another's attention on invariants and discriminations concerning the environment and thus "teach" him. He distinguishes (Gibson, 1966, p. 91) between knowledge derived from direct contact with the environment involving the utilization of perceptual systems and secondhand knowledge about the environment acquired through symbolic communication. The latter seems to be a capacity peculiar to man. The direct, perceptual experience can proceed with or without language and the "curious observer can always observe more properties of the world than he can describe" (Gibson, 1966, p. 282). One must directly perceive an object or event to know it, and not just something about it, partly because of the aspects that cannot be articulately communicated and partly because more perceptual systems have gotten involved in acquainting one with the object or event.

Symbolic communication is itself a form of stimulation and information and must be perceived in the same manner as other forms of stimulation. "No symbol exists except as it is realized in sound, projected light, mechanical contact, or the like. . . . All knowledge rests on sensitivity" (Gibson, 1966, p. 26). Although one aspect of language may be its code quality, much emphasized by sensation model researchers, Gibson insists that there is more to language than a set of associations and more to learning language than learning to associate the code with the object (Gibson, 1966, pp. 280–292). Language learning is "an expression of the distinctions, abstractions, and recognitions that the child is coming to achieve in perceiving" (Gibson, 1966, p. 281). The child gets information first through perception, without the aid of language. But once he begins to learn language it helps to consolidate his perceptual development by providing labels for the invariants and by permitting communication with adults. Adults talking to a child (or other adults, of course) can educate the child's attention to perceive certain differences and invariants. The person talking to himself can enhance the tuning of his perception.

There is an unlimited range of possible discriminations to which one might pay attention. Language inevitably produces selection of attention but does not necessarily coerce perception. Although language may direct one to finer differentiation, such as the Eskimos' names for snow, there is no experimental evidence to suggest that men perceptually dissect nature along lines laid down by their native language. "It is unlikely that perceptual learning is appreciably distorted by language categories, though it is likely that it can be facilitated by calling attention, verbally, to distinctive features of things" (E. Gibson, 1969, p. 159). Words and labels seem to have greater influence on the memory of perception and on which perceptions are discussed verbally than on actual perceptions. Studies on perception of color between Zuni Indians and Anglo-Americans, who have different ways of dividing up the hues in their languages, indicate that hue discrimination is not affected by naming habits (E. Gibson, 1969, p. 160).

Those who feel language does distort perception seem to be operating on the assumption that perceptual identifying is not separable from verbal naming (for example, Whorf) and the fact that no language completely and accurately codes the environment. Gibson feels that language may distort perception to the degree that it leads us selectively to pay attention to some stimuli more than others. And when we have knowledge about something only through secondhand, symbolic contact, our understanding is incorrect or distorted to the degree that the language itself incorrectly represents the environment. Gibson, however, does not see man as a prisoner of his language, nor does he feel men must be cut off from and misunderstand those whose language cuts up the world differently.

> The basis for agreement among men exists in the available stimulus information. Men often disagree but they are not fated to do so by their language or their culture. Disagreement is not caused by inherent differences in their habits of interpreting sensory experience—habits permanently fixed by the words they use. A man can always re-educate his attention. For that matter, a man can invent new words for something he has seen himself. He can even get others to see what he has newly seen by describing it carefully, and this is a fortunate man (Gibson, 1966, p. 321).

This is a hopeful orientation. However, it raises some question as to why some people are more able than others to perceive things not provided for by the language and to trust their own perceptual experiences and why some people can go a lifetime surrounded by information and never perceive it because of language produced perceptual selection. We hope our own work offers some insight into the influence of social interaction on information perceptiveness.

The Gibsons' perceptual systems model is very promising. It solves a number of problems growing out of our sociological work that the sensation model does not handle as well. The suggestion that information can be acquired independently of language and perhaps in contradiction to it may look deceptively simple, but it has profound implications for models of social change and social involvement, which we discuss in subsequent chapters. The idea of the human organism in resonation with information in the environment is precisely the perspective we need to link the environment with the body in our own model of biosocial resonation. The emphasis on contrasts in information and on perception as in part a search for clarity and certainty support our own conclusions on the importance of these dimensions in social information processing, and these two aspects are developed as part of our overall model. We like the Gibsons' conceptualization of the role of language better than any other we have seen, and we incorporate this, too, into our model.

There are, however, some shortcomings of the model that prevent us from embracing it entirely. Gibson's model does not satisfy us with his treatment of memory and expectations. We would like to know how his perception and recognition differ in brain neurophysiology from memory and recall. We suspect that part of the problem is in the overabundance of labels. If we simply talk about information obtaining, retaining, and processing we might be better off than trying to distinguish the brain neurophysiology of perception, expectations, recognition, memory, and recall. Such terms seem to be subjective labels rather than accurate statements of brain processes, much in the same manner that various labels for emotions are subjective rather than distinguishing different physiological processes. Gibson has not adequately developed the role of symbolic articulation of predictions into his discussion of expectations. He has overreacted to the concept of memory in perception to the point that he has distorted his own model.

Although his perceptual systems model handles insight from gradual unfoldings in perceptual exploration very well, his emphasis on continuity through time of the perceptual insights process makes it difficult to explain sudden perceptual insights. Gibson attempts to explain such insights by using the classic example of the chimpanzee in a cage with a long stick and a bunch of bananas just beyond his reach outside the cage. After many futile attempts to reach the bananas with his hand, the chimpanzee suddenly seizes the stick and rakes in the bananas. This is usually explained in terms of the association of neural traces. Gibson suggests that the chimp perceived the "rake-character" of the stick (Gibson, 1966, pp. 273–274). That may be so, but the question is how did he perceive it, and why all of a sudden? To suggest that it was appropriate to the task, as Eleanor Gibson might, doesn't help much in understanding the mechanisms of such insight. We do not think the Gibsons have found an adequate way to explain the "a-ha" experience from their perspective. For sudden insights and for reflective thinking detached from the ongoing situation, the sensation model's association of traces still offers perhaps more useful explanations.

The absence of any one completely satisfactory model of thought, learning, and perception has made it necessary for us to present these two different, broad theories together, because each seems to handle some things very well and others not at all well. Perhaps some compromise between them is the answer. In the meantime it will be necessary to watch the developments in these areas.

Implications for Some Sociological Notions

ANNA AND ISABELLE

The Gibsons' perceptual systems model might be applied to the oft-cited cases of Anna and Isabelle, which sociologists suggest are evidence of the importance of social interaction and language in learning and especially in learning social customs (see Toby, 1964, pp. 250–257; Vernon, 1965, p. 77). Both Anna and Isabelle were illegitimate children, each isolated by her relatives until she was discovered at about the age of six and taken into public institutions. Anna was isolated alone in a room with little stimulation of any kind and undernourished. Isabelle was isolated in a dark room with her deaf-mute mother. When found, neither was capable of symbolic communication, although Isabelle could use gestures. Both were very limited in their response capacities and demonstrated minimal perceptual development. Anna was so apathetic to sound stimuli that it was uncertain whether she could hear or not. Isabelle had little awareness of the relations of objects. Anna did not receive expert attention in public institutions and advanced slowly, learning language slowly, mainly communicating in phrases just before her death at the age of ten and a half. Isabelle received concentrated, expert attention and soon learned language; thereafter she developed very rapidly and was nearly normal two years after her discovery. The usual sociological interpretations revolve around observations that "until Isabelle's speech and language development, she had all the characteristics of a feeble-minded child" and, that these two cases proved an opportunity to "observe *concretely separated* two factors in the development of human personality which are always otherwise only analytically separated, the biogenic and the sociogenic factors" (K. Davis, 1947, p. 437, emphasis Davis'). Although these studies, at least in the case of Isabelle, do demonstrate the utility of language, it should be realized that language provided a means to fill the child's perceptual development gaps by calling attention to the invariants of the environment and providing secondhand perceptual experience. A good deal of the behavioral improvement may have been the result of perceptual development and increased capacities owing to the new, vastly richer en-

vironment provided by social interaction, not simply the fact that the
child could think and talk with words.

Sociologists frequently use these studies to suggest that Anna and Isabelle before they were found and socially embraced were examples of
what people would be like if there were no social participation or language. But these girls were not simply without language and social contact; they were also in an unusually deprived natural environment. There
was little opportunity to explore and experience outside of their
darkened rooms. What we are observing in Anna and Isabelle is a complex consequence of sensory deprivation, lack of environmental contact at
crucial points of physiological development, possibly malnutrition, a lack
of social contacts, and lack of language. We most emphatically are *not*
seeing the concrete separation of biogenic and sociogenic factors. The organism by nature does not develop in a vacuum but must be considered
while it is resonating in its normal environment. It is incorrect to say
that what we see happening to a vegetating body in isolation is the true
or complete picture of the organism's basic nature. It seems to us that the
proper use of the stories of Anna and Isabelle is to illustrate the idea that
social patterns are not instinctive but are learned through interaction
with other people. The role of language, social symbols, and social training in a human being's ability to perceive effectively and to manipulate
his environment would better be illuminated by examining cases of social
isolation in which the isolate had free movement in a natural environment.

PERCEPTION AND NORMS

The socialization process is frequently described as the internalization of
cultural norms (following Parsons especially, see Parsons and Bales, 1955;
Toby, 1964; Bredemeier and Stephenson, 1962). The notion of internalization, though a valuable one, seems to suggest a certain compulsiveness
and irresistability similar to conditioned responses. The role of continued
perception in modification of and monitoring of the cultural norms one
practices has not been adequately explored in sociology. The dramaturgi-
cal or interactionists' position (such as Irving Goffman, Gregory Stone)
that meaning is constantly changing and emerging from each social encounter seems to be a plausible suggestion from the point of view of the
Gibsons' model. We might suggest that this is true of all social norms,
that our image of them is constantly being validated and modified by
ongoing social interaction. These social norms could be viewed as invariants in which one may discover new dimensions and differentations
over the years. Socialization might more properly be viewed as a contin-

ual unfolding and validating perceptual process that is never complete for a given norm. From this point of view, changing social behavior is not so much the struggle between the conscious mind and the unconscious, internalized norm, but rather the perception of new, invariant relations pertaining to social norms and the nature of things. The periods of vacillation may be the result of uncertainty from the lack of clarity as to the correct invariant relation or the more advantageous pattern to follow rather than the nagging of old, internalized patterns. However, to the degree physiological accommodation has been made to the social norm, producing physical modification or cyclical adjustments (such as to number of meals and their size and time of serving), the changing of social patterns may require considerable effort and establishment of new physiological patterns. Further work is certainly needed to clarify the relations between perception, socialization, and physiological processes.

Variations in perceptual development in social participants seem inevitable as a result of different experiences, and these variations may distinguish social groups from each other. We can expect people to have various areas in which they are perceptually developed and others in which they may be aware of few invariants. Perceptual skills may be generally applicable, but some capacities may not be; for example, mathematical skill does not seem to make one necessarily more rational than others in nonmathematical undertakings (Berelson and Steiner, 1964). At one extreme we may find people whose perceptual capacities are poorly developed and who have recognized comparatively few differentiations and invariants and are capable of few levels of abstraction. These people may turn out to be action oriented, tending to pay attention primarily to the ongoing situation and the stimulation of the moment. At the other extreme we may find people who have developed sufficient perceptual skills to be able to recognize many invariants, at least in areas of their interests, and who are capable of high levels of abstractions. These people are more likely to use reflective thought as well as direct observation of the situation. Such differences could have considerable influence on the aspects of the social milieu one responds to, and on one's relation with the social group. One may proceed at a different level of independence from the organization or be inclined to different kinds of groups.

Summary

Two general models of information obtaining by the human organism have been discussed: the widely accepted sensation model and the fresh, new, perceptual systems model.

There are two forms of learning that in living situations occur together but which have been analytically separated in the models we have been discussing: (1) learning of behavior and (2) learning of information. These two distinguish between learned responses to the information and the acquiring of information about the environment. There does not seem to be one single, acceptable model to handle both forms of learning and information processing; thus for the time being we will watch developments in both and utilize each separately as tentative explanations of the forms of information processing they handle best.

The sensation model suggests that the sense organs pick up from stimuli meaningless sensations and transmit these to the brain, where they are recorded in neural configurations through changes in the nerve cells. When the individual encounters a similar situation, the similar sensations are compared with the remembered sensations and recognized. This is perception. Perception requires memory of past sensations.

The sensations are synthesized in the brain into meaningful images by being associated one with another in similar situations. Language is learned by association with sensation configurations. In this model, information is a property of the neural syntheses of sensations in the brain and not a property of sensations or of the environment.

The sensation model learning theories revolve around conditioned responses, with reinforcement and drive reduction (or some similar notion) as the reasons for the retention of learned behavior. The emphasis is on learning new forms of behavior (as in operant conditioning) and on learning to perform old behaviors to different stimuli (as in classical conditioning). Learning is inferred from changes in behavior. Thus the emphasis is on learning behavior rather than learning information. The conditioned-response learning theories go a long way in explaining how behavior comes to take a particular form, why one responds to a particular stimuli, and, by calling attention to the nature of the reinforcement, why some behaviors are abandoned sooner than others.

Although advocates of this model often feel that they can explain all forms of learning, including information learning, in terms of reinforcement and conditioning or association, we find their arguments not entirely convincing.

The perceptual systems model focuses on information learning and suggests that information is a property of the environment in the relations of energy that stimulate sense receptors. The information is actively sought through exploratory behavior in which various properties of objects and events are discovered. These collections of properties are called invariants and are perceived directly in the environment as a result of contrasts and inhomogeneities.

Perception of invariants is a gradual process, increasing in accuracy with repeated and varied experiences with the situation and increased capacity to differential dimensions of the environment. Memory is not necessary for perception of information, which can be picked up directly from the environment. Representations of the information are produced in the brain, but these are neural representations and not picturelike projections on a screen. No association between these representations is necessary to produce meaning or information.

Language provides labels for perceived invariants, and language is itself learned through perceptions as invariants. Language provides means of secondary information exchange and for calling attention to invariant properties and improving discrimination. Although language can focus attention and lead to overselection of what is attended to so that information is distorted, language does not necessarily determine perception. All people can perceive environmental information directly, independent of language. Some do so to greater degrees than others. Incorrect information about the environment incorporated into a language can be discovered by individuals directly perceiving the environmental information. As we have pointed out, not everything perceived is ever expressable in language terms. Each person knows a good deal more than he can communicate.

Attention is seen as more important to information learning than reinforcement. Information is retained because it increases clarity, reduces uncertainty, or provides meaning. Perceptual learning is seen not only as the obtaining of information but also as the development of the perceptual systems' capacities to differentiate and to discover invariants. The development of the perceptual systems depends on both maturation of the body and training. This involves some learning of behavior in the refining of the use of the exploratory motor activity, but this is not a model for explaining changes in learned behavior or for "action."

In this work we prefer the perceptual systems model and utilize it within its limitations; however, the sensation model, despite its shortcomings, still has much to recommend it and handles some observed information processing behavior the perceptual systems model does not.

CHAPTER IV

Autonomic and Neuroendocrine
Processes and Changes
in Susceptibility to Disease
in Biosocial Resonation

The Autonomic and Neuroendocrine Systems as the Basis of
Physiological Responses to Information Processing

Information processing is capable of producing changes in the physiology
of the body which modifies one's susceptibility to disease and subsequently provide additional information for processing. The perception
of the physiological changes in one's own body have, for the most part,
been discussed by both scientists and laymen in terms of subjective labels.
The limitations of such labels as accurate designations of empirical physiological phenomena is finally being understood. Although the subjective
reports are critically important in understanding why physiological processes are modified in some situations and not others, we would be wise
to examine the physiological processes themselves from a perspective free
from the distortions of the vocabulary of the subject.

Emotions and stress have been and are still the most frequent subjective vocabularies applied to these perceived physiological changes. Sometimes emotions and stress are treated separately, sometimes together.
Emotional stress is a common label for the kinds of physiological activities we are discussing, and it tends to emphasize the similarity, if not the

96

sameness, of the physiological responses subjectively labeled stress and emotions (see Arnold, 1967, p. 124; Lazarus, 1967; Gellhorn and Loofbourrow, 1963). As we have concluded in Chapters I and II, there is no reason to use the terms stress or emotions for discussing the relations between information processing and physiological processes because there does not seem to be any real difference between them as physiological responses to information. Nor does there seem to be any great difference between the physiology of various emotions. If there is a specific physiological pattern for each emotion, it is much too subtle to be of any interest to us in predicting changes in susceptibility to disease.

It appears now that the physiological processes involved are variations of the autonomic and neuroendocrine systems. Emotions and stress responses seem mostly to be variations of the activity of the sympathetic division of the autonomic nervous system, with some emotions associated with parasympathetic activity (Gellhorn and Loofbourrow, 1963; Schachter and Singer, 1962; Mandler, 1969). What is important to us here is not so much the subjective content of the emotion but the degree of intensity and configuration of physiological activity. There is a complete continuum of autonomic and neuroendocrine activity from very mild levels to very severe reactions that might even cause death (Oken, 1967). Whether the subjective content of the experience is positive or negative is irrelevant except in predicting which situations will produce the various intensities of response. The attempt by some psychological stress researchers to distinguish between emotions and stress on the basis of positive or negative subjective content of the emotion, with stress applying only to negative evaluations (see Arnold, 1967; Lazarus, 1966) seems futile to us. Susceptibility to disease is modified to the same degree by the same physiological changes whether the changes are accompanied by positive or negative subjective affect.

Wolf and Wolff's 1947 study of Tom with a gastric fistula is a classic, early study demonstrating the two-dimensionality of the physiological response to information. They watched Tom's stomach during a variety of moods and emotions but found only two patterns, one in which the stomach wall was turgid with blood and very red, and the opposite, when it was pale. These conditions correspond with parasympathetic-sympathetic influences on the stomach (Schachter and Singer, 1962). We adopt the position, which seems currently to have considerable support, that the visceral physiological response to and in resonation with information processing is a nonspecific, general response that a wide variety of information and subjective experiences can produce. This general response is composed primarily of autonomic nervous system responses, especially the sympathetic, and neuroendocrine responses, primarily adrenocorticotropic (ACTH) hormone from the pituitary and adrenal cortical steroid hormones (see Gellhorn and Loofbourrow, 1963; Appley and Trumbull, 1967; Glass, 1967; Oken, 1967; Schachter and Singer, 1962).

THE AUTONOMIC NERVOUS SYSTEM

The autonomic nervous system is part of the central nervous system and controls visceral body functions, some entirely and some in part. It is activated mainly through the hypothalamus, brain stem, and spinal cord, although the cerebral cortex and other portions of the brain may influence it. It often operates by visceral reflexes in which impulses from the viscera and some internal sensory receptors are received in the autonomic system and appropriate responses transmitted by reflex back to the organs. It has two major portions: sympathetic and parasympathetic.

The sympathetic fibers arise in the spinal column from the thoracic and first two lumbar segments (thoracolumbar). Parallel to the spinal column within the body cavity are two chains of sympathetic ganglia, one on each side. The sympathetic fibers go from the spinal cord to the ganglia, up and down through the ganglionic chain, and out to the innervated organs, glands, and the autonomic plexes such as the cardiac, the celiac (below the diaphragm and above the stomach), the hypogastric, and a number of others (see Gray, 1959, p. 1059; Guyton, 1961, p. 259).

The parasympathetic fibers arise in the midbrain and medulla, leaving the brain with some of the cranial nerves (III, VII, IX, X), and in the second, third, and sometimes the fourth sacral segments of the spinal cord. The vagus (X) nerve is the most important cranial source.

The autonomic nerves contain both efferent and afferent fibers. The sympathetic nerve fibers at their post-ganglionic endings secrete norepinephrine, and perhaps small amounts of epinephrine. They are said to be adrenergic, from adrenalin, which is another name for epinephrine. The parasympathetic nerve fibers secrete acetylcholine at their nerve endings. Acetylcholine is the substance secreted at skeletal-muscle nerve endings, as well as by preganglionic sympathetic nerve fibers. They are called cholinergic nerves. These different secretions act on the innervated organs to produce the respective sympathetic or parasympathetic effects.

In describing the physiological influences of these two systems, one has to take note of effects they have on each organ and system. It is commonly assumed by laymen that these are two, mutually inhibitory systems, which is not entirely true. For one thing the sympathetic system influences or innervates some organs that the parasympathetic does not (for example, sweat and apocrine glands; blood vessels of the lung and muscle; skin; bone; blood coagulation and glucose levels; basal metabolism, which may increase up to 150%; adrenal cortical secretion; piloerector muscles, which make one's hair stand up; and the adrenal medulla). The parasympathetic system has some innervations the sympathetic does not, for example, the ciliary muscles of the eye (Guyton, 1961; Chusid and McDonald, 1962). In addition, the two systems must sometimes act together to produce an effect. For example, the parasympathetic system produces penis erection, and the sympathetic produces ejaculation. To add to the complexity, norepinephrine and epinephrine may both result from sympathetic responses, but each may have different effect upon the process or organ. Among the organs mutually influenced are the pupillary muscles of the eye; lacrimal, submaxillary, sublingula, and parotid glands; mucous membranes of the nose, palate, and mouth; heart; larynx; trachea, bronchi, and lungs; esophagus, stomach, and intestines; bladder; sex organs; and perhaps portions of the kidney, liver, and abdominal blood vessels—the sympathetic at least influences these three (Guyton, 1961, p. 263; Gray, 1959, p. 1059).

The autonomic nervous system requires much lower frequencies of nervous stimulation to maintain full activation, about one-tenth that required for full activation of the skeletal muscle nerves. Both the sympathetic and parasympathetic are constantly active, providing visceral tone. For example, sympathetic tone of some blood vessels keeps them half-dilated; further stimulation of the sympathetic system constricts and a decrease in stimulation dilates the vessels. The sympathetic-induced secretion of epinephrine and norepinephrine from the medulla of the adrenal gland (as contrasted with the adrenal cortex, which secretes corticosteroids) is important for maintaining sympathetic tone. For the most part, this tone maintenance is a homeostatic feedback control process.

The sympathetic system responds generally to what is called a mass discharge (Guyton, 1961, p. 269). Large portions of the system are stimulated simultaneously. However, it does occasionally activate isolated portions of the body. For example, release of heat through sweating and increased skin blood flow may occur without activating the rest of the system, dilation of blood vessels to active muscles only, and local reflexes involving only the spinal cord. The parasympathetic system, by contrast, is relatively specific in its influences, acting primarily on specific organs. There is, however, some association; for example salivary and gastric secretions can occur independently but often occur together.

The sympathetic mass discharge is sometimes referred to as the "fight or flight" system. The parasympathetic system is more related to food ingestion, stomach and intestinal gland secretion, peristalsis of the stomach and other aspects of the digestion system, and with postpranial relaxation and relaxation in general.

For comparative purposes let us provide a short list of some of the physiological influences of each. When the sympathetic system is activated the pupil of the eye dilates; heart rate increases; lung bronchi dilate; peristalsis and stomach and intestine tone decreases; sphincter tone increases; liver releases glucose; kidney, ureter, and bladder releases are inhibited; blood coagulation rate increases; body metabolism increases; adrenal cortical secretion increases; mental activity increases; excitation of piloerector muscles; muscle blood vessels dilate; and abdominal blood vessels constrict.

When the parasympathetic system is activated the pupil of the eye constricts; heart rate decreases; lung bronchi constrict; peristalsis and tone of the stomach and intestines increases; sphincter tone decreases; kidney, ureter and bladder release are excited; salivary fluids are secreted, and so forth. These processes do not necessarily occur all at once, however.

The autonomic nervous responses, especially the cardiovascular responses, tend to be polyphasic rather than simply an explosion that is suddenly over. There is generally a compensatory change in the opposite direction after any reaction. The opposite reaction to brief, abrupt changes may be as acute as the original response. An example is vasovagal fainting, which is the second phase of a highly excited response (Malmo, 1967).

THE HYPOTHALAMUS AND THE PITUITARY GLAND

The portion of the brain that is primarily responsible for autonomic and adrenal cortical control is the hypothalamus. The hypothalamus is located in the central ventral portion of the brain. Growing directly out of the hypothalamus below it and connected to it by a narrow stalk (the infundibulum) is the hypophysis or pituitary gland (Gray, 1959, p. 879).

The hypothalamus is organized into two reciprocally inhibitory zones, the anterior-lateral and posterior-medial. The anterior-lateral zone inhabits sympathetic autonomic responses and the output of adrenocorticotrophin (ACTH) from the pituitary, thus inhibiting release of hormones from the adrenal cortex; the posterior-medial portion facilitates these same processes (Bovard, see commentary in Oken, 1967; Peele, 1961).

The hypothalamus has connections with the limbic structures of the brain, which are related to emotional behavior. Apparently, the amygdala (a limbic structure) and the hippocampus (a closely related brain structure) are involved in determining when the hypothalamus stimulates the adrenal glands and autonomic system. They seem to be electrically active in novel events and in the assessment of error and success in activities, among other things (Pribram, 1967; Oken, 1967). The evidence seems to indicate that feedback occurs between the hypothalamus and the cerebral cortex, with habituation to information accompanied by a decline in the adrenal cortical responses (Gellhorn and Loofbourrow, 1963). The interrelations of the hypothalamus and other brain structures is very complex and only partially understood.

In addition to the multitude of physiological processes the hypothalamus controls or influences through the autonomic nervous system and pituitary secretions (including such basic processes as water, fat, protein, and carbohydrate metabolism; food intake; body temperature; and reproduction), it also contributes to sleep-waking mechanisms, strongly influencing cerebral cortical electrical rhythms in company with the brain stem and the thalamic reticular activating system (Peele, 1961). Its functioning varies with the degree of wakefulness and excitement; it produces increased sympathetic discharges and cortical electrical rhythm asynchrony, and it recruits previously inactive neurons in the cortex of the brain when extreme excitation occurs (Gellhorn and Loofbourrow, 1963). Some consider the hypothalamus the chief center of affective aspects of human life (Chauchard, 1962; Gellhorn and Loofbourrow, 1963).

The pituitary gland is also divided into anterior (adenohypophysis) and posterior (neurohypophysis) portions. The posterior portion releases two hormones into the blood stream as a result of nerve impulses from the anterior hypothalamus: antidiuretic hormone or vasopressin, which makes the kidney tubules permeable to water and without which little water is reabsorbed into the body, and oxytocin, which is a powerful stimulant on the pregnant uterus, especially toward the end of pregnancy.

The anterior portion of the pituitary is governed primarily by a series of blood vessels called the hypothalamic-hypophyseal portal system. Neurosecretory substances, such as corticotrophin releasing factor (CRF), are produced in the hypothalamus and carried through the portal system to the anterior pituitary, where they stimulate the secretion of specific hormones. The hormones of the anterior pituitary are of greatest interest to us in terms of the physiological responses to information. It produces a growth hormone that acts directly on practically all body tissues. It also secretes five hormones; the function of each is to stimulate a specific, target organ. These latter five are thyrotropin, which stimulates the thyroid gland; three gonadotropins, the follicle-stimulating hormone and luteinizing hormone, both of which act on the ovary and the luteotropic hormone, which acts on the ovary and the mammary gland; and the very important hormone variously called corticotrophin, corticotropic hormone, and adrenocorticotropic hormone (ACTH), which stimulates the adrenal cortex to secrete greatly increased amounts of cortisol or hydrocortisone, and to a lesser extent corticosterone and adrenal androgenic hormones (Guyton, 1961; Peele, 1961; Oken, 1967).

THE ADRENAL GLAND

The endocrine glands include the pituitary, thyroid, parathyroids, islets of Langerhans, and gonads, as well as the adrenal gland. They are called endocrine because they secrete their products, called hormones, into the blood stream rather than having ducts carry the hormone to a particular organ. Although all these glands are important in maintaining resistance to disease, the adrenal and pituitary glands seem to be the most important and most responsive to information processing. At least they have received the most attention by stress and emotion researchers.

The adrenal has two functionally distinct parts, which are independent organs in fishes and more primitive vertebrates but which are fused in the human gland. These are the cortex, which forms the outer portion and makes up the greater part of the gland, and the medulla, which forms the inner portion (Gray, 1959). The adrenal *cortex* produces several steroid hormones, including cortisone, corticosterone, aldosterone, and the hormone important for our purposes—variously labeled cortisol, hydrocortisone, and 17-hydroxycortiscosterone. Aldosterone, which affects water and electrolyte metabolism, may be released as the result of substances produced in the kidney (Oken, 1967). Among the physiological processes influenced by these adrenal cortical hormones are carbohydrate, protein, and lipid metabolism; electrolyte and water metabolism; quantity of red and white blood cells (erythrocytes, lymphocytes, and eosinophils); the structure and function of lymphoid tissue important to immunity. They augment hydrochloric acid and pepsinogen secretion of the gastric mucosa and trypsinogen secretion of the pancreas; they affect inflammatory and allergic phenomena—both cortisol and cortisone are antiinflammatory, preventing inflammation from physical, chemical, or bacterial substances and counteracting allergic hypersensitivities, which are similar to inflammation (White et al., 1959; see also the discussion of Selye's findings, 1956, on adrenal function in inflammation in Chapter II).

The normal adrenal cortex is very important to the maintenance of physiological homeostasis, which might otherwise be disrupted as a result of contacts with various noxious stimuli. The adrenalectomized animal or person has difficulty maintaining homeostasis when even mildly stimulated. The person's own internally produced hormones, such as thyroxine and vasopressin, may produce death in doses much smaller than normally tolerated. For the adrenalectomized, anything but mildly noxious stimuli may prove fatal. "It appears that diverse types of noxious stimuli impose upon the tissues of the body a markedly increased requirement for adrenal cortical hormones" (White et al., 1959, p. 924; see also Oken, 1967).

The adrenal *medulla* embryonically originated from neural tissue (ectoderm), whereas the adrenal cortex developed from glandular tissue (mesoderm). The medulla developed from primitive, sympathetic ganglia cells, and it remains under the control of the sympathetic autonomic system. It is, then, not surprising that its two distinct hormonal secretions are the same as those secreted by postganglionic sympathetic nerves: epinephrine or adrenalin and norepinephrine or noradrenalin. These two hormones are structurally very different from the steroid hormones of the cortex, being related instead to tyrosine, and they are called catecholamines. The proportions of the two hormones secreted is under control of the hypothalamus through the sympathetic nervous system (White et al., 1959). Their influence on various organs depends, in part, on the type of receptors sensitive to epinphrine and norepinephrine: alpha receptors, which react with both epinephrine and norepinephrine, and beta receptors, which react only with epinephrine (Stein, 1967).

Epinephrine, through the liver, can mobilize glucose into the blood stream and increase carbohydrate metabolism and glycogenolysis in muscles. It dilates the arterioles of the heart, brain, and skeletal muscle, and it speeds heart rate and increases its output. Oxygen consumption and carbon dioxide production increase with elevated body temperature. It can relax the smooth muscles of the gastrointestinal tract while producing constriction of the pyloric and ileocecal sphincters. It also dilates bronchial musculature. Norepinephrine primarily constricts arterioles and raises blood pressure, with much less influence than epinephrine on blood glucose and heart rate (White et al., 1959; Kety, 1967). Both cause an increase in circulating free fatty acids (Oken, 1967).

Although the influence of the catecholamines on the periphery of the body is relatively well understood, their role in the brain is still a puzzle. Norepinephrine is one of several amines found in relatively high concentrations in the brain, localized in the hypothalamus and other areas of the limbic system. Drugs that deplete the brain of amines are depressants (for example, chlorpromazine), and those which permit the accumulation of amines in the brain are antidepressant, possibly producing euphoria or hyperactivity. All the drugs having a significant effect on moods have one or the other of these effects on brain norepinephrine (Kety, 1967; Woolley, 1967). Kety (1967) suggests that norepinephrine in the brain contributes to alertness, pleasure and euphoria, anger, and fear. Other amines in the brain, such as serotonin or dopamine, are also involved. LSD and psilocybin, both hallucinogenic, have marked structural similarities to serotonin. Phenylketonuria, a genetic defect in converting dietary phenylalanine to tyrosine, seems to produce mental retardation as a result of an excess of phenylalanine in the body, which competes with the serotonin and catecholamines in the brain (Woolley, 1967).

One interesting note, and a possible source of confusion to the nonphysiologist reading the literature on stress research, has to do with the affects of artificially administered epinephrine. The nerve endings of the sympathetic nervous system primarily secrete norepinephrine and some epinephrine, but artificially administered epinephrine produces sympathetic like responses, whereas artificially administered norepinephrine does not (White et al., 1959; Schachter, 1967). As little as $\frac{1}{2}$ cc of a 1 : 1000 solution of epinephrine injected into the bloodstream produces increased heart rate and systolic blood pressure, the redistribution of blood flow to the muscles and brain, increased respiration, and increased sugar (glucose) levels (Schachter, 1967).

It appears, then, that perceived information produces changes in the central nervous system, including the hypothalamus, which initiates autonomic discharges and stimulates the pituitary to secrete hormones that in turn stimulate the appropriate endocrine glands. Some of these endocrine secretions and neurohumors, once secreted, are carried to the brain through the blood stream and further excite the brain or stimulate specific parts of the hypothalamus, thus influencing the nature and intensity of the response and accuracy of perception (Gellhorn, 1968). The neuroendocrine system is known to be extremely sensitive to a wide range of informational and environmental stimulation with perhaps the most important being the adrenal cortical activity (Brady, 1967). Hypothalamic activity, cerebral cortical arousal, muscle tone, and sympathetic discharge are all correlated. Even the conscious intention to flex an arm, though not carried out, can initiate autonomic vascular responses similar to those that occur in actual movement (Gellhorn and Loofbourrow, 1963; Gellhorn, 1968).

These systems in the biosocial resonating person are in a constant state of dynamic fluctuation, sometimes maintaining tone and varying hardly at all, at other times stimulating vigorous activity in the organ systems. Always there is the constant mutual influence between the body and the environment. As Opler puts it, "the total organism and its reactive mechanisms, including limbic system, CNS, and so forth, constantly responds, sometimes adversely for its survival to the total conditions under which it exists" (1967, p. 212).

TYPICAL METHODS UTILIZED TO MEASURE AUTONOMIC AND
NEUROENDOCRINE RESPONSES

The measurement of these general physiological responses is not a simple matter. One uses a single measure at his peril because these responses are not monolithic events with all the same physiological processes always occurring in the same proportion and directions for all people. For pragmatic reasons it is sometimes necessary to use only one measure, but to be accurate one should use several at once, particularly if one is measuring processes known to vary relatively independently of each other (Appley and Trumbull, 1967; Shapiro and Leiderman, 1964).

Peripheral Physiological Measures. There are a number of devices, mostly electronic, used to measure on the outside of the body physiological changes, which are then used as indicants of various internal changes. These include electromyographic (EMG) measurement of muscle tension and electroencephalographic (EEG) measurement of cerebral cortical activity. Autonomic responses are measured by galvanic skin response (GSR) measurement of changes in skin conductance, skin temperature, cardiovascular measures such as heart rate and blood pressure, and respiratory measures such as rate and depth of breathing (Malmo, 1967; Weybrew, 1967).

GSR is a popular measure, presumably because of the ease with which it can be used and the unobjectionable nature of the apparatus for the subject. It is usually used as a measure of arousal and autonomic activity. Some workers conceive of GSR as indicating the intensity of subjective experiences without differentiating these subjective states (see Shapiro and Leiderman, 1964, pp. 110–111). The GSR varies significantly with sleep, alert wakefulness, and activity in a simple task. It is frequently used in conjunction with heart-rate measurement because these two measures have a low correlation together and thus offer additional information about the physiological changes of the subject (Shapiro and Leiderman, 1964).

An example of creative use of peripheral measures is found in the work of Friedman and Rosenman (1960), who used a modified Reid-type polygraph (lie detector) to measure respiratory rate and changes in response to tape recordings. They also observed body movements and expressions, including teeth clenching and hand clenching (subject held a rubber bulb in his hand).

As useful as they are, we must bear in mind that external measures of physiological responses do not always present an accurate picture of internal states. Stein (1967) measured respiratory rate externally and brochiolar size internally. He found that the characteristic asthmatic respiratory rate of shortened inspiration and prolonged expiration usually associated with bronchiolar obstruction or contration was found in asthma resulting from pain or fear without bronchiolar size reduction or obstruction.

Internal Physiological Measures. Oken (1967) prefers measures of internal processes, for example, measurement of hormone levels in the blood or excreted in the urine. He feels that the peripheral measures are more subject to minor environmental shifts and idiosyncratic, individual variations than the internal measures of hormonal activities.

The most popular internal measure of the response is the measurement of changes in secretion and excretion of adrenal cortical hormones, especially 17-hydroxycorticosteroid (17-OHCS). Gellhorn and Loofbourrow (1963) feel that the liberation of ACTH and increased secretion of adrenocortical hormones into the blood and their excretion in the urine are adequate indicators of the impact of the situation on the hypothalamic system. Mason and Brady (1964) also favor use of plasma and urinary 17-OHCS as indexes of pituitary-adrenal cortical activity. A second common internal measure of the general response is the use of blood and urinary levels of epinephrine and norepinephrine—the catecholamines—as indicants of sympathetic-adrenal medullary activity. The 17-OHCS and catecholamine blood plasma and urine levels are remarkably sensitive to subjective experiences (Mason and Brady, 1964).

There are some problems, however, with these hormone measures. Measurement of blood levels of the hormones may be good for discovering rapid changes in the secretion of particular hormones, but these changes in levels are difficult to interpret or to compare. For example, blood levels of epinephrine reflect both the rate of secretion of the adrenal medulla and the rate of its disappearance from the blood as a result of liver metabolism or excretion by the kidney. Variations in rates of removal of epinephrine can produce errors in interpretation of secretion amounts and rates (Kety, 1967). In addition, the half-life of epinephrine (the period of time it takes for half a quantity of the hormone to disappear) is short compared with the corticosteroid's, making accurate assessment of quantities and rates more difficult. Urinary measurement of epinephrine and its metabolites and blood levels offer some indication of higher concentrations, although they are of little value in timing the changes precisely. The blood and urinary measurement of norepinephrine is even more inaccurate because a considerable amount of the norepinephrine secreted by nerve endings is taken back into these nerve endings without passing into the blood stream (Kety, 1967).

Other measures of internal processes include measurement of electrolyte balance, various metabolic products and processes, and changes in white blood cell levels and morphology—lymphocytes and eosinophils (Weybrew, 1967; Selye, 1956).

It is important to keep several things in mind when using these methods. One factor is that there is considerable variation between individuals in the nature of their physiological response to a particular situation. These variations cannot be adequately explained without paying attention to the person's subjective definition of the situation. However, given a situation a group of people have subjectively defined the same way, there are still variations in the intensity and configuration of various autonomic and neuroendocrine system responses between individuals. Yet a given individual may exhibit considerable consistency in the configuration and intensity of autonomic and neuroendocrine responses to given subjective experiences. Consequently, when measuring the physiological responses of groups in given situations one must be very careful to remember that the basic pattern sought is found in each individual's response configuration. Too many studies try to discover "typical" human physiological patterns for given situations by comparing individuals and looking for the pattern common to all in the given situation. Such studies often yield conflicting and confusing findings because individual pattern variations are ignored. There are some interesting and carefully done studies examining the degree of convergence between physiological patterns of people in the same situation working together. These usually take account of individual patterns and focus on their modification in social interaction (Lazarus, 1966, 1967; Appley and Trumbull, 1967 b; Malmo, 1967; Oken, 1967).

Given the polyphasic nature of the autonomic response, it would seem desirable to measure continuously the entire response sequence in a situation. Without it, there is always the danger that the configuration measured for an individual represents only a segment of a polyphasic response. One could make serious errors in classifying if one assumed the reaction to the original response was that person's response (Oken, 1967).

Finally, we must be extremely cautious about assigning subjective states to the person on the basis of physiological responses, or conversely, of assuming to know the physiological configuration when only the subjective evaluation is known. Although such correlations can occur in a very general way, as a rule they must be ascertained for each individual. At this point it seems necessary to make it a practice to measure both subjective and physiological variables together, using appropriate methods for each (Gerard, 1964; Cohen, 1967; Lacey, 1967).

The Biosocial Resonation of Autonomic and Neuroendocrine
Systems with Information and Social Participation

ON THE SPECIFIC RESPONSE ORIENTATION

In Chapter I we comment on the limitations of the specificity approach
in psychosomatic research, in which specific situations and subjective
states were thought to produce specific illnesses. We also discuss and reject, for our purposes, theories of emotion that suggest that each subjective emotion corresponded to a unique physiological configuration. Although the evidence has not supported these positions and they have
fallen in disfavor in general, they are still alive, and some modification of
them may yet prove to hold part of the correct picture. Those who favor
the specific approach tend to focus on the similarities between physiological responses of many people to a particular situation and minimize the
differences in physiological patterns between individuals. There is a tendency to imply that everyone responds similarly to similar situations or
subjective evaluations (Lacey is an exception to this tendency).

One of the more provacative studies from this orientation was done by
D. Graham et al. (1962) in which they were able to induce urticaria
(hives) and hypertension in hypnotized patients by suggesting certain attitudes. To produce urticaria they told patients they felt they were being
treated unfairly but could do nothing about it. They were helpless and
innocent victims. To produce hypertension they told each subject that he
was about to be attacked and hurt painfully, that he must be constantly
on the lookout. These suggestions seem very similar to the kinds of attitudes Wolff (1953) tied to the body's protective reaction patterns (see
Chapter II for a discussion of Wolff). However, we must remain somewhat skeptical until the physiological links between the suggestion and
the response can be demonstrated to produce only one pathology, that
they are not capable of producing a number of physiological changes and
pathologies which are not being observed, and until it can be reasonably
established that this same response occurs in everyone who holds that attitude.

Lacey is generally considered a major figure in this orientation, and his
work is more sensitive to the advances of physiological psychology that
led to the rejection of the specificity approach in the first place. He summarizes the evidence into two conslusions: (1) a large number of physiological processes are simultaneously activated to arousal by stimuli, probably by separate but intimately related pathways; and (2) these processes

show only moderate intercorrelations (Lacey, 1967). These conclusions seem to be rather well established (see Appley and Trumbull, 1967 b; Gellhorn and Loofbourrow, 1963). The disagreement seems to revolve around the degree to which these physiological processes are aroused simultaneously. Are they almost always aroused simultaneously in the same configuration for given individuals in a wide variety of situations, or are they rarely aroused simultaneously in the same configuration, with similar configurations corresponding to similar situations?

Lacey believes that the evidence indicates that electrocortical, autonomic, and behavioral arousals can be considered as relatively independent. EEG activation need not be related to active behavior. Normal EEG's have been found in comatose patients, and normal behavior has been found with very-low-background EEG activity. The physiological variables usually correlate with behavioral arousal, but there are exceptions. Even when they do correlate together, they do not respond as a whole in the sense that all of them show equal increments or decrements of activity. He agrees with our earlier emphasis that intraindividual correlations of physiological processes using several measures is the proper approach, rather than using a few measures or focusing on interindividual comparisons.

Lacey says:

> I propose that activation or arousal processes are not unidimensional but multidimensional and that the activation processes do *not* reflect just the intensive dimension of behavior but also the intended aim or goal of the behavior . . . the nature of the transaction between the organism and its environment (Lacey, 1967, p. 25, emphasis his).

He suggests that similar situations involve similar configurations of physiological and behavioral arousal. He proposes the concept of situation stereotypy, in which classes of similar stimuli or information produce a configuration of physiological responses more or less specific for that particular class of situations for that person. The specificity is evidently in large measure the result of the various physiological processes of the behavior required or engaged in, in the situation and the goals involved.

The physiological processes we focus on in this chapter are those of the autonomic and neuroendocrine systems. Lacey's model incorporates variations in somatic, cerebral, and behavioral activity as well, noting the correlation but relative independence between them. In order to find a specific pattern of physiological response to a situation, it may be necessary to focus on all of these. Such information may be of interest to physiological psychologists, but trying to catalogue physiological variations of the whole body for every conceivable situation classification does not seem a practical approach to examining and predicting influences of social experiences on physical health for large numbers of people. We suspect that much of Lacey's situation specificity would evaporate if he focused only on the autonomic and neuroendocrine systems and subjective situations.

One of Lacey's (1967) most oft-cited findings deals with the sensitivity of the cardiovascular system, specifically the heart rate and blood pressure, to the nature of information processing. He found that attentive observation, which he called environmental detection, and reflective problem solving, which he called environmental rejection because one is not paying attention to the information in the environment at that moment, were differentiated by the cardiovascular activity accompanying them. He used several physiological measures and found that all of them, with the exception of the measures of heart rate and blood pressure, showed physiological arousal for both environmental detection and rejection. However, environmental detection was accompanied by cardiac deceleration and stabilization, with either a decrease in blood pressure or much less of an increase than expected with physiological arousal. Environmental rejection, on the other hand, was accompanied by cardiac acceleration and increased blood pressure. When these two information processes were balanced experimentally, the cardiac and blood pressure responses were essentially zero, whereas other physiological measures showed great activation. The cardiac deceleration, or environmental detection, was accompanied by reduced reaction time and increased sensorimotor readiness. "The decelerator seems to be wide open to his environment, for reception of input and for the release of simple responses to these inputs" (Lacey, 1967, p. 36). However, cardiac deceleration was not always proof of attention, nor its lack of inattention.

This dichotomy is similar to Pribram's (1967) participatory-preparatory dichotomy and has some things in common with Witkin's field-dependent and field-independent dichotomy (Cohen, 1967). It has often been taken as evidence (see Lazarus, 1966) that there are specific physiological responses for various coping or problem-solving activities or for various subjective responses to a situation. Lacey's findings indicate that there is only a simple dichotomy in heart rate and blood pressure responses. One response occurs when a person is paying attention to the environment, the other when he is thinking about the solution to some problem. Lacey's findings indicate no evidence that there are different specific physiological responses to the various *contents* of what is being paid attention to or the problem being solved or the solution selected. Oken (1967) found this same dichotomy in his research, and he interprets it not as two distinctive patterns of response but rather as differing degrees of arousal. He points out that although many people think epinephrine raises blood pressure, small doses actually produce a drop in diastolic blood pressure as a result of vasodilator properties. Environmental detection could be mild arousal and environmental rejection more pronounced arousal.

Oken (1967) believes that physiology studies have adequately worked out the dimensions of the nonspecifically induced, more general physiological responses, and physiologists are now turning to the subtle specificities found in the data on these responses. He feels that the nonspecific, general responses make up the major portion of responses to information but exhibit variations between individuals, with possibly subtle variations for different situations, emotions, and subjective states. The variations for different emotions and situations, if they occur, have yet to be established. As Oken (1967, p. 61) puts it, "our knowledge of specific patterns remains very meager. There are no glamorous major insights, no 'breakthroughs' to report."

Before leaving the problem of specificity we should take brief note of Horowitz' suggestion (Horowitz et al., 1964) that some of the physiological specificity may be due in part to psychological acts. His evidence indicates that small acts such as muscle twitches may be considered as part of larger psychological acts, and he suggests the possibility that changes in heart rate, GSR, and other physiological processes may be similarly directly induced by conscious, goal-directed thought. Research has shown that students of Zen can be taught to identify the occurrence of their own EEG alpha rhythm, and even to attain some degree of control over it (Nowlis, see discussion in Weybrew, 1967, p. 60). Horowitz feels that this line of research has received too little attention.

Throughout this work we primarily consider variations in nonspecifically induced, general responses and their relation with disease susceptibility, information processing, and social interaction. We will wait for more conclusive and useful evidence on specificity before incorporating it into our model.

THE NONSPECIFICALLY INDUCED GENERAL
PHYSIOLOGICAL RESPONSES

In contrast to the specific response orientation, there is the position that there are only a few nonspecifically induced physiological responses revolving around the sympathetic-parasympathetic dichotomy of the autonomic system for the multitude of situations and attitudes (Gellhorn and Loofbourrow, 1963; Schachter and Singer, 1962). Those who favor this position call attention to the differences in individual physiological configurations in similar situations and subjective states, emphasizing that for each person the physiological configuration aroused is relatively stable and limited to only a few forms, which occur in essentially the same manner for that individual in a large variety of situations and subjective states. There is much more intraindividual consistency in physiological responses to information than between individuals. The individual's physiological-reaction profile may remain unchanged for several years (Malmo, 1967), the pattern of his profile being the result of both social participation and genetic inheritance, for example, density of innervation of the carotid sinus (Lacey, 1967). These physiological responses are general, involving many organ systems and processes rather than influencing only one system, such as the stomach, skin, or heart. The information provoking them is determined by the individual's subjective evaluation of the situation (Appley and Trumbull, 1967 b; Oken, 1967; Wolff, 1953; Mandler, 1967; Lazarus, 1967).

Some Endocrinological Aspects of the Nonspecifically Induced General Physiological Responses. Oken (1967, pp. 49, 56) believes that the evidence shows that an individual's level of adrenocortical steroid secretion tends to "remain within a range characteristic for him." Mason and Brady (1964) studied 17-OHCS levels in the urine in a number of situations. They found that clearly defined, individual differences in mean corticosteroid excretion in the urine sustained over long periods of time was characteristic. In their study of leukemic children they also found that the parents could be characterized as chronic "highs," "middles," or "lows," in their levels of mean 17-OHCS excretion and often showed "remarkably little fluctuation within their own narrow range" (Mason and Brady, 1964, p. 21). They believe the evidence indicates that a subject's mean 17-OHCS levels could be quite reliably predicted on the basis of social-psychological variables, such as tension-relieving activities and other habitual behavioral responses.

Oken (1967, p. 46) says that "almost any situation of affective arousal leads to a rise in 17-hydroxycorticosterone" and "many affects are associated with the common features of a general stress response." Adrenal corticosteroid levels have been found in patients anticipating surgery to be best correlated with global rather than specific affective involvement; in acute schizophrenics, to overall affective arousal rather than one emotional state; and in depressive patients and others, to the intensity of emotional distress in general (Oken, 1967). Gellhorn and Loofbourrow (1963) think that the affective charge is responsible for increased ACTH secretion from the pituitary and subsequently the increased 17-OHCS associated with emotions and psychological stress. 17-OHCS secretion is so consistently associated with subjective arousal that it is frequently used as the sole indicant of subjective arousal (a practice not recommended).

The catecholamines—epinephrine and norepinephrine—have been associated with psychological stress almost as frequently as 17-OHCS. Some have tried to link norepinephrine to anger and epinephrine to anxiety, but Oken (1967) points out that there is no unitary release mechanism for norepinephrine, as there is for epinephrine; thus we must be careful about trying to dichotomize the two.

Autonomic Aspects of the Nonspecifically Induced General Physiological Responses. Although no one organ system completely controls behavior, the central nervous system and the endocrine system are essential to the integration of information with physical activity. Gellhorn and Loofbourrow (1963) believe that the hypothalamus, limbic, and reticular systems of the brain are at the center of the integrative process. The neocortex has abundant connections with these systems and is essential for their effective operation. This hypothalamic-limbic-reticular hub has two pervasive influences. One is called ergotropic and involves the arousal and mobilization of the body, primarily through the sympathetic system. The second influence is called trophotropic and involves energy-conserving processes that relax the body and work primarily through the parasympathetic division of the autonomic nervous system (Pribram, 1967).

The ergotropic response is a combination of sympathetic responses and the somatic activity associated with it. It involves creating favorable conditions for maximal performance of the somatic nervous system through cardiovascular adjustments, increases in blood sugar, delays in fatigue, increased tone of skeletal and respiratory muscles, and cerebral cortical arousal. In the latter case the motor cortex and extrapyramidal motor neurons (responsible for the praxias discussed earlier) are excited, enhancing motor activity (Gellhorn, 1967, 1968; Gellhorn and Loofbourrow, 1963).

The trophotropic response is the combination of the parasympathetic responses and its associated somatic activity. There is a close relation between feeding and the trophotropic system. This system involves enhanced gastrointestinal functions, excretion of wastes, enhanced restitution of cellular functions, slowing of the heart rate, pupillary constriction, increase in the tendency to sleep, synchronous potentials in the EEG, and a general decrease in responsiveness and activity of the somatic nervous system (Gellhorn, 1967, 1968).

Trophotropic responses are related to approach behavior, which seeks increased contact with the stimulus, such as in empathy, and can result from gentle stroking. Erogotropic responses are related to withdrawal behavior (Gellhorn, 1967). These two are found in simple animals as the flexor reflex and the extensor thrust and in rather undifferentiated form in infants born without cerebral hemispheres. The cerebral hemispheres add differentiation and greater sensitization to the information and stimuli. The notion of an approach-withdrawal dichotomy is an old one, going back at least to Allport's early work in 1924 in which he suggested that pleasurable emotions were related to the parasympathetic system and the unpleasurable to the sympathetic system (Malmo's modern work on mice is along this line; see discussion in Oken, 1967). However, Gellhorn feels that this is an oversimplification. For one thing, some unpleasant subjective feelings, such as sadness and resentment, are related to parasympathetic responses, and some pleasant emotions, such as euphoria, are related to the sympathetic (Gellhorn, 1968; Gellhorn and Loofbourrow, 1963).

When one of these systems is excited, the other is generally diminished in response, but there are complicated interrelationships between them. The ergotropic is the main vehicle for arousing the body and the trophotropic for relaxing it, but both may be elicited from the same neural structures. Very slight changes in the state of excitation of the subcortical structures, such as the hypothalamus, can cause significant changes in ergotropic-trophotropic balance and alter emotional reactivity.

What is usually called emotional arousal or emotional stress is a state of ergotropic activity (Gellhorn, 1968). There are also emotions or subjective-feeling states associated with the trophotropic response (Gellhorn, 1968), but this is overlooked or ignored with surprising frequency in discussions of emotions or emotional stress. Perhaps this is in part an artifact of the old emphasis on "emotions" as a degree of activation or arousal.

Tuning of the Ergotropic-Trophotropic balance. The shifting of the autonomic balance so that either the sympathetic or parasympathetic system is dominant is called tuning. Tuning can be a major distinguishing property of a person's particular autonomic-neuroendocrine response configuration. The autonomic balance or tuning in a particular person can be the result of genetic inheritance or of experiences. When either the sympathetic or parasympathetic system is utilized with sufficiently greater frequency, changes in brain neurons (discussed earlier in Chapter III) are produced, which make those neurons increasingly responsive to stimulation. In such cases the responsiveness of the more-utilized system is increased. Experiences can reversibly modify the balance or produce permanent changes (Gellhorn, 1967, 1968; Gellhorn and Loofbourrow, 1963). There appears to be a normal curve of distribution of the population in terms of sympathetic or parasympathetic dominance, with the majority having a balanced response (Malmo, 1967). Whether there is a balance between the two divisions of the autonomic system, or a dominance of one by the other, has far-reaching influences on body states, responsiveness to information, and subjective moods.

The "tuned" person tends to respond disproportionately with the tuned system to stimuli that in the balanced person elicits both sympathetic (ergotropic) and parasympathetic (trophotropic) responses in some cooperative configuration. The "tuned" person may also respond with the dominant system to stimuli that in balanced people produces activation of the system whose responsiveness is decreased in the particular person. For example, gentle stroking of animals normally produces a parasympathetic or trophotropic response, but in the sympathetically tuned animal, petting can produce rage, which is a sympathetic or ergotropic response (Gellhorn, 1967, 1968; Gellhorn and Loofbourrow, 1963).

There is a similarity between metabolic, autonomic, and somatic functions in states of marked activity such as exercise and anger on the one hand, and relaxation, sleep, and depression on the other. If one of these two general configurations of physiological conditions, activity or relaxation, appears predominantly or invariably in a given individual, it is an indication of ergotropic-trophotropic imbalance or tuning (Gellhorn, 1967).

Gellhorn suggests that autonomic imbalance is related to abnormal cortical patterns and perhaps to some forms of abnormal behavior. The normal function of the brain depends upon a relatively narrow range of hypothalamic activity. Restoration of the autonomic balance appears to have a marked therapeutic effect. Gellhorn believes that the psychotherapeutic technique of requiring the patient to emotionally relive a traumatic experience works in this way. Extreme excitation followed by exhaustion seems necessary. Under these circumstances a new ergotropic-trophotropic balance can occur. This new balance may or may not be normal, however. Extreme subjective arousal in any human experience can result in a new state of tuning or its removal and can be accompanied by marked behavioral changes ("He's just never been the same").

From our discussion we see that there is an individual, specific response profile, fairly stable over time, that involves the very broad and far-reaching effects of the autonomic and neuroendocrine system, especially the adrenals, and occurs in each individual in response to a wide variety of subjective evaluations of information in situations. It is determined in part and can be modified in part by social participation; it is also an integral part of a person's on-going social experience. There appear to be at least three dimensions of variability that must be kept in mind in studying individual autonomic and neuroendocrine profiles: (1) responsiveness in terms of stability and lability of the steady-state autonomic activity, "its predisposition to impulsive reaction to input" (Pribram, 1967, p. 13); (2) the pattern of response of the physiological components (Pribram, 1967); and (3) the balance or imbalance—tuning—of the autonomic system.

The form of the physiological response, such as the state of tuning, can be modified by social interaction. There are too few studies of social situations in which a large number of physiological measures have been used for us to be able to describe the fluctuations in physiological patterns in resonation with social activity (Kaplan et al., 1964). However, there is enough evidence to indicate that such resonation almost certainly occurs. This is a fertile new area into which researchers are just beginning to venture.

The verbal discussion of events for which the person subjectively feels fear, dread, anxiety, or anger may greatly increase free fatty acids in the plasma (blood fluid minus the corpuscles) (Back and Bogdonoff, 1964). Wolf (1963) found nausea and cessation of gastric motor activity when discussing pregnancy with a young woman, and when mentioning the horrors of the jungles and the Japanese with a soldier hospitalized during World War II. The anticipation of dreaded events that have been experienced before seems to produce physiological responses as great as when exposed to the event itself (Stern, see discussion in Oken, 1967).

The unavailability of either situationally relevant behavior or an adequate response to information can produce an epinephrine response (Mandler, 1967) or a general physiological response (Engel, 1962). If the volume of information important to a person is too great for the person to handle (Engel, 1962) or is new and unexpected, it may produce a stress or general physiological response (Oken, 1967). As Oken (1967) points out, novelty is one of the most consistently effective stressors.

Gerard (1964) studied the relationship between gelvanic skin response and agreement or disagreement of others with the subject's convictions. His results were essentially the same as those of C. E. Smith in a 1936 study. They found GSR higher when the subject disagreed with the majority than when he agreed. Those subjects having greater self-confidence had greater physiological reactivity to both conformity and deviance from the majority than those having low self-confidence. Evidently, the more self-confident people try harder than less self-confident people to increase their attractiveness to others when in agreement and to reject others when in deviance. Interestingly, on convictions very strongly held, there was little GSR response by the subjects, which is perhaps a result of having previously considered and eliminated the counterarguments. This would suggest that disagreements over values one believed in but was not completely convinced about would produce greater physiological change than disagreements over values one was thoroughly convinced about. If this is the case, the convinced person should have somewhat better health than the less convinced, other things being equal.

Shapiro and Leiderman (1964) studied three male groups and found that GSR and heart rate were related to success in leadership roles. The more successful the individual was as a leader, the higher his GSR and heart rate. If a leader unsuccessfully initiated an effort, there was a drop in his heart rate.

Concerning the possible influence of mothers on their infants' physiological profile Caudill (1958) cites Benedek's work on the emotional balance between mother and child. He asks:

> Does the child, in accordance with the quality of the relationship to the mother, develop patterns of physiological response that are similar or even attuned to hers, or patterns that are in counter directions? Does such a patterning, if it exists or persists, have anything to do with the emotional and perhaps physiological resonance that the individual experiences with some persons later in life and not with others? (Caudill, 1958, p. 21)

The research on convergence of physiological responses among group members suggests that the mother-child relationship may indeed have such influences. Leiderman and Shapiro (1964, p. 195) cite evidence that group influences tend to change individual physiological responses toward some intermediate level, and that a co-varying physiological response pattern creating a sort of physiological empathy may result from an affectively appropriate interpersonal relationship. In psychotherapist-patient interaction, rapidly falling speech muscle tension in both the therapist and patient followed praise by the therapist, and both displayed continued speech muscle tension when the therapist criticized the patient. The heart rate of patient and therapist have been found to vary together in relation to the affective tone of the session, for example, anxiety, hostility, depression (Kaplan et al., 1964). Caudill (1958) cites studies of a rowing crew in which social solidarity was directly related to similarities in physiological responses to the racing experience. The degree of division of labor, Caudill suggests, may indicate the degree to which similar physiological responses are appropriate for social groups to function effectively. For example, in football teams in which there is a division of labor there will be of necessity differing physiological responses, for example, the "cool" of the quarterback versus the aggressive excitement of the defensive linebacker.

Despite the fact that 17-OHCS mean excretion level is usually stable for given individuals, social situations of a rather special nature can produce temporary changes, and long-term research may find some permanent changes. For example, Mason (cited in Mason and Brady, 1964) in 1959 studied B-52 jet bomber crews. He found that three crewmen who were working closely together in the back of the plane all ran elevated levels of 17-OHCS excretion levels of 13 mg/day, as compared with the mean normal of about 7 mg/day. On nonflight days, the excretion levels in these men were quite different from each other and were substantially lower than 13 mg/day. Similar results were observed in a study of young adults in groups of 7 to 13 who volunteered and were studied in a hospital ward. The results indicate that small-group living can influence endocrine functioning. Members of some groups showed a very narrow range of variation in corticosteroid levels, with perhaps one deviant; other groups showed wide ranges of individual variation in similar situations. Mason and Brady suggest that social explanations probably hold the key to these group differences.

Kaplan, Burch, and Bloom (1964) using GSR studied nursing students in which they paired the girls in three categories. In the first group, girls were paired with other girls whom they liked and felt liked them, as indicated by a sociometric questionnaire. In the second group, girls were paired with girls they were neutral toward; in the third group girls who disliked each other were paired. The girls met for 20-minute sessions each day to discuss topics they did or did not agree upon. The researchers found that physiological covariation depended upon the "degree of simultaneous and consensual affective investment in the stimulus field by the participants in social interaction" (Kaplan et al., 1964, pp. 100–108). They suggest that this physiological covariation can be measured and used as an index of consensual affective investment in studies of social interaction. The negative pairs covaried significantly more than the positive pairs, who covaried more than the neutral pairs. The negative-pair members apparently covaried more than the others as a result of their greater sensitivity to the behavior in the interaction.

Back and Bogdonoff (1964) compared plasma free fatty acids (FFA) between "natural" groups of existing friends brought into the laboratory and groups made up of strangers. The task required one member to take the lead and to make a judgmental decision, then for the rest of the group to indicate whether they agreed. In the natural groups, being a leader did not produce increased FFA but not being agreed with as a leader did. In the groups of strangers, being the leader, being agreed with, and being the best performer all produced increased FFA. In the natural group, conformity and cooperation were believed to be the dominant influence and deviation from the group the most arousing. In the group of strangers the dominant dimension was individual achievement, in which case pressures to conform or to assume group leadership was arousing. Back and Bogdonoff (1964, pp. 38–39) showed that "the degree of autonomic activity could be modified by the condition of interaction between the members of the groups" and that one might be able to make inferences about the meaning of group and cohesion by observing differences in autonomic activity of group members. They reaffirm the importance of discovering the subjective meaning of the situation to the individual in order to correctly explain findings.

Participation in small social groups has been found to influence the galvanic skin potential, plasma FFA, and the urinary excretion of 17-OHCS.

From these leads, it seems altogether likely that CNS-mediated changes in a variety of endocrine and autonomic functions will be discovered in the next few years under conditions of strong affect engendered in group situations (Leiderman and Shapiro, 1964, p. x).

Measures of physiological covariation in groups may prove significant not only in understanding why susceptibility to disease varies between social groups but also as valuable adjuncts to social measures of fluctuations in group consensus and solidarity (Kaplan et al., 1964; Back and Bogdonoff, 1964).

The Physiological Responses to Information and General Susceptibility to Disease

We might arbitrarily divide the influences of the general physiological responses to information on physical disease into three categories: (1) general changes in physiological processes that alter the body's resistance to disease agents; (2) pathological changes in the body that result directly from the general responses; and (3) changes in the responsiveness of the central nervous system that increase the possibility of accidents and error. These processes, in conjunction with natural, innate and acquired immunities, such as antibodies (see Wilson and Miles, 1964), form a general configuration whose essential elements are common to all people but whose particular form is different for each person. This configuration represents the person's capacity and probability of success in resisting the onset of disease in his given milieu. We refer to this configuration as his general susceptibility to illness.

Medicine has had a tendency to focus on the acute or semi-acute infectious diseases resulting from exposure to virulent microorganisms from outside the body. But the most common microbial diseases in man today arise from microorganisms that are ubiquitous in the environment and persist in the body without normally causing obvious harm. They produce pathologies only when the person infected has some experience which alters physiological processes (Cassel, 1970). Cassel suggests that stimuli which produce changes in the pituitary and adrenal cortical processes, although not necessarily producing a manifest subjective or emotional disturbance, "can produce important physiological changes and alteration in susceptibility to disease manifestations" (Cassel, 1970, p. 194).

Clearly, the presence of bacteria or other microbes (viruses or fungi) are in itself not a sufficient cause of disease and the most well-known defenses of the body such as antibodies are not necessarily always the main protection against infections. Local tissue changes are important to susceptibility to infection. A classic example is the tubercle bacillus. The acid-base or electrolyte balance is crucial in holding this bacteria in check. Situations producing increased adrenocortical hormones have been found to be positively associated with the disturbance of electrolyte balances and tuberculosis (Wolff, 1953; Selye 1956 c). Another way the electrolyte balance may be upset is the result of increased levels of the catecholamines and the direct neurogenic influences on renal (kidney) blood flow, which changes urinary output and produces other electrolyte balance modifications (Oken, 1967).

In our earlier discussions of the physiology of the general responses we list many of the physiological processes influenced by the hypothalamus, pituitary, autonomic nervous system, and adrenal glands. Virtually every physiological process of the body can in some way be influenced by the activities of these systems. Many of these are first-line defenses, such as the electrolyte or acid-base balance and antibody and white blood cell activity. Increased doses of adrenalcortical hormones can reduce or even block antibody formation, resulting in temporary loss of immunity to the microbes the antibodies normally handle (Guyton, 1961). The white blood cells (lymphocytes and eosinophils) and lymphatic tissue such as the lymph nodes are reduced in numbers and effectiveness by adrenocortical secretions (Selye, 1956 a). The ability to reduce or increase inflammation and some allergic reactions depends in part on adrenal cortical secretions (see discussion of inflammation and Selye in Chapter II). Changes in blood coagulation properties may also occur (Guyton, 1961). In addition, metabolic rates, cardiovascular conditions such as heart rate and blood pressure, neural activity, digestion and alimentary tract activity, and a number of other processes, all important in the defense and repair of the body, are influenced in the ways noted earlier in this chapter. Most of the negative effects mentioned can be recognized by the alert reader as consequences of the sympathetic-adrenal activity, rather than of the parasympathetic. These negative effects have been commonly associated by researchers with stress.

These physiological changes reduce the ability to recover if they occur or continue to occur during an illness.

SOME PATHOLOGIES RESULTING DIRECTLY FROM
THE GENERAL RESPONSES

There are a number of ailments that can be produced or largely produced as a result of activity of either of the two broad dimensions of the general responses, sympathetic or parasympathetic. Some of these seem to be related to the state of autonomic tuning, discussed previously. For example, hypertension can result from a sympathetically tuned (sympathotonic) nervous system. In such cases sympathetic discharges can also lead to constriction of the renal blood vessels, ventually producing renal ischemia. If this condition continues, eventually the kidney metabolic changes become independent of sympathetic stimulation and will remain hypertensive even if the sympathetic discharges are discontinued (Gellhorn and Loofbourrow, 1963). Unusual responses to being startled including the requirement of a longer period to return to normal, could also be the result of sympathetic tuning (Malmo, 1967; Moss, 1968).

Asthma, arthritis, peptic ulcers, and even colds have been related to parasympathetic tuning. Interference with parasympathetic discharges by sympathetic hyperactivity has been known to eliminate, at least temporarily, each of these (Gellhorn and Loofbourrow, 1963).

Peptic ulcers deserve special attention because both the sympathetic and parasympathetic systems can produce them. Parasympathetic activity can increase the flow of gastric juices (acids, enzymes, etc.) at excessive levels that overwhelm the protective elements of the stomach and duodenum (a portion of the small intestine leading immediately from the stomach), such as the normal alkalinity of the digestive tract and the mucus protecting the stomach lining. Sympathetic and adrenal activity, on the other hand, can reduce the quantity of the protective mucus, sometimes almost completely, and thus permit the existing digestive juices to dissolve the stomach lining. Although sympathetic activity reduces acid production and stomach motility, adrenal glucocorticoids can increase the secretion of acid and pepsin (Guyton, 1961; Robert, 1968; Gray, 1956).

In contrast to the stable dominance of the autonomic system by either the sympathetic or parasympathetic system in tuning, one may have an unusually labile autonomic system characterized by fluctuations in responsiveness between and within the sympathetic and parasympathetic systems. This lability can produce gastrointestinal spasms, irregular heart rate, headache, nausea, dizziness and may occur in various organs in various intensities (Gellhorn and Loofbourrow, 1963; they call it the autonomic-affective syndrome).

The general physiological responses seem also to be related to irregularities in the menses, even amenorrhea (Osofsky and Fisher, 1967; Cleghorn, 1968); nausea, vomiting, fevers, epilepsy (Gellhorn and Loofbourrow, 1963); and increased levels of FFA and cholesterol levels, important in producing cardiovascular disease (Caffrey, 1967).

The general responses, particularly sympathetic-adrenal activity, can have destructive effects at crucial periods of a person's growth and development, effects that produce permanent damage or weaknesses as well as episodes of acute illness. Apparently, the older fetus can be effected by stress in the mother so that at birth it is lighter, more restless, more irritable, and prone to gastrointestinal motor disturbances, such as loose stools and difficulty in retaining breast milk, than babies of mothers not experiencing stress (Sontag, 1948). During the first 4 to 8 weeks the lack of tender care of the infant seems to disrupt adrenal function through the central nervous system, which can produce a number of pathologies including deprivation dwarfism. This dwarfism is the result of the catabolic (destructive) effect on the epiphysial cartilage in the bones by adrenal corticosteroid hormones. These same hormones produced in large amounts by disturbing childhood experiences can have detrimental effects on the brain, producing atrophy and in some cases seizures. Severe disturbances in childhood may later even influence susceptibility to senile psychoses. In general, the earlier the brain is exposed to excessive amounts of corticoids the more damage seems to be done, and both physical stress and social-psychological stress during infancy may predispose the individual to the premature onset of aging. Subjective distress during adolescence, especially among females, can disturb thyroid function and produce hyperthyroidism (Cleghorn, 1968).

SOME INFLUENCES OF THE GENERAL RESPONSES ON THE
CENTRAL NERVOUS SYSTEM

Throughout this and the preceding chapters the influence of the physiological components of the general responses on the CNS has been discussed as a part of the resonation between the body and information. To avoid redundancy we do not repeat the evidence here. However, it is clear that adrenal hormones, autonomic activity, hypothalamic activity, and related hormonal secretions have profound influence upon the brain. Recalling the evidence presented earlier on brain amines, one is struck by the extreme sensitivity of the brain to sympathetic responses to information. Under extreme excitation, there is actual disruption of the cerebral cortex electrical functions, making rational thought impossible. At the other extreme, parasympathetic activity can be accompanied by apathy and unresponsiveness to otherwise alarming information. The brain is highly sensitive to adrenocorticosteroids, which can cause mental disturbances that in turn can cause elevation of adrenocorticosteroids (Cleghorn, 1968; Gellhorn and Loofbourrow, 1963). Under such circumstances the individual's capacity to perceive correctly the situation in which he finds himself may be impaired; his capacity to anticipate possible problems and avoid accidents may be reduced; and his physical coordination may be altered temporarily so that the possibility of physical trauma or mistakes that produce or encourage disease is much increased.

His misperception of the situation can influence his social behavior so that it becomes impaired to the point of becoming deviant. Many behavioral illnesses are related to the functioning of the adrenal glands and autonomic system. These illnesses include senile psychoses, autonomic-affective syndrome (which is a mental disorder also), anxiety, paranoid schizophrenia, and manic-depression (see Gellhorn and Loofbourrow, 1963; Malmo, 1967). To this we can add anxious overactivity associated with hyperthyroidism; apathy found with Addison's disease (an adrenal disorder); cognitive and affective disturbances with Cushing's syndrome (a disorder of the pituitary and adrenal, Cleghorn, 1968), as well as many others.

Gellhorn and Loofbourrow (1963) suggest that mental disorders could well be grouped in two categories, one associated with sympathetic arousal and tuning and the other with parasympathetic activity and tuning. They suggest that there are encouraging relations being uncovered between various psychoses and hypothalamic conditions. For example, manic phases are accompanied by increased secretion of adrenaline and noradrenaline, and both of these secretions are decreased in the depression phase. The 17-ketosteroids are significantly increased in paranoid but not in nonparanoid schizophrenia (Gellhorn and Loofbourrow, 1963).

Our primary emphasis in this work is on the relations between physical health and information processing. Although mental health could well be included, it presents special conceptual and theoretical problems of its own that are beyond the scope of this work. Nevertheless, we believe that the basic framework of this model will prove fruitful for examining mental disorders as well.

SOME THOUGHTS ON THE MEASUREMENT OF
GENERAL SUSCEPTIBILITY

It appears that the most practical way to measure general susceptibility is in terms of fluctuations and clusterings of incidence and prevalence of diseases of all types over time in particular situations or milieus. This is certainly much easier than trying to identify every antibody and physical weakness a person has. But susceptibility can change without one's contracting an illness or an illness significant enough to be reported. One way partially to overcome this is either to follow one individual for some time or to compare large groups of people in the same situation, perhaps using diaries to record minor ailments and thus taking advantage of statistical probabilities. A fruitful initial research hypothesis might be that information perception that arouses a general response may be detrimental to health through the modification of general susceptibility, producing fluctuations in incidence and prevalence of diseases of many types for the person or group studied. The study of many diseases in a group permits prediction and testing of fairly large groups in a short period of time, because one does not have to wait for one particular disease to emerge in a large enough, workable subsample. One makes predictions on which subsamples will have the higher incidence and/or prevalence of disease during biosocial resonation with a particular situation. Observation need only apply to the situation and perhaps its immediate aftermath because the changes we are interested in will usually occur during the situation itself.

Some Notes on Subjective Interpretation of Visceral Physiological Processes

Because many different situations and affective states may be accompanied by the same general physiological response pattern, the "meaning" to the person of a general response must come from something other than that response itself. Schachter (Schachter and Singer, 1962) has suggested that the situation, particularly the social situation, determines the "meaning" attached to a particular visceral physiological response involving sympathetic and/or parasympathetic autonomic systems.

His (Schachter and Singer, 1962) work is based on responses to artificially injected epinephrine (adrenalin), which produces sympatheticlike activity, into subjects in a laboratory. A stooge was instructed to express anger or lighthearted euphoria (fooling around by tossing wads of paper at a waste basket, joking, etc.). The subjects were divided into three groups, those that were told the nature of the injection and what physiological changes they could expect to experience, those injected but not told what to expect, and those given a placebo. On the basis of their responses he formulated his model, noting that those who knew why they felt as they did were less influenced by the behavior of the stooge than those with the injection who had no explanations for their feelings (see also Schachter and Wheeler, 1962; Schachter, 1964, 1967).

Stein (1967) criticizes Schachter for failing to take into consideration the rapid rate at which epinephrine is removed from the blood stream by the body. Many of the injection's effects might have subsided before the experimental manipulation took place. He also feels that Schachter should have taken the influence of the experimental situation on the subject's physiological state into account. Scotch (1967) is not, as we are not, satisfied with Schachter's designation of certain behaviors as anger, euphoria, or joy in his study. However, a number of psychophysiological researchers endorse Schachter's perspective, including Gellhorn (1968) and Kety, who says:

> The data furthermore sustain a generalization that supports an important thesis of Schachter: the release of a catecholamines is related to the intensity rather than to the quality of affect, while the nature of the affect depends to a considerable extent upon cognitive factors and the past experience or present situation of the individual subject. (1967, p. 105)

See also Malmo (1967, p. 1046) for a similar view.

A rather interesting study by Kopa et al. (1968) and continued by Grastyan (1968) further illustrates the significance of the situation in determining how an animal or person responds to physiological stimulation. They implanted an electrode in the thalamus of cats. The cats were conditioned by electric shock on a grid to leap to a small ledge in the cage for safety. When the cat was on the grid, stimulation through the electrode produced the conditioned response. When the cat was on the ledge, stimulation of the electrode had a relaxing effect on the cat, even though the same neutral point was being stimulated.

There is evidence that social participation influences whether one interprets his body states as illness and what he says about them. Among the more well-known examples is Zborowski's oft-cited study of differences in pain responses among American ethnic groups, with Italians and Jews likely to perceive and express more pain for the same condition than are Irish and Anglo-Saxon patients. Zola similarly found that different ethnic groups report different amounts of symptoms for the same disease when seeking medical care. In Koos' study of Regionville, the same physical states were defined as symptoms of illness by upper-class people and as normal by the lower classes (Scotch, 1967).

Physiological changes a person wishes to explain can come from many sources. Infrasound, very-low-frequency sound waves, produced in storms can be felt miles from the storm and can increase accident and school absentee rates (Green and Dunn, 1968). Some people may interpret the physical feeling produced by infrasound as a "feeling in my bones" that something is about to happen. High levels of noise are widely recognized as a source of psychophysiological disturbance (Chauchard, 1962). Noise and vibration are capable of increasing the heart rate, decreasing blood pressure and respiratory rate, and influencing other physiological processes (Weybrew, 1967). Some sounds, such as those of the woods or the sea, may be physiologically as well as psychologically soothing.

Changes in sequential or cyclical physiological activity, such as menstrual and diurnal cycles, and biosocial activity cycles, such as meals, work periods, sleeping times, and holidays, have been little studied in relation to behavior and physiological interrelations (Trumbull and Appley, 1967). Subjective feelings of "all's well" may be dependent in part on the continuity of these rhythms. Those who cannot adjust their biological rhythms to different conditions may experience disruption of the neural-temporal organization of physiological processes (see discussion by Prescott in Cohen, 1967). The polyphasic nature of the autonomic response may also have implications for social patterns. Subjective as well as physiological well-being can be enhanced by institutionalizing such things as coffee breaks and vacations to coincide with the parasympathetic phase following a period of sympathetic excitement. Continued high levels of activity without provisions for these down phases may be a source of considerable disruption, especially in workers in high-risk jobs such as air traffic controllers and surgeons.

Physical states of arousal or depression, whatever their precipitating factor, may be taken as intuitive or spiritual guidance and may be used as a substitute for reason. People say things like "my heart tells me," and "I feel good about it. . . ." When there is a lack of adequate information on which to base an act that must be taken (and sometimes even when there is adequate information), one may resort to his "feelings" or interpretations of his physiological processes for guidance in selecting an alternative (Vernon, private communication, 1969). Given the great amount of inarticulate information one has learned and the possibility that the physiological responses are a part of biosocial resonation to the information in the situation, this process may produce pretty fair judgements. However, because physiological processes are not very differentiated and because subjective interpretations of them are based on the situation, there is also the possibility that one's own desires and the exigencies of the situation will simply be validated.

Physiological responsiveness may contribute to making something "meaningful." The "meaningless" experience is the one that doesn't "turn me on." For some people when they no longer "feel anything" for their spouse means that they are no longer "in love" and there is no longer any reason to be married. It might turn out to be important for the individual's social involvement and the solidarity of the group, as well as the health of the individual, that there exist social processes capable of physiologically arousing participants and teaching neophytes to be so aroused.

Summary

There are general physiological responses to information, meaningful to the individual, that vary along sympathetic-parasympathetic lines. Which of these two directions a response takes and its intensity depend on the subjective meaning of the information for that individual. The general responses are a collection of physiological responses that mainly involve the autonomic nervous system and its organs of innervation; the neuroendocrine system, especially the adrenal gland; and the hypothalamus and pituitary gland. The proportions of these physiological elements in the general response and the degree to which each changes in response to exciting or depressing information vary between individuals and are the consequence of both inheritance and social experiences. The general response tends to be relatively stable in configuration for a given individual but varies considerably between individuals.

One important dimension of variation between individuals in their general response pattern is the tuning of the sympathetic-parasympathetic system. Most people have a balanced, autonomic resting point in which neither the sympathetic nor parasympathetic is aroused. However, the tuned person has as a base line of autonomic activity a chronic state of sympathetic arousal if sympathetically tuned or parasympathetic arousal if parasympathetically tuned. Accordingly, responses to information may be amplified or muted for the tuned person in comparison with the normal.

The general responses have direct influence upon the individual's susceptibility to disease. Contacts with information that produce a general response, particularly if it is intense, produce sympathetic or parasympathetic tuning or chronic arousal; these contacts can produce changes in that person's susceptibility to disease and may cause pathology directly.

CHAPTER V

The Biosocial Resonation
of Individuals in
Social Communication Networks

We have focused on the physiological aspects of biosocial resonation; we now shift our attention to the social dimensions. In this chapter we examine the relations between interpretations of perceptions and subjective involvement with the social groups or organizations in the social milieu. We also speculate on the influences on disease susceptibility that various types of involvement have. In this and the following chapters we are seeking concepts that embrace the bulk of social-subjective phenomena having a high probability of producing general physiological changes. These categories are *not* to be used as indicants that a physiological response has occurred, but are to be used in conjunction with physiological measures or indicants of illness. They are designed to be guides to the populations of people most likely to experience general physiological responses in sufficient magnitude or duration to produce significant alterations in susceptibility to disease and as a guide to formulate questions when examining these subjects.

Information Incongruities in Social
Communication Networks

From birth onward man is immerged in social interaction and, consequently, in social communications. Although he may acquire considerable information through direct perception, much of what he pays attention to is determined by the communication networks in which he participates. However, the values and norms he learns can come from nowhere else than these social communication networks. Thus much of the information encountered and the bulk of subjective interpretations are derived from the communication networks in which one participates. Consequently, exactly when a general physiological response to information will be experienced depends in large measure on these networks.

THE SOCIAL COMMUNICATION NETWORK

As Dewey emphasized, society exists in and through communication; common perspectives—common cultures—emerge through participation in common communication channels . . . Despite the frequent recitation of this proposition, its full implications, especially for the analysis of mass societies, are not often appreciated. Variations in outlook arise through differential contact and association . . . people in different social classes develop different modes of life and outlook, not because of anything inherent in economic position, but because similarity of occupation and limitations set by income level dispose them to certain restricted communication channels (Shibutani, 1967, p. 164).

Shibutani refers to common communication channels as social worlds. In modern societies mass media, electronic communications, and rapid transportation have made it possible for people geographically dispersed to communicate effectively. "Culture areas are coterminous with communication channels; since communication networks are no longer coterminous with territorial boundaries, culture areas overlap and have lost their territorial bases" (Shibutani, 1967, p. 165). One may have strangers for neighbors. There are a great variety of social worlds in modern societies. These include communal-like relations such as social elites, ethnic minorities, and "the underworld"; occupational and professional associations; and special interest "worlds" such as sports or stamp collecting. Each has its own means of communication, from special interest publications and electronic media programs to annual meetings and grapevines. Each of these social worlds is delineated by the limits of effective communication rather than by territorial distribution or formal group membership (Shibutani, 1967). Scott and Lyman (1968 a) suggest a similar concept of speech communities in which people who associate and talk together may be considered as a unit.

Social communication networks are people transmitting and modifying a particular configuration of information composed of language vocabularies, conceptions of the natural environment, arbitrary values and norms, and preferred patterns of interaction. They form a structural continuum from well-defined role relations in highly visible organizations to very informal and transient communication encounters. They may vary in size from a clique or family to a whole society. They may be coterminous with a role structure, as in a family, or extend far beyond any formal role structure to include anyone receiving the network's information. They may contain, be contained by, and overlap other communication networks. Communication networks are all linked in a worldwide information community, forming an interconnected fabric of human social activity; consequently they have no boundaries.

This lack of boundaries is one of the unique properties of social phenomena that has frequently been overlooked because of enthusiasm for organic analogies applied to societies and its parts, for example, the work of Parsons. Communication networks can be cut up analytically into many different patterns and then labeled, but it must be remembered that these are labels of convenience and not designations of units with boundaries. A very complex interconnected network might be labeled a society. Interacting patterns that occur within it might be labeled unions, industry, and military. Someone might challenge this and say that they really form a military-industrial-union complex. Another person might point to international unionism. From our point of view all these labels are correct, since all apply to recognizable communication on networks. Instead of dividing social phenomena into levels of complexity with less-complex systems fitting into the more complex like boxes, we are concerned with the interconnection between communication networks.

There is another reason why it is inappropriate to attribute boundaries to patterns of social relations. People participate sequentially and simultaneously in many different social communication networks. If the organic analogy of organs and membranes is applied to social phenomena, then it can only apply where the people as a rule, like cells in the mammal, remain in only one role position and engage in only one function. But people have many roles and functions in diverse social systems. Thus the notion of boundaries and membranes in social phenomena can be sustained only if people are ignored and the abstract role structure alone considered. From our point of view such abstractions are as much a true representation of social phenomena as a bath sponge is a representation of the living saltwater sponge. Although the concept of boundaries may be attractive to some, we feel that it prevents us from grasping the truly unique properties of social phenomena.

The worldwide information community is characterized by constant fluctuations in communication patterns and in the information communicated, with the reverberations of these multitudes of changes producing both temporary and permanent changes in interelated communication networks. Some networks are more dependent on each other and form clusters in varying degrees of resonation, as in a given society. Resonation here refers to the degree that changes in one communication network produce accompanying modifications in others and the degree to which these modifications in turn amplify or alter the changes in the first. Hart (1957) conceptualizes social change in a similar manner. He calls attention to the cultural complexes such as the economy, family, and religion that are the components of a society. The overall pattern of change in a society depends on the degree of interdependence between the various cultural complexes undergoing change. To observe social change, Hart contends, we should focus on the various cultural complexes, the processes of change taking place in each, and the interrelations of changes between them.

Social change and variation of social properties are changes in the activity of people. Culture is whatever people believe and do; it is not separable from people. Biosocial resonation emphasizes that social information exchanges and physiological activity cannot be separated but must be conceptualized as a resonating whole. Efforts to separate social and physical [for example, Swanson (1967) separates organic, individual, and social into independent and mutually constraining phenomena; Parsons (1961) separates the behavioral organism, personality, social, and cultural systems] only encourage the development of concepts that ignore the importance of people and their biology, such as culture. Culture is information that depends on human communication for its existence, and it is susceptible to interpretation and modification in every social interaction (see Shibutani, 1967 for a similar view). Culture must be reaffirmed constantly from day to day through social and environmental interaction. There are few social "roles" for which the "script" is firmly established, rigid, not requiring improvisation by the role player, and not taking some of its form from the emergent qualities of the situation (McCall and Simmons, 1966).

A person's information repertoire is an amalgam of information from his complement of networks and direct perceptions. Information from one network is frequently tested for validity in others in which the person participates or through direct contact with the environment. If a communication network's information is continually confirmed to the person's satisfaction, it becomes part of his perspective of his world. In time it may become so familiar and taken for granted that it becomes a part of the background of experience, without much attention being paid to it.

Through the processes of reaffirmation in direct contact with the social and natural environment one may encounter information that invalidates the information communicated through a particular network. The natural environment may appear different or normative behavior may not occur as one was told to expect. In such cases, the invalidating information may either disrupt a person's confidence and support for the communication network providing the apparently erroneous information or lead to the rejection of the phenomena or person that did not meet one's expectations. In either case, some configuration of a general physiological response may be produced.

There is ample opportunity to encounter conflicting information in modern societies, which are characterized by their heterogeneity of communication networks. When members of a particular network participate in others, they are more likely to encounter sources of correction, deviance, innovation, or autonomy. This can produce more viable social communities in greater harmony if modifications in the information and patterns of the communication network is permitted, or it can lead to greater isolation of a network from those communicating conflicting information. If the participant arrived at the insight invalidating the network's information from direct observation of the environment, the network's participants may either permit correction of the information configuration, isolate the person, remove him, or try to call into question the credibility of his observation.

In this chapter we are concerned with modifications in the person's subjective involvement with his social communication networks when he has experienced invalidation of some of its information. In the next chapter we are concerned with the processes of change that occur in the network as a result of changes in involvement.

THE INVALIDATION OF INFORMATION THROUGH THE SUBJECTIVE
EXPERIENCING OF INFORMATION INCONGRUITIES

What is the general property of subjective information interpretation that seems most likely to produce a general physiological response? We suggest that it is the subjective experiencing of information incongruities, that is, contact with invalidating information. Information purporting to describe natural conditions can, in principle, be verified or invalidated by direct or empirical observation. Secondary information from those trusted to make direct observations, such as scientists, may serve as well as one's own direct observation to verify or invalidate information. Some information supposedly deals with the natural environment but is not verifiable in principle, such as some myths, folklore, religious pronouncements ("there is a heaven"), and other supernatural information. The validity of social norms and much of the supernatural information are verifiable only by persuasion, by consensus, by conflict such as wars, or by pseudoempirical verification in which natural phenomena are said to be evidence of the "truth" of the supernatural or normative.

However, promises and sanctions attached to a community's norms can be empirically perceivable and verifiable. These promises and sanctions may include serenity, material gain, social approval, imprisonment, and the like. Even the "wrath of God" is interpreted in terms of observable troubles. These observable promises and sanctions are part of one's expectations. Their failure to materialize is an information incongruity that can invalidate a piece of information from a communication network and lead the participant to question the validity of the rest of that network's information complement. One's continued willingness to accept a social community's norms and information about the environment depends upon his subjective perception that they "work," that is, that he can predict the environment and the behavior of others. When a person encounters information that he subjectively interprets as invalidating the information he has learned and is normally in contact with in his social relations, he will attempt to correct the incongruity so that subjectively there is congruity.

The degree of integration within and between communication networks may be conceptualized in terms of the proportion of participants experiencing subjective information incongruities, the proportion of a network's information involved, and the degree acceptance of the seemingly invalidated information is a requirement for network participation.

Subjective information incongruities is the largest category we have found for handling social-subjective phenomena likely to produce a general physiological response, and the rest of our model revolves around this notion. Subjective information incongruities are basically the mismatch between neural organizations produced by continuing perceptions of invariants and by one's perceptions in a given situation. Subjectively it is incongruity between what was expected and/or desired and what was actually experienced or learned. We feel that there are at least six categories of information within which incongruities may be experienced:

1. Expectations of nonsocial natural phenomena based on direct perception previous to the current encounter and direct perceptions of that same natural phenomena in the current situation.

2. Expectations of nonsocial natural phenomena derived from social interaction where others have directly called attention to the phenomena or have provided secondary experience through verbal descriptions and direct perception of the same natural phenomena in the current situation.

3. Expectations about social behavior, particularly normative behavior, based on previous direct observations and/or verbal descriptions, and direct observation of social behavior in the current situation. This may produce judgements of people (for example, they are deviant) or norms (for example, people don't behave that way).

4. Situations one has been taught socially to avoid or to seek and the situation experienced. One finds himself either in a situation he has been taught to avoid or is unable to get himself into a situation he has been taught to seek. This includes taboos, sin, and folklore proscriptions, as well as normative goals.

5. Social statements about the natural world or about appropriate normative behavior by two or more communication networks the person comes into contact with in a situation.

6. Information believed to be available and subjectively believed to be necessary for understanding or deciding actions in a given situation. The information may be available but not to that person at that time, or there may be no adequate information in human societies on that matter.

Incongruities in each of these categories are discovered through active perception of one's world and through the assessment of information accuracy and its effectiveness in manipulating or predicting activity in the environment.

The importance of information incongruities in human behavior has been noted by a number of workers. Festinger's (1957, 1963) theory of cognitive dissonance is a major example. Festinger assumes, as we have, that people find information consistency desirable and engage in behavior in efforts to maintain consistency. He is most concerned with the consequences of behaving in a way inconsistent with one's knowledge—doing things one "knows better" than to do—particularly when justifications of these actions fail. He sees the dissonance that arises in such actions as a motivating factor, and he examines dissonance-reducing behavior as it applies to this sort of information incongruity. We are interested in information incongruities on a broader scale. Festinger focuses more on the explanation of behavior, whereas we focus on predicting changes in susceptibility to disease.

Zajonc (1968), based on Festinger's model, suggests a number of propositions and ideas about dissonance that are similar to and support our own. He sees the sources of dissonance as inconsistent sensory perceptions, inconsistent social requirements or definitions, communication conflicting with what one knows, disconfirmed expectations, insufficient justification to support one's behavior, and "post-decision dissonance," which occurs when the choice made has negative consequences and other alternatives available turn out to have positive consequences. He sees two sources of dynamics in dissonance: pressure from interaction with the environment to bring one's cognitions into correspondence with "reality", and the tendency to maintain consistency among cognitions. From our point of view, the tendency toward congruity between "reality" and one's information about it is the result of ineffective efforts to explain or manipulate the environment. Only when such contacts are subjectively evaluated as ineffective or when one is looking for effective information will there be a tendency toward congruity between "reality" and one's information. One can live an entire lifetime with remarkably little correct information about "reality." However, in the long run, there is probably a tendency for collective human knowledge to approximate "reality" more closely. Zajonc (1968) sees cognitive dissonance as a noxious state people attempt to avoid, with severity of noxiousness related to the subjective importance and relative number of cognitions involved. Cognitive dissonance is reduced or eliminated only by adding new or changing old cognitions, thereby favoring one side or the other in the dissonance or changing their relative importance or degree of contradiction.

Merton's (1957) model of anomie suggests, among other things, that various forms of deviant behavior, such as what he calls innovation, retreatism, ritualism, and rebellion, can be the result of incongruities between the social norms concerning desirable goals to be obtained by the proper means and the information one encounters concerning his opportunities or capacities to utilize successfully the proper means. Merton suggests that the limitations of access to proper means are as socially determined as the designation of certain goals and means as desirable are.

When discussing the higher rates of suicide among Protestants compared with Catholics, Durkheim commented on the development of the freer spirit of inquiry among Protestants, which he saw as a cause of the higher Protestant suicide rate:

> Reflection develops only if its development becomes imperative, that is, if certain ideas and instinctive sentiments which have hitherto adequately guided conduct are found to have lost their efficacy. Then reflection intervenes to fill the gap that has appeared, but which it has not created. Just as reflection disappears to the extent that thought and action take the form of automatic habits, it awakes only when accepted habits become disorganized (Durkheim, 1951, pp. 158–159).

Thus even the suicide rates in Durkheim's classic study in part might be explained in terms of the encounter with information incongruities.

Mechanic (1962, 1968) has for some time advocated the focusing of sociological attention upon discontinuities as a source of social stress. In 1962 he said:

From the larger structural point of view it is quite possible to study not only responses to discontinuities, but also the discontinuities themselves that are likely to induce stress in particular groups of persons . . . (p. 207).

In 1968 he said, "In recent years there has been increasing concern and interest among behavioral scientists in discontinuities in social systems resulting in stress response" (p. 307). We suggest that the essential aspect of such discontinuities is the subjective interpretation of information as incongruous and that virtually all social discontinuities can be classified as such information incongruities.

UNCERTAINTY AS THE SUBJECTIVE STATE ACCOMPANYING
EXPERIENCING OF INFORMATION INCONGRUITIES

Uncertainty cannot occur in an environment of complete congruity between neural representations of information and perceptions. Uncertainty can only occur when incongruities in information are experienced. Uncertainty offers us the most readily observable clue to those people whose interpretations of information in a particular situation involve an incongruity and may involve a general physiological response and thus changes in susceptibility to disease. However, uncertainty, like incongruities, cannot be taken as evidence that physiological changes have occurred. It is only a clue to guide our attention to populations having the greater probability of physiological changes. These physiological changes must be measured directly.

Uncertainty and information incongruities are experienced as a whole. That is, uncertainty is what one subjectively articulates while experiencing information incongruities. The uncertainty may be very mild, such as, "Now where did I put my socks?" It may be invigorating, such as, "Who do you think will win the ball game Saturday?" Or it may be distressing, such as, "Don't you love me anymore?"

The subjective intensity of uncertainty may be understood in terms of the risk involved in that situation. Risk is the subjective estimate of the value of the gains or losses involved and the probability of their occurring. We might expect general physiological responses to be more likely to occur at greater intensity as the degree of risk in uncertainty increases. Whether positive or negative subjective emotions are involved makes no difference.

Uncertainty has many social roles. Without it there would be no questions, no problems, and no curiosity about the unknown (Gross, 1967). It seems to be important for human motivation and enjoyment of life. Uncertainty may be purposely maintained through limited access to information in order to assure continuing participation by members in a communication network. Students work for uncertain grades and business-men for uncertain promotions and profits. Uncertainty is necessary in com-petitive situations to maintain incentive for action. If the outcome is known there is little incentive for either the winners or the losers (Moore and Tumin, 1949).

There are areas of information in which uncertainty is necessary for continued interest, and others in which it cannot be tolerated, such as one's self-concept (Sherif and Harvey, 1952). On the other hand, sports is an area in which uncertainty is absolutely necessary as far as the outcome of contests is concerned. Some of these sports, such as mountain climbing, car racing, gambling, and ballooning, involve high-risk uncertainty. The positive feelings accompanying successful participation in sports, espe-cially high-risk sports, may in part result from positive evaluations of one's own capacities to handle uncertainty. With the universal possibility of experiencing uncertainty, it is little wonder that man has made a sport of defying the uncertain or seeks through milder sports for "safe" areas in which to test his uncertainty-handling capacities. Burke (1965) notes the heightening of sensory awareness of individuals in situations of high-risk uncertainty (rather like "getting high" on excitement). Nevertheless, we maintain that there are a very great many areas in which incongruity and accompanying uncertainty are not at all welcome. Either way—positive or negative, unexpected or actively sought—uncertainty can be expected to produce various changes in general physiological responses.

Social communication networks might be seen as a means of control-ling and reducing uncertainty, which may be accomplished by specializa-tion and development of expertise, with each member dependent on every other's expertise and higher status allocated to those with the ex-pertise to handle the higher-risk uncertainties. It is no accident that med-ical doctors are highly esteemed. The viability of communication net-works may be evaluated in terms of their continuing capacity to handle adequately various kinds of uncertainty for participants.

Perhaps one of the greatest challenges life offers man is not only to re-duce uncertainty in knowledge about his environment and likelihood of survival but to be able to live fully aware of the enormous amount of un-certainty and lack of security in human existence. This is also true of his ability to live with the relativity of his norms or moral ethics.

SOME EXAMPLES OF SIMILAR VIEWS IN STRESS LITERATURE

A number of stress researchers have suggested situations producing stress that are similar to the types of incongruities we listed previously or that involve uncertainty. Levine and Scotch (1967, p. 167) believe that there are at least three different types of stress situations: "(1) those in which the organism is blocked by a specific barrier or constraint to the attainment of a goal; (2) those in which it is presented with conflicting expectations; and (3) those in which heavy and unpleasant loads are applied to the organism."

According to Engel (1968) neurophysiological evidence indicates that when the central nervous system is failing in the task of processing input, the body mobilizes its emergency biological defense systems. He believes that central nervous system failures occur when input relevant to the organism is too great in volume (overload), the brain has no "program" or response to input available (incongruence), or the information cannot be handled promptly and efficiently so that the organism has no relevant behavior. When these situations occur the limbic structures with the hypothalamus mobilize the body.

Ostfeld suggests that there are four characteristic events that increase blood pressure in man:

> (1) the outcome of the event is uncertain; (2) the possibility of bodily or psychological harm exists; (3) flight or fight may be considered, but they are not appropriate forms of behavior; (4) the person involved must maintain a vigilant attitude until the event is concluded (1967, p. 16).

Antonovsky and Katz (1967) classify life crises into four categories: physical trauma, change in the general environment, changes affecting primary interpersonal relations, and changes in status, such as type of employment. Mandler (1967) believes that when the person has available no situationally relevant behavior, anticipation and ambiguity will produce epinephrine responses or distress. Almost all of these can be reconceptualized in terms of incongruities accompanied by uncertainty.

In Marks' (1967) perceptive discussion of the types of "social factors associated with chronic emotional stress," personal and social disorganization are of central concern.

> Indices of disorganization or stress would consist of evidence in an individual's life history, or his current activities and attitudes, or disharmonious relationships among his statuses and roles, reference groups and aspirations. Such relationships might take the form of sharp *discontinuities* in the individual's social relationships, life style or cultural milieu; *conflicts* among the values of the various groups of which he is a member and *discord* in his interaction within the groups; *conflicts* among the roles he plays in these various groups, *discrepancies* between his general social status and the normative life expectancies deriving therefrom on the one hand, and his personal reference groups and aspirations on the other. Status crystallization, relative depri-

vation, marginality, culture conflict, disengagement, alienation, and *anomie* appear to be the most useful in directing the choice of specific areas to be investigated in assessing the integration of the individual personality, the integration of the individual within the social system and the integration existing among the various elements of his social milieu. With reference to the last of these, a lack of functional integration or congruity among elements of a social system will be reflected in conflicts within the individual, and will alienate him from the system, its norms and its values (pp. 54–55, emphasis mine except for *anomie,* which is Marks').

"Incongruities" could easily be substituted for the words we have emphasized in Marks' statement. Clearly, both of us are concerned with the same property in social behavior. And both of us have come to a similar conclusion, a very exciting one, that these incongruities in social behavior produce both stress or physiological changes *and* alienation of the participant experiencing it from that social situation. To this end we have developed a typology of involvement that is based on the subjectively experienced congruities and incongruities in the information from the communication network.

A Typology for Subjective Involvement with Social Communication Networks

One essential dimension of our typology of involvement is the degree to which the information available in a given communication network has been appropriated by a person. That is, how much of it has he learned, accepted as correct, and incorporated into his social behavior and self-concepts. The second dimension is the degree to which one subjectively evaluates the information learned in a communication network as accurate and effective in his milieu. Accuracy and effectiveness are decisions based on the experiencing of congruities or incongruities in various situations. One may decide information is inaccurate or ineffective after only one highly disturbing encounter, or it may take many separate situations over time for the person to conclude that the information is indeed faulty. There are four types reflecting two things at once, the subjective evaluation of the congruity of the communication network's information and the degree of rapport or subjective involvement the person feels with that network. From the network's perspective, they also reflect the degree to which a person fits within the network, that is, his degree of conformity and affection for it. Like most typologies, these are analytical categories rather than designations of sharply delineated boundaries. One could construct several continua out of this typology, such as degree of autonomy.

TYPES OF SUBJECTIVE INVOLVEMENT
WITH A COMMUNICATION NETWORK

Information Repertoire Perceived as Congruous When Utilized in the Communication Network and Its Environment	Information Repertoire Dependent upon the Communication Network	
	Yes	No
Yes	Identification	Autonomy
No	Alienation	Anomie

The identified person finds the network's information accurate and effective for him and accepts it. His world is to him the way the information indicates. When he follows the norms of the network and uses its information to manipulate the environment, he is satisfied with the results. The identified person feels involved with the communication network. He feels rapport and affection for the people with whom he communicates in the network. His self-concept includes his status and roles in the network and is built in part upon the responses to him by other members of the network with whom he communicates. If asked to answer the question "Who am I?" he is very likely to mention his network roles. Identified people are more likely to identify themselves in terms of roles and positions in the networks in which they participate and less likely to see themselves as unique individuals independent of any communication network and to be aware of their personal attributes not included in the network's information. Other members of the communication network see the identified person as conforming and supporting the communication community and are likely to offer considerable approval and other positive sanctions. The identified person is the ideal member from the point of view of active participants of the communication network.

The alienated person finds the communication network's information he has accepted is inaccurate and ineffective for him. Information incongruities have led him to conclude that the world is not as it is described by network members, that he cannot effectively manipulate the environment by using information they have taught him, and/or that conforming to the norms of the network does not produce the results he has been taught to expect. He is dissatisfied with the information from, and has ambivalent feelings toward, the network. He is negatively involved. Much of his behavior and information may still be derived from the network and completely satisfactory alternatives may not have been discovered yet. He may vacillate between trying to change the network, finding some other alternative, or just living with the dissatisfaction he feels. His self-concepts are likely to be somewhat ambiguous and unclear. The actively participating members of the network, especially the identified ones, are likely to be troubled by those who are alienated. They do not see the alienated as ideal members, and may try to "straighten them out," remove or isolate them from communication channels, or accommodate them by making some changes in communication patterns and content.

The autonomous have developed a configuration of information and norms peculiar to them. This does not necessarily mean that they are odd people but that they have built a repertoire of information based on what they have found to work and to accurately represent the environment. They may incorporate large amounts of information from the particular network, but this information will be rearranged and qualified to fit their interpretations of the environment. They are detached from the particular network and are able to view it quite objectively. Autonomous people are able to move in the communication network comfortably and to get what they want from it. They understand the network, and their own information complement includes the means of relating with active and identified members of the network comfortably. Identified members may find autonomous persons tolerable and utilize them in mutually constructive ways. However, autonomous people may seem somewhat uncomprehensible to many identified people who cannot perceive the autonomous person's perspective. To the identified, the autonomous may seem somewhat unpredictable and a bit eccentric but a "good" neighbor as a rule and one who often comes up with surprising insights. An alienated person may find the autonomous good listeners who can understand the problem of nonworking information that bothers the alienated and may also be able to provide useful suggestions for reconciliation with the complex, introduction to a more compatible complex, or the development of the alienated into autonomous people. Autonomous people are more likely to identify themselves in terms of their perceptions of their own unique configuration of properties and capacities independently of any roles or positions in communication networks in which they might participate.

The anomic are people who do not comprehend the communication network's information and cannot interact effectively in that network. They may not be able to comprehend because of physical disabilities. They may never have been taught (because of lazy or absent parents, for example). They may have been taught by members of the communication network who themselves did not adequately comprehend the network's information content. The network may have changed without their being able to change with it. They may be isolated from communication channels as members of some disfavored group. They may have come into the group from another communication network in which they learned norms and information that do not work in the present network. They frequently do not even know where to go to learn about the network's information: they cannot locate the communication channels. They are uninvolved with the network. However, they may have learned information elsewhere that is accurate and effective for some parts of the environment other than the given communication network. The members of the network hold varying views about anomic persons, differing on the degree to which the anomic are dependent upon the network, such as immigrants, mistreated children, or deviants. (Not all deviants are anomic. They may be alienated, autonomous, or identified with another communication network.) As a rule, network members will condescend to help the anomic or will seek to control them to prevent them from disrupting the network's communication flow and interaction. The anomic person's self-concept is derived from somewhere other than the particular communication network unless he is forced to participate in it and to accept the label, such as retarded, applied to him by the network's members.

Identification is the most common type of involvement. It is generally subjectively preferred because of the security, certainty, and human support it provides, as well as the feelings of living a meaningful life. People who are socialized into a communication network are identified if the socialization is effective. Thus most people start out in life identified with a network to some degree. Identified people are generally less likely than the alienated or autonomous to perceive incongruities in the network's information or to attribute incongruities, if perceived, to the network. Alienated persons may be overzealous, attributing incongruities to the network inappropriately. Autonomous people are more likely to find and incorporate positive alternatives into their information complement after experiencing incongruities than the alienated are. Anomic people are least likely to perceive incongruities between the network's information and the environment since they understand none of the network's information and do not have access to its communication channels.

A sequential pattern is likely to begin when an identified participant of a network discovers incongruities and becomes alienated. He then either produces changes in the network to make it acceptable and eliminate the incongruity, leaves the network and becomes identified with another network that does not have that incongruity problem, or gradually develops autonomy. One cannot be alienated from a network with which one has not at some time been identified. The anomic person can never be alienated from the network, though he can be antagonistic toward it.

As a rule the autonomous people have developed their own perspective as a result of alienation. On rare occasions an autonomous person may have been taught to be autonomous by autonomous people. However, we suggest that even the autonomous person tends toward identification and will establish a new communication network if similarly minded people are available.

In determining involvement type, one must pay attention to the scope of the communication network being examined. Is this a small clique, a nation, a worldwide religion? Does it involve some or most of a person's information repertoire? Is it a primary group? The significance of identification, alienation, autonomy, and anomie vary considerably with the scope of the network involved. For the most part we are concerned with communication networks, whatever their size in numbers of participants, that account for a large proportion of the subject's information, attachments, and social activities. A person's subjective involvement should be evaluated for each of the major communication networks in which he participates if we are to predict which norms, values, and ideas will effect his subjective interpretation of a given situation. Each person's relations with communication networks are continually changing, presenting a dynamic mosaic of subjective involvement that must be reassessed from time to time.

Not only are these concepts useful in locating people whose social experiences and information contacts make them more likely to experience changes in susceptibility to disease, but they can also be used in conjunction with subjectively lifeless sociological concepts, such as bureaucracy, social change, institutionalization, and socialization, to improve our capacity to assess the subjective impact of the social activity described by such terms.

The Development and Maintenance of Identification Through Information Communication

Identification with a particular communication network can occur in two general ways. Most commonly it is the result of being born into the network. The communication networks of one's parents are those with which one is in contact from birth. Such membership usually includes exposure to other networks and the movement into some of them at various stages of growth as a result of the network's norms, such as going to school, monogamous marriage, or going to work. Various rites of passage such as baptism or graduation may also note the gradual movement of the person into more privileged positions of communication in the network as he matures.

A second and less-common route to identification is the result of contact with a communication network that is incongruous with one in which the person is currently participating, the subsequent alienation from the old network, and identification with the new one; or the alienation from the old and the exploration and eventual identification with a different, usually competing network.

In this section we focus primarily on the first, more common route to identification, some of the problems and processes for maintaining identification, and some of the characteristics we expect to find among identified people. The second route to identification is discussed in the section on alienation.

The recruitment of new members to replace those lost through death, alienation, or some other means is essential for the maintenance of a communication network. There is nothing intrinsic in communication networks that mandates their continuity, certainly not the simple fact that there is some degree of consensus on how roles are performed in the system. The recruitment of communicators and communicatees, the preservation of information content through socialization of communicating members into the identification state of involvement, and the development of information processes for handling incongruities common or anticipated in the network's milieu, all are essential in maintaining continuity.

IDENTIFICATION AND SELF

Children of participants are a major source of recruits. The infant immediately begins resonating with information in his milieu. As he grows he begins to imitate the sounds and behavior of people around him. Obviously, his social behavior, language, norms, and other information derived from human interaction can only come from people with whom he comes in contact. As a result of being born into contact with representatives of communication networks he may find himself in a particular religion, ethnic community, nation, socioeconomic status, and he is faced with certain occupational propensities. Turner (1956, pp. 322–323) suggests that children engage in nonreflexive role taking. They have little self-awareness and simply adopt the others' standpoint as their own. "This style continues to be a major source of values and attitudes of the individual," he says. Consequently, the child's information, especially his interpretations of social norms and their correct performance, reflects the interpretations of the network participants from whom they are learned. There probably is, but need not be, congruity between such interpretations and the consensus of the network's participants.

People from whom a child derives his knowledge of social behavior have been called orientational other by Kuhn (1967). The orientational others are those to whom the individual is most broadly and basically committed; those who provide him with his general vocabulary, including basic concepts; who continue to provide him with meaningful roles and other categories upon which his self-conception is based; and who provide him with communication that supports or facilitates changes in his self-conceptions (Kuhn, 1967, p. 181). Similar concepts commonly used are primary group and significant other. Foote (1967, p. 352) uses the term identification to denote the "full commitment to identities shared with others," which catches a good deal of what we mean by the term.

Independence from other people and communication networks, and especially the development of autonomy, requires the development of a self-image in which one sees himself as an object about which he can think, which he can correct, and which he can use as a basis for comparison and reference (Shibutani, 1961; E. Becker, 1962). "The individual with a self is not passive, but can employ his self in an interaction which may result in selections divergent from group definitions" (Meltzer, 1967, p. 23). As self-awareness develops, the attitudes of others are adopted as attitudes toward one's self and as third-party criteria for selecting alternatives—sometimes called the generalized other when norms of communication networks are involved. The third-party perspective of one's self permits selective reaction to audiences (Turner, 1956). This third-party criteria not only provides a reference point for conceiving of activity independent of the given audience, but also can produce an identified person who constantly monitors his behavior from the point of view of a network's norms. He may be capable of judging himself and feeling elation or remorse just as if some other member of the network had sanctioned his behavior. Such a person is more concerned with what "they" say, with doing what is "proper" in a given situation than in what he feels like doing, if indeed his feelings diverge at all from those prescribed for the situation by the network's norms.

The most likely type of communication network, outside of the family, with which one may identify in modern societies is the large-scale organization. As E. Gross (1970, p. 65) puts it, "The individual finds that in order to earn a living, or to obtain any long range goal, he must associate himself with some large organization, and usually quite a number of them, for all of his life in order to survive." He sees these organizations as "only strategies for the avoidance of stress through routinization" (p. 65), which supports our feeling that organizations persist because they are currently the most subjectively effective way of minimizing incongruities and uncertainty. Thus we would expect most people, especially adults, in response to questions such as "Who am I?" (Kuhn, 1953; McPartland and Cummings, 1958) to identify themselves in terms of their organizational roles and memberships. In turn, the communication networks with which one identifies at a given time may be determined by asking such questions. The language vocabulary the individual uses to explain and justify his behavior may also indicate the networks with which he identifies (C. W. Mills, 1967). McPartland and Cummings (1958) believe that the most appropriate self-identification is in terms of roles. They think, as we do, that such role identifications indicate social system involvement. However, they suggest that such identifications are associated with a lack of mental illness. We believe that the identification type of involvement may or may not be "healthy" depending on the amount of incongruity or uncertainty one must tolerate to be involved with a particular communication network.

Because of the similarities of the organizations making up modern societies, many organizations are capable of sustaining a person's self-concepts and are reasonably compatible with his information despite the heterogeneity of communication networks making up the society. Caplow (1964, p. 289) refers to pluralism, in which the organizations' values and interests may vary but the actual activity of the individuals in each are about the same, permitting easy mobility from one to another. Still, modern industrial societies offer a number of difficulties in maintaining a consistent identity or self-concept. The complexity and multiplicity of the communication networks with which one must deal and the degree of change and mobility make it challenging to handle all the different norms, roles, and choices and to reconcile them into a harmonious, congruous configuration (Ruitenbeek, 1964). Sherif (1952) thinks that the physical and social information acquired in childhood provide stability and consistency in a person's behavior as long as these social and physical information anchorages remain stable themselves. "As the physical and social anchorages become more unstable, more uncertain, the individual's personal bearings become more unstable, more uncertain" (Sherif and Harvey, 1952, p. 302). One of the major consequences of encounters with incongruities can be the disturbance of these anchorages and the disruption of one's self-concepts with accompanying uncertainty, insecurity, and inconsistency in one's behavior.

As one's contact with other communication networks expands and as he becomes more aware of the manmade, arbitrary nature of human norms and values—and thus of the relativity of all values—he will be less likely to be identified and thus less likely to identify himself in terms of the normative roles in which he participates. He would be more likely to formulate his self-image in terms of some configuration of properties, capacities, values, and activities engaged in that he sees as distinguishing him from other human beings (Becker, 1962; Shibutani, 1961), which is a mark of developing autonomy.

Reisman's types illustrate some of the different forms of involvement or identification with communication networks. Reisman (1961, pp. 241–242) considers his tradition-, inner-, and other-directed types as having a good social-psychological fit with their societies. They "respond in their character structure to the demands of their society." They "fit the culture as though they were made for it, as in fact they are." The identified participants in different networks may have much in common, but they may also be quite unique in their style of relation to the network, depending on the nature of the information and communication patterns of the network.

EMOTIONAL INVOLVEMENT AND SENSITIVITY OF THE IDENTIFIED

The range of phenomena that "excite" or otherwise produce subjective responses, positive or negative, in an identified person tends to be limited to those phenomena taken into account in his communication network's information complements. There may be some esoteric personal experiences that provide each person with some unique sensitivities, but in the main the sensitivities of the identified person are developed and stimulated by interaction in his communication networks. Consequently, identified people may be somewhat bland in comparison with autonomous persons because the range and refinement of their sensitivities may be spotty and sharply circumscribed. Their life styles may be rather routine and inflexible, tending to follow the "in" fashions, music, and recreation favored by members of their network. They may expend considerable energy attempting to be "in the know" about the "latest" in their networks, because information access marks status. Because of their limited sensitivity, identified people may have difficulty "taking the role" of others outside of their own communication network cluster or feeling sympathy and empathy with them, and they are more likely to be suspicious and intolerant of such people.

The identified participant, in the extreme, pure type, is intensely involved with the communication network and is highly ethnocentric, defending the organization from critics and feeling uncomfortable outside the sphere of the communication patterns of the network. His role or "job" in the network may even become an absolute good-in-itself for which the person would die rather than permit to be disrupted or fail in his duty (Burke, 1965, p. 204). The network is generally seen as benevolent, and all failings are seen as problems of individual inadequacy or outside meddling. He "loses" himself in and expresses himself through the network's communication activities and vocabulary. For him the communication network takes on religious overtones, with some of its norms, practices, and symbols seen as sacred or absolute. He is capable of intense subjective and physiological responses to sacred and taboo elements of the network (Caplow, 1964; Maslow, 1954).

This involvement provides an opportunity for the intense feelings of religious devotion, patriotism, and "spiritual" ecstasy that can accompany group excitement. Through such involvement one may experience merging with something he feels is larger, more powerful, and more meaningful than himself. The network's symbols may come to represent and even reproduce these feelings of devotion (Rose, 1969). We would expect all of this to be accompanied by arousal of the sympathetic physiological response, which may be in large measure responsible for the subjective elation or "high" experienced. These sorts of experiences are generally considered very valuable by human beings and serve to make life meaningful and to mark major events in their lives. Such experiences are often one of the major inducements of communication networks to encourage identification by its participants. The feelings of companionship and rapport with other people in the network, considered as brotherhood or brotherly love, provide feelings of warmth and security that do not seem to be duplicated in any other way.

As a rule, when groups of people who have highly congruous information repertoires find each other and establish a communication network, such rapport and involvement may emerge. Argyris (1957) believes that there may be a fusion of the individual and a complex organization if the person finds his objectives expressed in and through the organization. Whyte (1956) describes the "organization man" who seems to be identified with the complex organization in which he is employed. The organization men seem to enjoy conforming and having the organization direct much of their lives (see also Caplow, 1964). The identified person may follow the network's norms so vigorously that it is difficult to interact with the person in any other context except as a network member. He is likely to develop an image of the ideal member based on the network's norms and to judge himself and others in terms of this image, striving consciously and persistently toward it. Such members are much less likely to "be themselves" and develop interests and relate to people in ways other than those prescribed in network information.

A major difference between autonomous and the identified people lies in this area of subjective responsiveness to the symbols, group gatherings, and feelings of brotherhood in communication network interactions. The identified person feels a sense of obligation or duty toward the norms of the network and may suffer mortification or guilt if he breaks them. Autonomous people may be highly ethical and very sensitive to other people, but their moral code is their own, although it may coincide with some of those of a given network. However, they feel no obligation to obey norms of a network they do not accept, though they may follow the norms because it is convenient to do so in that milieu or if it permits freedom of movement and activity that otherwise would be denied them.

From our point of view identification is neither good nor bad. How it is evaluated depends on the values of the judge and the properties being evaluated.

PRESERVATION OF IDENTIFICATION BY INFORMATION PROTECTION IN COMMUNICATION NETWORKS

Once identification has been established, it must be preserved from disruption caused by contacts with incongruous information; if contacts occur, information and communication channels must be established to prevent the incongruities from disrupting identification. There are two dimensions involved: (1) the probabilities of incongruities being encountered and (2) the capacity of the network to handle such encounters, thereby preserving identification, including the preparation of the member to accept the existence of the incongruities without disruption of his self concepts and behavior.

The probability of encountering incongruities in a communication network's information involves at least four factors. The first is the heterogeneity of information and norms in a given milieu. By heterogeneity we mean the quantity of incongruous information, values, and norms found in the communication networks associating in a particular milieu, including incongruities within a particular network's information. In modern societies communication networks contain, are contained within, overlap, and communicate with other networks. The variety of networks resonating together and the rapid rate of change increase heterogeneity, which enhances the probability of incongruities being encountered. Even in situations in which a given communication network dominates, such as a church in a small community or an isolated Indian tribe in Central America, internal information heterogeneity may expose incongruities in the network's information. For example, the more uncertain the success of the practical information of the communication network, the more alternative suggestions for handling the problem may be found in the same network; whereas the more effective the information is in producing the desired results, the more it will be accepted by all of the network's participants. In healing practices in Sierra Madre it was found that the more effective a cure was, the fewer alternative cures were suggested (Werner, 1970). Thus suggestions may proliferate in areas in which the network's information is ineffective. Perception of these conflicting suggestions, or dissatisfaction with the effectiveness of them all, may lead one to question the validity of the network's information. These conditions also reflect the second factor, which is the degree to which direct contact with natural environmental conditions incongruous with the communication network's information is unavoidable.

The third factor is the degree to which the communication network's norms encourage or require activities that may entail contact between participants of incongruous communication networks. The national requirement of military service brings together in intimate contact participants of many incongruous networks operating within the nation. The norm of many networks, that one should seek a college education, is another example.

The fourth factor influencing the probability of encountering incongruous information is called isolation. Isolation is accomplished by using norms to prevent awareness of and contact with incongruous information in other networks, and to prevent access to information within the network that may be incongruous with the network's more widely shared information. With the growing volume of information being carried by a wide variety of media, from printed matter such as newspapers, magazines, and books to electronic media such as telephones, television, recordings, and movies, the accessibility of material from a wide variety of communication networks is as close as the drugstore newsstand, the public library, and the television in the living room. Here, self-selection based on a network's suggestions about what to read and watch and how to interpret what is read and seen provide a filter to prevent incongruities from being experienced. Such norms controlling information content are the major means available to network members for preventing contact with incongruities.

Moore and Tumin (1949) point out that for the organization to function effectively it must control information. Some communication of misinformation by participants is inevitable but not intentional, because of the imperfect understanding of any person or group of all of a network's information. Still, the communication network's participants have ample reason to desire limited information access. To do so preserves privileged positions through the secrecy of insiders having privileged information. It protects network information and norms through the ignorance of alternatives and of the magnitude of normative violations, maintaining the picture that deviation is inconsequential. If the true extent of deviation were known and if it were large, it might destroy the consensus on which the norms are based. Communication networks can prevent experimentation by maintaining ignorance of the correct consequences of independent action as against conforming to group norms. This information control produces large areas in which a member has inadequate information and must rely upon the "superior" knowledge and resources of other members of the network for answers and resources. This strengthens loyalties and encourages identification with the network. The discovery by the person of his own ignorance, the knowledge of what it is he does not know may be the beginning of the development of autonomy or at least prepares him to acquire new knowledge.

We can expect that the communication network will be more responsive to participants and members of associated networks to the degree that these people have access to the particular network's information. This is partially because communication is easier, involving common vocabularies, and partially because the norms of the networks with which the particular network clusters can be brought to bear when there are normative incongruities. Because information communication channels are increasing and becoming more accessible in modern societies and because disclosure of communication network information, voluntarily or otherwise, is becoming more common, we can expect the responsiveness of network members, particularly those in more central information control positions, to increase also.

Such information distribution and subsequent modifications of information and communication networks may in time lead to a greater homogeneity of information within a given cluster of networks. In addition, as information flow increases we can expect shifts in power and status group occupants. Power will be more widely distributed, and those who control information distribution or produce new information will be among the elites. However, in the early stages of such increased access to communication network's information, we expect an increase in contact with unresolved incongruities. This period of breakdown of isolation and increased exposure to incongruities may produce considerable disturbance in subjective well-being and disease susceptibility.

The Insulation of Members Encountering Information Incongruities. Despite all precautions, some contact with incongruous information is nearly inevitable. If the communication network is to maintain a member's identification after such an encounter, adequate explanations or justifications of the incongruity must be developed. We have applied the label "insulation" to such explanations and justifications.

There are at least five forms of *explanation* of an incongruity to discount its existence or legitimacy: (1) the fluke—the perceived event that indicates an incongruity is a fluke or exception not to be taken seriously; (2) temporary perceptual distortion—the perception of the event was distorted because of some natural or personal condition at the time ("How many drinks did you say you had?"); (3) incompetence—the failure of practical programs or suggestions of the network is caused by some shortcoming of the participants or their failure to follow the procedures correctly; (4) sabotage—incongruity experienced when activities of the network are not successful may also be explained as the work of some other people or forces working against the network members, such as the Communist conspiracy, evil spirits, the establishment, or the CIA, to name a few popular boogey men; and (5) discounting the source—the rejection of the source providing the incongruous information as unreliable, questioning the integrity and intentions of the source ("You can't believe anything he says because everybody knows he is just a . . ."). Undoubtedly there are many other forms of explanations.

There are dozens of *justifications* for incongruities experienced, depending on the nature of the information the network communicates; for example, the discovery of practices and information in a given network that are incongruous with what most participants have been told in communication within the network can be justified as necessary secrecy to accomplish goals the participants approve, such as military secrets in times of war or denial of an impending merger between companies while it is being negotiated. Encountering of incongruities between parts of a particular religion's dogma or between the dogma and other forms of information such as scientific findings might be justified as a "mystery" that tests the participant's faith and will be explained in God's own due time.

We can expect larger proportions of the network's communications to deal with these explanations and justifications as the heterogeneity of the communication networks in which the given network participates increases or during periods of social change. These justifications may be accompanied by active efforts to proselyte or to persuade participants in other networks of the correctness of the given network's information.

The information control of communication networks does not necessarily require a cynical elite looking with contempt upon the masses. Such control can be the result of network participants themselves being unable to handle information incongruities, with the network's information and communication channels providing means for handling the incongruities and/or the accompanying uncertainty. When queried on a given incongruity, they may simply be reciting the information they themselves use to handle these same incongruities.

If a participant rejects these controlling norms, explanations, or justifications provided in the network, he may be disapproved of by other members and denied access to certain kinds of information and their accompanying rewards. For the identified members, conformity in others is valuable and necessary for the continuity of the information and communication networks upon which they rely (see Homans, 1961). In extreme cases, the communication network may be passing inaccurate and ineffective information encumbered with many justifications, explanations, and controls to participants who are dependent upon the information for protection from incongruities and accompanying uncertainty. Yet these people may be learning information that makes them potentially more vulnerable, because the manufactured incongruities of the network are added to the inadequacies and uncertainties of ordinary human existence that the network exists, in part, to reduce. Conceivably, if there were judges wise enough, we could rank the various communication networks in the world in terms of the volume of effective and accurate information each contains for understanding and operating within the environment with a minimum of uncertainty; the minimum of unnecessary manmade incongruities or uncertainties that exist only to preserve identification with the network; the maximum of information distribution (and consequently power) among participants; and capacities of the members to increase the congruity of the network's information with the environment and with other networks with which it clusters.

If, despite all of the network's effort, a participant recognizes incongruities invalidating the network's information, the probability of his rejection of the communication network still depends in part on the risks in higher uncertainty such a rejection would entail. Would rejecting the communication network expose the person to even more situations for which he has inadequate information or resources than if he accepts the network and ignores the incongruity or explains it away? What would happen to the social anchorages for his self-concept? We suggest that the probability of a person admitting an incongruity and acting upon it depends on the availability of acceptable alternative networks with which he can identify. It also depends on adequate development of the individual's own information repertoire and self-concept so that he has sufficient information, personal norms, skills, and resources to be able to survive in the cluster of networks without dependence on the continuity of the particular network in which the inadequate information was discovered. We expect the identified participant, as compared with the autonomous, to have greater difficulty living with uncertainty, particularly normative or moral uncertainty, which Fromm (1941) thinks is experienced as a "terrible" aloneness. The more identified person may be expected to prefer absolute values, pat answers, and firm conclusions, with considerable distress occurring when faced with normative uncertainties and no desire to experience moral "aloneness" by leaving the network.

Identification in a particular communication network can be very healthy, or it can make one very vulnerable. However, as a rule, we expect communication networks to reduce perceived incongruities and their accompanying uncertainty and thus benefit the health of the person by minimizing arousal of the general physiological responses in sufficient intensity or duration to produce changes in susceptibility to illness. Even a communication network containing large amounts of inadequate information can be effective in this regard if its isolation and insulation techniques are effective and if its information is sufficiently accurate and effective to permit viable survival (see development of this property of communication networks in Chapter VII).

The evidence concerning identification and health is, at best, suggestive. Wilkins (1967) indicates that in isolated groups, such as Antarctic researchers, positive orientations toward the goal, mission, or task of the group is important not only for the group's work but for the individual's capacity to remain free from psychological problems in the confining situation. Hinkle, after studying 24 female office employees concluded, "Those who fit most comfortably into given niches, who by background, temperament, and physical characteristics seem best suited to the situation in life in which they find themselves, seem to do better in terms of their overall health" (cited by Thurlow, 1967). Hinkle (1958), studying Chinese immigrants, found that subjects who had few illnesses experienced relatively little conflict or anxiety, but had little "insight" and less awareness of emotional problems. They tended to be emotionally insulated in interpersonal relationships, being relatively insensitive to the needs of others. Leighton et al. (1963) state that people who conform to culturally acceptable means-ends patterns tend to be mentally healthy. Cassel (1970, pp. 195–196) notes that individuals deprived of "meaningful human contact or group membership" are higher risks for schizophrenia, accidents, suicide, and respiratory diseases. He also comments that the literature on hypertension covering some 30 years from many different countries shows that lower blood pressure has been consistently found in small, cohesive societies insulated from changes occurring in modern industrial societies. This evidence suggests that identification in communication networks, especially those more isolated from incongruities, may indeed be associated with lower levels of disease susceptibility.

On the other hand, identification with some communication networks in modern societies may increase susceptibility to disease. An example is the work of Freidman and Rosenman, in which they distinguish a configuration of behavior patterns and attitudes they call Type *A* that is related to increased risk of coronary heart disease. Type-*A* people are characterized as eagerly competitive and having an intense drive to achieve, a persistent desire for advancement and recognition, continuous involvement in a variety of activities with deadlines, a constant tendency to accelerate the rate of execution of physical and mental activities, and extraordinary mental and physical alertness (Freidman and Rosenman, 1959). Freidman and Rosenman (1963) suggest that Type-*A* patterns are common in modern industrial societies (see also Freidman, Rosenman, and Byers, 1964; Zyzanski and Jenkins, 1970; Jenkins, 1971). Coronary heart disease patients have also been found to be more committed to prevailing ethical norms (Caffrey, 1967). We could suggest that underlying the Type *A*'s behavior is the high-risk uncertainty we have discussed previously. Just what incongruities may be involved would have to be empirically examined, but it seems likely that many of them are related to the attainment of normative goals and the uncertainty of this attainment in the given networks.

In general, we expect modern heterogeneous societies to be associated with increased susceptibility to disease because of the greater probability of encountering incongruities and the large proportion of major social norms and goals that involve high-risk uncertainty to obtain or perform. However, to the degree that members of modern societies are also participants in communication networks that isolate and insulate them from many of the incongruities and provide them with security, brotherhood, and reassurance that their lives are meaningful and their activities important, we can expect them to be less susceptible to disease than other members of that society. This may explain in part Syme's (1970) finding that in terms of death rates Seventh Day Adventists seem less susceptible to many diseases than others in the same milieu.

Communication Networks as the Source of Alienation

The usual way of breaking free or losing the protection of the information from and participation in a communication network is through alienation that results from contact with and acceptance of information incongruities disqualifying some of the network's information. This is the very thing the identified members of the network most fear happening.

Alienation is an unstable situation, and people tend to move out of it. Usually they become identified with different communication networks or effect changes in the old network, making it more acceptable. They may become autonomous. But rarely do the alienated renew identification with the same, unchanged network, although prolonged contact between the alienated and the network members may occur.

ARE MAN AND SOCIAL ORGANIZATIONS BY
NATURE INCOMPATIBLE?

Years ago Fromm (1941) suggested that as men matured they had two choices, either to develop their independence or to give up their freedom and "escape" from independence and individual identity. In the latter case, "the individual ceases to be himself; he adopts entirely the kind of personality offered him by cultural patterns; and he therefore becomes exactly as all others are and as they expect him to be" (Fromm, 1941, p. 185). He believes that this is the choice the majority of normal individuals make in modern societies. Such people are probably identified in our terms. It is not so much the choice that interests us here but Fromm's tone. He seems to feel that individual independence is "good" and being identified with the communication network is "bad," or at least not as good. He is not the first nor the last to judge communication networks harshly and to praise independence, autonomy in our terms. A whole tradition of social criticism has developed around the values that independence or autonomy, continual development or growth, and original creativity are "good" and that identification with communication networks, conforming to them, not trying to be creative or to grow and *enjoying* it, are "bad."

The classic individualists are the thinkers of the Enlightenment who believed in progress and the infinite perfectability of man, his powers of reason, and his capacities to correct social institutions. Individualists tend to see communication networks as sources of limitations on the development of man's natural capacities. In practice, they have sought to minimize stratification and to eliminate networks they decide are restricting. For example, in the French Revolution the trade and craft organizations were eliminated and the family and church purposely weakened (Hobsbawm, 1962; Zeitlin, 1968).

The thinkers favoring the communication network are not much wiser in their enthusiasm. They tend to see man's own natural inclinations as the limiting influence on his development, with society rescuing him despite his natural resistance to control (Durkheim is an example). They sometimes see man as an empty vessel to be filled by society, as a nonhuman until he is properly socialized. Such thinkers have tended to defend order and stratification.

Both these groups, in our opinion, have over-emphasized the natural attributes of man. This suggests lingering belief in such notions as mind and spirit as sources of innate ideas or capacities. Both have failed to realize that man's capacities (including physiological) are the product of his inherited genetic properties and the socio-environmental milieu in which he is resonating. In our opinion we cannot correctly speak of human capacity or tendencies existing separate from communication networks. We cannot say human beings are better off in one sort of network than another because their natural capacities are inseparable from the information and communication patterns of their communication networks.

The list of workers who have felt that there is an inevitable conflict between the individual and social organizations reads like a Who's Who of Sociology. Park and Burgess believe that "personal evolution is always a struggle between the individual and society—a struggle for self-expression on the part of the individual, for his subjection on the part of society" (cited by Caplow, 1964, p. 38). Etzioni (1964, p. 41) calls this the organizational dilemma that can never be eliminated and thus is an inevitable source of strain. He thinks that alienation from social organizations is both inevitable and occasionally desirable. Merton (1957, p. 200) notes that the result of successful inducement to conformity by the organization produces timidity, conservatism, and technicism among the conformers. Veblen's trained incapacity and Dewey's occupational psychosis are forms of social training that prevent awareness of other alternatives, and they can be blamed on the social system. Merton (1957, p. 198) and Burke (1965) believe that such training will be a handicap to the person in times of change because he will continue to behave in terms of the old skills that are no longer adequate. Maslow (1968, p. 47) suggests that there is inevitable conflict between safety and growth, which is a dilemma for all men. Argyris (1957) believes that there is a basic incongruency between the mature person and the requirements of the formal organization:

> this inevitable incongruency increases as (1) the employees are of increasing maturity, (2) as the formal structure . . . is made more clear-cut and logically tight for maximum formal organization effectiveness, (3) as one goes down the line of command, and (4) as the jobs become more and more mechanized. . . . (p. 66)

He suggests two polar types of organization, the ideal formal organization and the ideal individual-need-centered group. In the former, an individual's personal interests are subordinated to the organization's existing prescriptions and interests; in the latter, the interests and prescriptions of the organization emerge from members' interaction.

Thomas and Znaniecki (1961, pp. 1292–1297) see this conflict as the "reconciliation of the stability of social systems with the efficiency of individual activities" (p. 1292). They suggest for a rather homogeneous and isolated communication network (Polish peasants) that the network requires the person to satisfy all his interests and have all aspects of his life encompassed by the network and that his individual development can proceed only to the stage the network permits. The rejection of some part of the network or its rapid change is apt to produce disorganization of the member "for the rejection of a few traditional schemes brings with it a general negative attitude toward the entire stock of traditions which he has been used to revere, whereas he is not prepared for the task of reorganizing his life on a new basis" (p. 1293). They say modern societies are characterized by "a plurality of rival complexes of schemes each regulating in a definite traditional way certain activities and each contending with others for supremacy within a group" (p. 1293). These conditions do "not correspond at all with the spontaneous tendencies of individuals," (p. 1294) so that a person's progressive development and creativity sooner or later make the schemes of the complex look insufficient.

Marx, the originator of the term alienation, defined it in terms of the separation of man from the fruits of his labor under capitalism; Weber and Simmel saw it in terms of the rationalization and routinization of complex organizations (Nisbet, 1966). Weber believed that rationalization and routinization in the form of monolithic, secular, and utilitarian bureaucracies destroyed emotionally meaningful relations in society and that they eliminated the enchanted in the social world (Nisbet, 1966). Weber's formal and Mannheim's functional rationality describe the typical mode of participation in complex organizations in which alienation (their definition) occurs. It is

> the type of rationality that prevails in an organization of human activities in which the thought, knowledge, and reflection of the participants are virtually unnecessary. . . . Their purposes, wishes, and values become irrelevant and superfluous. . . . What they forfeit in creativity and initiative is gained by the organization as a whole and contributes . . . to its greater efficiency (Zeitlin, 1968, p. 311).

Simmel also feared that the increase in universalism and objectivity in the bureaucracy would destroy opportunities for expressive personal involvement and for feelings of "wholeness" (Nisbet, 1966, pp. 305–310). Still, both Simmel and Weber recognized that alienation could be useful as a form of insight into one's environment and himself.

Such arguments can only stand if individuals and social systems can be separated. For some social scientists social organizations seem to have been reified into fire-breathing monsters out to devour the tasty morsel that is man's creative individuality. We take the position that men are their societies and vice versa. Conflicts of men who would be different are not with social organizations but with people who are fond of behaving as they are in a given communication network having a particular information content. All the conflicts described by the above authors can be translated into our notion of incongruities between the information in the network and that information directly perceived by the individual or learned in other networks in its cluster that are teaching incongruous information. Many times writers have condemned social organization per se for the inadequacies of the information content and communication patterns of a particular communication network. There is nothing in the nature of human interaction to prevent man, in principle, from knowing all things and incorporating this accurate, complete, and effective information into a worldwide society of homogeneous communication networks in which all people are creatively and happily identified.

In addition, how can we reconcile the cries of lamentation of the individualists that on the one hand everyone is sure to be alienated from the complex organization because of its "inhuman" restriction of man's "natural" capacities, while on the other hand they also lament that people are too happy in these organizations for their own good? As we noted earlier, members of modern societies must all engage in several complex organizations, and yet the evidence indicates that most people are identified with some communication network, though they may not like some other network in which they have found incongruities. We doubt that only routinization and rationalization can produce alienation as we have defined it, because many people seem content with, and even anxious to maintain, such routinization. Americans' distaste for assembly-line work may be more the result of incongruities between information of various networks and what one experiences—for example, what dignified work is, the physical capacities one has been taught to develop, the degree of fatigue one has been told is normal, and similar considerations—than the actual properties of 8 hours of repetitive work per se. Edward Gross' (1970) research indicates that complaints about working conditions, cafeteria food, and the like reflect occurrence of disturbances in the workers' life, but not necessarily in the work milieu. He concludes:

> that arduous working conditions will become more and more closely related
> to stress as the identification of the member with the organization declines.

In reverse, as identification increases, persons become increasingly tolerant of working conditions until, at an extreme, they may even take pride in their own toughness in handling such conditions (Gross, 1970, p. 85).

Thus, routine work dissatisfaction may be the result of alienation more than a "cause" of it.

Gouldner (1967), in a unique position, notes the malleability of human learning. He suggests that the capacity to be socialized into first one, then another communication network is a reflection of one's autonomy from social systems in general. He thinks that people are not completely dependent upon a given social system, even after being socialized into it, and that they can develop escape velocity from it. He sees the tension between social systems and individuals as the tension between a respect for one's own and others' privacy and a competing desire to include others; it is tension between social distance and sharing. This fits much better with our model, in which social systems are seen as people interacting in communication networks. Some of the tensions within a network may be incongruities of personal preferences for privacy and sharing. Gouldner (1967) believes that communication networks are moving toward a more complete integration or sharing between members, which could overrestrict the autonomy of some of its participants and impair their performance both within and without the network.

Gouldner believes that some balance between effective integration of the network and an inhibition of the network's supposed tendencies to overrestriction must be attempted. We require more objective evidence before we can be convinced this overrestriction is necessarily a property of all human communication networks.

We doubt that social organizations and men are natural enemies, eternally doomed to protect, fight, hate, and live off of each other. We do believe, however, that the information content of a communication network can cause unnecessary contact with incongruities and uncertainty. These could be reduced by modifying the information without reducing the effectiveness of the overall organized effort. This modification could lessen both the alienation and susceptibility to disease of the network's participants. An example of such information content that might be changed was found by Kornhauser who studied auto workers:

> It sometimes seems almost as if the pervasive emphasis on money, competitive success, and pleasures of consumption had been designed to produce frustration and undermine self-esteem among the disadvantaged and less successful (1965, p. 271).

Kleiner (1965; Kleiner and Parker, 1963) also found that the emphasis on status achievement produced insecurity concerning one's status. Galbraith

(1967) too believes that if people define products as necessary for health and happiness and as indicants of social achievement and community standing—as they are encouraged to in our society, they may suffer to the degree that they do not have these goods.

Edward Gross (1970) takes a position similar to ours on the debate over the costs to the individual of organization participation in terms of pressures on the individual and restrictions on his creativity. He notes, as we have, that the basis of individualistic-oriented theories is the assumption that human beings have certain needs they carry into all situations that confront them. Among the most popular are those suggested by Maslow: physical well-being, safety, social satisfaction, esteem, and self-actualization. From the individualists' point of view the organization opposes the expression of these individually unique needs, and various organizations "demand conformity, obedience, and dependence, and keep the person at an immature level" (E. Gross, 1970, p. 97). Because the needs press for satisfaction, this attempt to frustrate them produces various social, psychological, and psychosomatic disorders. "The result is a great battle between the organization and the individual to get the latter to alter his personality; of course, since the needs are unalterable, the person must fight back or collapse," (E. Gross, 1970, p. 98) the individual theorists maintain. The advocates of this point of view see individual needs as invariable and thus insist that social organizations must do the changing.

Gross (1970) offers the following criticisms of individualistic theories. First, they overemphasize the uniqueness of the problem as one of large organizations, whereas any form of organized activity requires discipline of participants and thus may generate conflicts. Gross points out that if one wishes to speak of tyranny, the tyranny of the small group such as family, clique, or fraternity may be even greater than that of a large organization tolerating little deviation. In fact, large-scale organizations may protect individuals from the arbitrary actions and constant demands of small groups by specifying obligations, whereas in small groups one is never sure when he is "done." Second, individualistic theories tend "to exaggerate the limitations of large organizations on personal freedom and on the sense of autonomy" (p. 100). According to Gross, the evidence on job satisfaction indicates that, overall, about 13 percent are dissatisfied. The evidence does not support the notion that the workers are miserable, alienated, and unhappy wretches. Third, there is some question about how universal the "need" of self-actualization really is.

The claim is made that self-actualization is universal. Actually it should be offered as a *conclusion* from many empirical studies rather than as a flat assertion. The claim could certainly be made that for most persons security and predictability, especially in their work, are more important than self-actualization (p. 101, emphasis his).

He notes that mental illness occurs throughout industry in all positions, including those where opportunities for creativity—the sacred cow of the individualists—are highest. Fourth, individualist theories overemphasize the importance of work to the individual. Many jobs require little change in the person and for many are of less importance than outside interests. Individualist thinkers tend to underrate economic rewards. "There is little evidence that money ever ceases to be a motivator, no matter what one's needs may be" (p. 102). Fifth, individualist theories have a strong democratic value bias. "If these theorists . . . simply said that one *should* provide workers with more challenge or autonomy, because that is consistent with democratic values, then one could not argue with them" (p. 102, emphasis his). But instead they argue that "traditional organization methods lead to dissatisfaction, anxiety, and aggression, or to dependency, conformity, and doing only a minimum of work" (p. 102). He suggests that anxiety may be useful in motivating the individual and that there is plenty of room for creativity in the organization, such as political power plays, restriction of output, or working harder so as to loaf half an hour. The individualists might argue that these are not desirable forms of creativity, which simply begs the question of creativity.

Gross suggests, and we concur, that discipline will inevitably prove distressing to some people. "Work in its organized form, then, is stressful, and yet is the major means that modern society offers for preventing or avoiding even greater stress" (p. 104). He suggests something sure to set individualists screeching, that some of the stressfulness of participation in social organizations could be reduced by teaching the young methods for dealing with the kinds of organizations in which they will spend most of their lives—what services they offer and how to obtain them, how to deal and live with authority and hierarchy, how to be able to do routine work when necessary, and the like. We agree very much.

The resources of complex organizations that are knowingly manipulated or utilized offer enormous possibilities for self-expression, creativity, and especially the solution of problems, which may well be the "highest" form of creativity, if values are to be applied. One important insight the young could be taught is the nature of the organization's reaction to creative solutions to problems. The scientist or innovator "can expect opposition, but that should not lead him to believe that such opposition is malicious or that conditions are necessarily better anywhere else" (E. Gross, 1970, p. 105). Rather, the organization generally assumes that it has solved its problems and may take a while to recognize the need to change. Training of the young could also prepare them for shifts in jobs and for demotions when they come, such as at the end of a career. Gross concludes: "There seems no alternative to organizations. They inevitably have built-in stress, and future research as well as the efforts of public authority should deal with attempts to keep such stress at a minimal level. What that minimum is, is not known. It is certainly greater than zero" (p. 105).

Through all this there are glimmers of "better" things to come. There is some possibility that a form of social organization is emerging out of the complex organizations in heterogeneous modern societies that has never been known before. In areas of governments and whole societies it has been called the cybernetic state (Schick, 1970) and the active society (Etzioni, 1968 a). Our existing bureaucratic-style organizations have emphasized internal efficiency and continuity. The new style of organization is oriented more toward external effectiveness in fulfilling the goals for which the organization was originally put together. In this new type of organized interaction participants will be more responsive to those that compose it and those it serves, partially because the means of communication will have developed to the point that the organization—or communication network in our vocabulary—can monitor "how it's doing" as its work progresses, partially because it will be more open to scrutiny by participants in communication networks with which it clusters. Much of the current social unrest in modern societies would probably never have materialized if such systems had existed earlier because problems would have been discovered before they produced widespread frustration and would not have required the development of special-interest pressure groups to correct them. This new type of communication network, supposedly, will be more receptive to change.

Thus to the question, Are man and social organizations by nature incompatible? we would answer, no. It is the incongruities in the networks' information content that produces alienation from communication networks.

Biosocial resonation makes no judgements about the developmental phases of man or their desirability. The theme of progress runs rampant through scientific literature on human behavior. Much of the individualists' thrust is based on the judgement that progress is good. We discuss why we reject the notion of progress in the next chapter.

Another theme seems to center on freedom. Briefly, we see freedom as subjective satisfaction with the array of choices one has before him. It could also be defined as the absolute number of choices at the same level of costs and risk concerning a given matter. It should be easily understood that a choice is not a choice unless one gives up something, perhaps many other choices, in order to select one. Being free is such a relative and subjective property that it hardly seems worth special attention apart from other subjective values. In our opinion, modern social societies offer enormous arrays of choices. That some people do not feel free may have more to do with information incongruities between communication networks, such as who has the "right" to what, than to any constraint upon the person by complex organizations per se.

To sum, our position is that man is more than any other creature a biosocial animal; to say that there is inherent conflict between the social and the biological or innate in man is like saying there is a fundamental conflict between the ingredients of a chocolate cake. We attempt to stay clear of values except for the value that physical health in humans is good. We judge social arrangements primarily in terms of their capacity to produce health. A quite different ranking of social behavior might be derived from other criteria, such as what gets the job done most efficiently.

ALIENATION THROUGH DISCOVERY OF INCONGRUITIES

Whorf (1940) calls attention to situations where rules have no exceptions in the experience of the actor. Because there are no exceptions, the rule is not recognized as a rule, or perhaps not recognized at all. It becomes instead a part of what Whorf terms the background of experience of which we tend not to be aware. Not until one has an experience that contrasts something with the given phenomena or points to irregularities in its occurrence can one become aware of it and formulate it as a rule. Of the experiencing of contrasts in social settings Shibutani says:

> People become acutely aware of the existence of different outlooks only when they are successively caught in situations in which conflicting demands are made upon them, all of which cannot possibly be satisfied.
> These conflicts are essentially alternative ways of defining the same situation, arising from several possible perspectives (1967, p. 167).

Such experiences may lead to subjective feelings of constraint by social systems (Dohrenwend, 1961). Burke (1965, p. 89) calls this process perspective by incongruity. Only when one is exposed to such incongruities do problems of social group loyalties arise.

The insights derived from discovery of incongruities can alter one's self-concept. Shibutani says, "It is possible for a man to alter his self-conception simply by noticing things he had previously overlooked (1961, p. 531). Chapman, Hinkle, and Wolff (1960) point out the importance of stable, intimate human relations, especially in the dependent years, and the grave effects of processes destroying one's hope and faith in other people. The constant invalidation of one's information can lead to disorientation, suspicion, and perhaps withdrawal. If invalidation is complete, the person experiences anomie. Scott and Lyman point out that "the constellation of significant others that systematically negates reality for an individual is engaged in producing persons who routinely place their world under suspicion" (1968 b, p. 186). This process can produce paranoiacs.

Alienation should be considered as a form of understanding derived from discovery that one's information complement is not accurate or effective. Despite the fact that it is subjectively uncomfortable and disappoints the members of the particular network, producing negative involvement, it is the opening of new horizons that may lead to greater understanding of the environment. Subjectively, one may feel disillusioned, angry, betrayed, degraded, or exploited. Strong satire cannot be written by the anomic, only by those who are alienated to some degree and are utilizing the insights from which the alienation in part was derived. Maslow, commenting on European Existentialists concerned with despair, anguish, and dread, says: "This high I. Q. whimpering on a cosmic scale occurs whenever an external source of values fails to work" (1968, p. 16). But he notes that psychotherapists have found that the loss of illusions, although painful at first, may be ultimately exhilarating and strengthening. Von Bertalanffy (1968, p. 25) also suggests that people may need some disruptions of steady states in order to establish new and hopefully better steady states.

Alienation, either from a particular piece of information or from a whole communication network, may be the first step to a more viable comprehension of the environment and to a greater sensitivity to and understanding of other people and their ideas and behavior. Unfortunately, this development frequently never materializes, and instead the person wallows in the agony and despair of living in a world that no longer excites his loyalties or provides him with a life style he considers meaningful. He may perform his tasks ritually and bother no one, simply withdrawiing his positive emotional involvement from the network and making his negative involvement apparent through his apathy. Although apathy is not necessarily an accurate indicant of alienation, it is a clue. Hostility is another clue that incongruencies are being experienced, with disappointment expressed violently and destructively.

A great deal could and has been said about the experience of alienation, the various forms and expression of alienation, and its various sources and possible solutions, but here we are interested primarily in presenting alienation as a form of negative involvement (see Tavis, 1969;

Ruitenbeek, 1964; Nisbet, 1966). A detailed critique of the multitudes of definitions of alienation would deflect us from our purpose, which is to indicate how alienation, as we have defined it, can produce changes in susceptibility to disease and to point out the various means of minimizing or preventing such changes through preventing alienation or minimizing its consequences.

There are several areas of activity in modern societies in which the potential contact with incongruities is high. We mention a few of these to illustrate the kinds of things we could look for in locating sources of incongruities and alienation and the means of protecting the individual from them.

The communication network in which one is employed is a major area of potential alienation. There are a number of possible sources of incongruities in the work milieu, including the possibilities of failure of the organization, uncertainties in career development, uncertainties concerning one's ability to perform the necessary tasks, uncertainties of acceptance by colleagues, and role and status incongruities.

Uncertainties concerning career development can be minimized by maintaining identification with other communication networks so that if incongruities between one's self-image and experiences at work occur, such as not being promoted, one can maintain his self-evaluations (E. Gross, 1970; Kornhauser, 1965; Caplow, 1964). For example, one may identify with a labor union, a political or religious group, a professional group, or in the case of potential rejection by one's colleagues in a profession, with clients, such as patient-oriented doctors and student-oriented teachers. The identification with a profession also provides some security from failure of an organization because one's work activities can be readily transferred to another organization. These alternative identities also pose potential problems for the communication network; the members of the network cannot be sure one will honor the requested restriction of certain information if he identifies with other networks, particularly networks from which the desired information is to be withheld.

The uncertainties of performing one's assigned task on the job, for example, inadequate capacities, have been reduced in part by that old bugaboo of routinization, which structures tasks so that one can be reasonably sure those hired can perform them (Gross, 1970). Kahn et al. (1964) notes that role conflicts and ambiguity in the work milieu are a source of subjective distress, especially if efforts to cope with it are unsuccessful. A major source of ambiguity and role conflict is the result of organizational requirements of work patterns, which lead to frequent contact with other organizations. Kahn et al. (1964) suggest that sheer reduction of the amount of interaction might reduce the occurrences of role conflict.

The family is another major source of potential incongruities resulting from, in part, the fact that so many communication networks provide so much information about marriage and what it will be like that the potential for encountering conflicts in marriage are enormous. For example, the romantic love myth leads people to believe that they should not only marry for love, but that they can expect love to increase with mutual understanding over the years. All the evidence indicates that the specialization of marriage roles and outside responsibilities lead to little gain in mutual understanding and perhaps even a growing apart over the years (Udry, 1966). Social background differences may produce clashes over everything in the marriage including finances, child-rearing practices, and even recreation. There are a number of normal crisis periods in marriage, none of which modern societies prepare the couple to handle very well, such as the honeymoon and period of adjustment to each other; the birth of the first child, with the shift in social relations in the family and the tremendous altering of financial resources, time for each other, and restrictions on social life; the menopause; the last child's leaving home; and retirement of the man (Udry, 1966; Blood and Wolf, 1960). In addition, individual families may develop practices for reducing uncertainty for some members at the expense of others, such as the "double-bind" in which a child is encouraged to do something and then criticized when he does it or is given two requirements that are incongruous with each other so that both cannot be fulfilled and punishment is inevitable (Berne, 1964; Croog, 1970); or the use of one child, possibly a disturbed one, as a scapegoat for other problems in the family (Croog, 1970). Many of the problems in the family, however, do not arise from incongruities within the family but from other networks with which one is involved (Croog, 1970). Croog also points out that sickness among family members may be stressful to other members because of "the incompatibilities between the demands of the sick role and the demands of the usual life roles in which the sick person has been engaged" (1970, p. 42). Given the fragile nature and lack of resources of the modern, isolated, nuclear family, sickness can greatly increase the family responsibilities of other members of that family.

In modern societies perhaps the major period in a person's life when incongruities are likely to be encountered is the period of adolescence, when he is leaving home for school or entering the adult world of work and marriage. This is considered by some (Udry, 1966; Meier, 1964) to be the first major crisis in a person's life that is a part of the normative structure of modern societies. The communication networks in which the adolescent has been raised seek to maintain the youngster's involvement through this period, expecting him to be weaned from his dependency on his family, to establish a new family, and to become identified with some occupation available in the society. In modern societies this is a period of discontinuity, when a person must suddenly shift from dependency to independence. The family's support for the person, even in cases of failure, may continue after he leaves home but cannot prevent his being ejected from other communication networks in which he might fail. Thus the adolescent must learn to live with competition, judgements of himself, and occasional failures without disintegrating as a person.

The adolescent communication network, or teenage subculture as it is called, provides some protection from the uncertainties of the transition. Unfortunately, the protection provided may be so effective that successful transition is hampered. The person may not experience or learn to handle competition and independence and never learn to make his own decisions or accept the consequences for them. The teenage subculture does provide opportunities to express independence from one's parents, usually in areas of no great consequence, such as clothing, hair styles, music, and recreation, to any of the major communication networks in which they have been raised. Yet adolescents are not experienced and confident enough, as a rule, to be able to handle the criticisms of their parents and other networks alone; thus they seek approval of their choices in the teenage communication network. Consequently, their "independent" choices are more often based on what the subculture indicates is the proper way to protest parental control and to establish their own capacity for decision making.

This period is one of the unnecessary areas of high-risk uncertainty in modern societies. Gradual development of capacity for judgement, decision making, and living with successes and failures could be obtained through the development of norms that permit and encourage people to assume responsibilities for socially significant activities at various stages of physical development. We could learn much from the age-graded structure of some "primitive" societies (see Eisenstadt, 1956).

Teenagers and young adults have long been known to be the group proportionately most likely to convert to new religions and to ferment political unrest. It is in this period that a person tries out his communication network's information in some larger arena and discovers whether it is accurate or effective to his satisfaction. If it is not, he will begin to look around and to experiment with other networks. Thus this is a period when proportionately we would expect to find the most alienation in modern societies (Eisenstadt, 1956; Udry, 1966; Parsons and Bales, 1955).

SOME SPECULATION ON THE POSSIBLE EFFECTS OF
INCONGRUITIES AND ALIENATION ON HEALTH

The alienated are generally more likely to be susceptible to disease than any of the other forms of involvement. Their alienation indicates that they have encountered a disruptive incongruity. This in itself would make them likely candidates for illness according to our model. However, they are also more likely to encounter additional incongruities and uncertainties, finding ineffective the isolation and insulation from incongruous information formerly provided by the communication networks with which they were identified. Thus we can expect disease episodes to cluster about periods of alienation and to decline when the person becomes identified with some other network, becomes autonomous, or in some other manner resolves the incongruities.

Incongruities and alienation can be viewed not only from the point of view of a given individual but in terms of the proportion of numbers in a given communication network experiencing incongruities, the importance to the person of the incongruities experienced, and the integration of communication networks. An effort to measure incongruities in clusters of communication networks in terms of social integration is found in the work of Gibbs and Martin (1964) on suicide. They measured status incongruities in terms of proportions of people in each role who also occupied certain other roles. For example, they examined the proportions of married people who also held various occupations. Those occupations having low levels of married people were considered more incompatible with marriage roles than those having higher levels. "Incompatible statuses are those configurations that are infrequently occupied" (p. 26). They offer as a major theorem: "The suicide rate of a population varies inversely with the degree of status integration in that population" (p. 27). Their six postulates on which this theorem is based deal with role conflicts derived from status incongruities and with the reduction in stability and durability of social relationships that resulted from nonconformity to socially sanctioned expectations when participants experienced role conflicts. They found evidence supporting these propositions.

Jackson (1962) did a secondary analysis of the data from *Americans View Their Mental Health* (Gurin et al., 1960). He used 16 closed-answer, symptom questions from that study, which had also been used in the Midtown Manhattan Study (Srole et al., 1962) and the Stirling County Study (Leighton, 1963). Using psychophysiological symptoms reported by the individual as an indicator of stress, he sought to test the hypothesis that the "degree of status consistency is inversely related to psychological stress" (p. 470). He found that those with inconsistent statuses experienced dissatisfaction with social relations, unstable self images, and rewards not consistent with aspirations. He believes conditions possibly arose from conflicting expectations associated with the inconsistent statuses. In a study of occupational, educational, and racial-ethnic backgrounds he found the following status inconsistencies directly related to symptom rate: (1) racial-ethnic rank superior to occupational or educational rank; (2) for males, occupational rank superior to educational rank; and (3) for females, educational rank superior to husband's occupational rank. He also found that a low-achieved status or an ascribed status superior to the achieved status was directly related to somatic reports. King and Cobb (1958) found evidence that inconsistency in education and income statuses due to social mobility were associated with arthritis (low education and high income, or high education and low income). The influence of status inconsistencies on physical health can be explained in terms of incongruities between self-evaluations and expectations developed in one communication network and experiences and evaluation of one's self as indicated by responses to him in interaction in other networks.

Changes in and worsening of cardiovascular or gastrointestinal conditions have been found in those who have experienced the exit from their milieu of someone close to them (Myers et al., 1968). Although object loss is not as significant in somatic illness as some have thought (Imboden et al., 1963; see the work of Schmale, Engel, and others), still the disruption of communication networks and the flow of supporting information could be severe in such cases, exposing one to all kinds of uncertainties.

Rahe and Ransom (1968), using their "Schedule of Recent Experience," measured the intensity of life change over the previous few years for a subject and found a buildup of life stress prior to the onset of a variety of physical illnesses. Curiously, they also found a nearly symmetrical falling off of stress intensity after the illness experience. They suggest that "life-changes resulting from illness experience are virtually equal in timing and intensity to those life-changes having a causal influence on the illness" (p. 344). Troubled life situations occurring at the time of acute illness have also been related to slow recovery (Imboden and workers, cited by Mechanic, 1968, pp. 320–321).

Hinkle (1961) found that periods of illness clustering could be predicted by rating subjects according to whether they found a particular year highly satisfactory or highly unsatisfactory. Hinkle believes that his evidence from this and other studies shows that there is a very significant relation between a person's evaluations and reactions concerning his life situations and the number of illnesses he experiences. He found that people tending to be unhealthy more often evaluate a given milieu as depriving, threatening, overdemanding, or involving conflict than do healthy people. Hinkle and Wolff (1958), in a study of 3000 industrial workers over 20 years, found evidence of illnesses clustering in relation to reactions to situations encountered and to various characteristics of the person himself. They found that one quarter of the people had over half the illnesses, and another quarter of the people had fewer than 10 percent of the illness episodes. This clustering of illnesses is, of course, what we would expect as a result of changes in general susceptibility to disease because of physiological changes accompanying the general physiological responses during periods when incongruities are being experienced. Whether, indeed, information incongruities are the source of the dissatisfaction and life stresses described in these studies requires further study, but the indications seem favorable.

Engel (1968) has conceived of a "giving up–given up" complex that accompanies situations where a person's social and psychological activities and devices are not effective or available, leaving the person with a feeling of inability to cope with the situation. While he searches for a solution, there is a disruption of one's behavior and of his sense of mastery which alters one's view of himself and the environment. This notion is based on clinical experiences. He further characterizes the response into helplessness—when one believes others are responsible for his plight—and hopelessness—when he blames himself for his plight. During these periods physiological processes of the body are altered, which increases susceptibility to disease. Schmale and Iker (1966), in biopsies of 31 out of 41 women scheduled for examination, correctly predicted cervical cancer on the basis of recent feelings of hopelessness or high potential for hopelessness. This potential was determined by subjective reports of chronic hyperactivity and "devotion to causes with little or no feeling of success or pleasure, irrespective of actual accomplishment" (p. 715). Thurlow (1967) reviewed some of the above work of Hinkle, Engel, and Schmale, and he concludes that disharmony with the environment is a general process relevant to disease etiology. We suggest that closer examination of these phenomena may well indicate that information incongruities could satisfactorily explain the occurrence of the disharmony and the change in disease susceptibility. Our concept of alienation embraces both the occurrence of an information incongruity and the subjective discontent accompanying it.

Some Probable Properties of the Autonomous

Autonomy as we have defined it has not been studied or discussed any-where near the degree that alienation and identification have. Much of the work that goes under the label of autonomy has more to do with or-ganizational properties, such as the degree of restrictiveness of rules and deviance from them, than with the subjective states of individuals inter-acting within the communication networks. Much of the rest of the work reflects as much the wishful thinking of individualist-oriented behavioral scientists as concrete observation. There is relatively little firm evidence about autonomous people, how they got that way, and the relation of au-tonomy to disease susceptibility. The probable reasons for this lack are the relative rarity with which we expect to find autonomous people to study and because most people are in some ways autonomous and in other ways identified, anomic, or alienated.

As a rule we can expect that as long as the networks in which they par-ticipate have many communication media and alternative channels of communication the autonomous as a group will have more correct infor-mation about the environment than other types of involvement. If the autonomous members participate in networks where information is tightly controlled and access is limited to the identified, some identified persons may know more correct information than any autonomous per-son in that communication network, unless of course the autonomous person was once one of these highly informed identified members. As a rule, the autonomous are open to more information from more sources and thus are more likely to get a balanced perspective and information repertoire, but this cannot be assumed to always accompany autonomy. Autonomy can provide a valuable source of perspectives and new infor-mation that can lead to greater congruity between the network and the environment. Autonomy can also be a source of much misinformation and ideological nonsense that may lead networks in the other direction to greater and more unnecessary incongruities. Autonomy is not a "good" in and of itself.

As a pure type we suggest that the following properties characterize the autonomous, but we emphasize that concrete people may never actually exhibit all these properties. The autonomous people are much less de-pendent for their own stability than the identified or the alienated mem-bers are on the continued stability of communication networks. They are, consequently, much more tolerant of change and can better weather disruptions. Presumably, they will also experience less change in general susceptibility to disease during such periods than the identified or alienated members. We may expect the autonomous person to have developed a set of ethics that provides him with a perspective for behavior and that gives meaning to his life, but which may be an amalgam of his own ideas and some of the norms of various networks. These ethics may or may not be approved by the networks in which he moves.

One generally becomes autonomous first by being alienated. As a result of alienation and the explorations involved in discovering a sufficiently accurate and effective information repertoire on which to base his autonomy, the autonomous person usually becomes aware of the relativity of human norms. Though he may not recognize all the norms and values in his life as such, his awareness that there are several alternative normative ways to behave in a certain situation is one of the major bases of his autonomy. With that information and understanding, it becomes nearly impossible for a communication network to completely involve him or to make him feel duty bound or guilty for not performing some normative pattern which he recognizes as an arbitrary, manmade, not "God given" or absolute norm or moral. He may seem immoral or unpredictable to the identified participants. However, he may not be degenerate at all; he may simply be operating on a different but "humane" set of values. He may well be operating in terms of values that are on a higher level of abstraction than those of identified people. He must reconcile the many normative approaches to situations he has observed and may thereby discover some underlying theme in the norms governing the situation that permits him both to handle the situation and to criticize the unnecessary aspects of the several competing norms covering the situation.

Not only does the insight into the relativity of norms free the autonomous person from some forms of communication network influence; it also exposes him to many of the "realities" of life, such as the lack of certainty about many events, so that he is frequently required to live with fewer illusions to comfort him. The uncertainties surrounding incongruities between his information and the environment must be handled, in many cases, through his own resources and values. He must be able to live with some uncertainties. The terror of having to live essentially "alone" with such knowledge and of depending heavily on one's own resources is what sends many would-be autonomous people scuttling back to the warmth and security of identification. As Jonathan Swift said in *The Tale of the Tub,* "Happiness is a perpetual possession of being well deceived." For many, euphoric obliviousness is much preferable to the insights of autonomy.

As a rule, autonomy is the broadening of one's perspective. He is aware of many alternatives and thus, with more information and norms to re-combine, more capable of creativity. He is also more capable of tolerance of those who behave differently because the relativity of values is recognized. The autonomous person is more likely to solve problems because he has more information from which to work and is less restricted in his use of information. Because of his broader awareness and greater tolerance of other normative systems he enjoys and finds delight and invigoration in a wider variety of situations, networks, and people.

This broadening of perspective among the alienated may be accompanied by confusion, inconsistent responses to situations, and unpredictability when it first occurs. Such a person is probably not a good problem-solver, though he may fancy himself as creative. This instability continues until the alienated person develops some consistent norms and self-concepts around which to orient these newly perceived perspectives (Warshay, 1964). However, autonomy can be developed without dissolving everything into ethereal fog and then trying to crystallize something meaningful out of it if one selects from among the alternatives discovered at each experience of incongruity and consolidates the selected ones into one's information repertoire so that the repertoire metamorphoses over time.

A number of workers have noted this broadening of perspective and the opening of perceptiveness that accompanies and frequently precedes autonomy. Maslow (1968) notes that self-actualizers are able to see the environment in fresh ways without depending on existing words and categories, are less likely to distort their perceptions to make them congruous, and have an openness and spontaneity concerning new experiences. Similarly, Berne (1964) notes that autonomy is characterized by awareness, perceiving and enjoying the present, spontaneity in expressing feelings through the available opportunities, capable of intimacy and candid communications, and free from the compulsion of game playing (in the sense for which Berne is famous). Hughes, on the thinkers of the 1890s, says:

> Indeed, it was their very certainty of "enlightened" values (however much they might jibe at them) that enabled them to strip away so mercilessly the illusions with which these values had become encrusted. Their own psychological security—their confidence in such unstated assumptions as humane behavior and intellectual integrity—had given them the inner strength to inaugurate an unprecedented examination of conscience (1961, pp. 426–427).

A necessity for development of autonomy is a comprehension of oneself as a unique person with specific attributes. The particular set of values of the autonomous person provide the basis for this self-concept, along with his appraisal of his capacities from success and failure in acquiring and using information and manipulating the environment. Although he knows the roles he plays in social organizations, he is less likely to use them in identifying himself. Autonomous people generally have high self-esteem and confidence without which they would have difficulty facing directly many of the incongruities in their information and the uncertainties in life they must consequently accept. However, the autonomous, in our opinion, are not so self-ruling or self-rewarding that they can comfortably live apart from other people without approval, friendship, and rapport. They do, however, like some privacy (which we doubt is a desire limited to the autonomous) in part, we suspect, to get away from judgments by identified members. Because of their own configuration of information and norms, they resist socialization into communication networks. Like Maslow's (1968) self-actualizers, our autonomous people often conform superficially to conventional norms but privately have no commitment to them.

The autonomous person selects the communication networks in which he participates on the basis of the congruity of the network's information with his own. He may participate actively, even identify by group membership, and have the same intense emotional experiences from group excitement that is so precious to the identified, but through all of this his values determine his behavior and, should an incongruity occur between the norms of the network and his, he will follow his own. He may also participate in a network because of the resources it provides him or for some other instrumental reason.

According to Gouldner (1967) the individual may maintain autonomy in at least three ways: (1) withdrawing from the network and participating in one more satisfactory; (2) diversifying sources so that what is needed can be obtained from a number of different networks; and (3) reorganizing the system so that it is more compatible with one's autonomy. He suggests that tensions arising between the network members and autonomous people indicate that those creating the disturbance have not yet been controlled or excluded but will be. The tension may also be a harbinger of a new pattern of information within the network.

The communication network has at least three alternative strategies for reducing the tensions created by autonomous persons, and all of them involve information control: (1) withdrawing as much as possible from interaction with other communication networks and driving autonomous persons away with demands that are incongruous for them, such as demands for high involvement; (2) engulfing all the networks with which it clusters, for example, industries' efforts to control suppliers, politicians, religious sentiments, and other possible sources of incongruous information; (3) the delegation of responsibility for information, communication, and tasks essential to the network to those participants who are identified and minimally autonomous (Gouldner, 1967). If a person is to remain autonomous and still participate within the network he must demonstrate that his autonomy is either not a threat or is of considerable value to the network. Either way, he is unlikely to ever be admitted into positions with the most complete access to the network's information and communication channels.

Autonomous people should be able to reduce incongruities by developing capacities and knowledge so that they can rely on their own competence and understanding. We expect them to be able to make their own decisions and to be willing to accept responsibility for the consequences. Many people cannot handle this form of uncertainty and must assign responsibility to some outside force, such as to God if they succeed or to the devil or the establishment if they fail.

Although we do not agree with Maslow that self-actualization is a need or that its attainment should be evaluated as a good, his studies and descriptions of people whom he considers self-actualized are instructive in understanding what some of the attributes of the more "wholesome" autonomous person might turn out to be. What the less "wholesome" autonomous person might be like will not be explored except to say that they might be exploiters, cynics, wheeler-dealers, or con men, who use the norms and information of the identified members to exploit them while only appearing to conform themselves. It must be remembered that we are more concerned with types of involvement and their relation to disease susceptibility; evaluating the behavior of each is no concern of ours. Which autonomous people are wholesome must rest on the values of whomever is judging.

Maslow (1954) sees self-actualization as an uncommon lifetime achievement. Among 3000 college students he found only one student who could be called a self-actualizer. Maslow concluded that in our society self-actualization is not possible among young, developing people.

Maslow listed as the qualities of self-actualizers "more efficient perception of reality and more comfortable relations with it." They are able to recognize fake, dishonest people and organizations and yet they are also able to live with this knowledge without fear or anxiety. They seem to be able to see through opinions to see what is there.

They are able to accept themselves with all of their shortcomings and the nature of things without being "crippled" by shame and guilt. They have spontaneity in thought and actions. Their behavior is simple and natural. Although they may be unconventional in their norms and ideas, their unconventional behavior is not high.

Apparently recognizing that the world of people in which he lives could not understand or accept this, and since he has no wish to hurt them or fight them over every triviality, he will go through the ceremonies and rituals of convention with a good humored shrug and with the best possible grace (Masow, 1954, p. 209).

However, convention is lightly adhered to or ignored in situations the self-actualizer considers basic. Frequently, they are not worried about how others react to their spontaneity. They have a continued freshness of appreciation; they are capable of mystic experiences, an "oceanic" feeling; they are capable of great empathy and sympathy; they have deeper and more profound and intimate interpersonal relations; they are democratic; they are able to decide on their course of action with little confusion in their life styles; they possess an unhostile sense of humor, and they don't enjoy laughing at the misfortune of others; they are creative. They resist enculturation. They do not feel that it is necessary to receive approval from or identify with the culture, and they resist molding by the culture. They are only somewhat conventional. For example, they make no great effort to be fashionable. They are not authority rebels in the sense of impatience, but rather they exhibit a calm, long-term concern.

Their value system is based on acceptance of their definition of themselves and their social life. Their sex life is coupled with love; they don't seek sex for its own sake but as an expression of love.

Self-actualizers are problem centered, focusing their lives on problems outside of themselves rather than being self-centered. They like privacy and solitude and are not troubled by it; they are detached. They find it easy to be aloof, reserved, or serene from the situation. They are relatively independent from the culture and environment. They also have a high state of self-awareness.

Levinson (1965) describes an approach similar to Maslow's in which 14 senior members of the Menninger Foundations Clinical Staff described some 80 people whom they felt were among the most mentally healthy they had encountered. The qualities these 80 people had in common are again instructive. They all had a wide variety of sources of gratification, were flexible under stress, could alter their behavior and outlook in order to solve a problem, recognized and accepted their own limitations and assets, did not depreciate their talents and skills nor try to hide their weak spots from themselves, and treated other people as individuals. They were interested in others and in their problems, and they responded to them. They were active and productive, and they sought to use their energies to do something rather than to be somebody.

Reisman's definition of autonomy supports our own.

The "autonomous" are those who on the whole are capable of conforming to the behavioral norms of their society—a capacity the anomics usually lack—but are free to choose whether to conform or not (1961, p. 242).

Along similar lines, Gurin et al. (1960) indicate that the mentally healthy were able to handle stress situations flexibly and rebound from difficulties. Their work, along with Bradburn and Caplovitz (1965), presents two forms of worry, a "healthful" concern and involvement and a self-defeating one that frets over unchangeable circumstances. Bradburn and Caplovitz found the higher income and education group more responsive and sensitive to the environment, whereas Gurin et al. found this same group had greater feelings of inadequacy, worried about more things, and yet were happier. Gurin believes that this group was more involved with life and more aware of their own attributes.

We expect that autonomous people are more similar to other autonomous people in other communication networks with which their own clusters, and even with the autonomous in different cultures and societies, than with the identified, alienated, or anomic persons in their own networks (Maslow, 1968). Kornhauser (1965), for example, found both satisfied and dissatisfied workers at all levels of the organization, and those satisfied on all levels were similar to each other, as were the dissatisfied, on all levels.

It should be noted in passing that all independence from a communication network is not autonomy. One who imagines himself to be Napoleon is not autonomous, because the members of his network will not treat him as Napoleon and his information will be ineffective in that network. To be autonomous one's information complement must be effective in the communication network in which he moves.

Even the autonomous person, we suggest, tends toward identification with a communication network composed of participants like himself that involves information to which he subscribes. Thus new networks might arise as a result of the communication between the autonomous in various networks. The humanistic psychology of Maslow may be an example of the kinds of information content around which a communication network of more autonomous people might develop. Maslow (1968) considers humanistic psychology as a prelude to a transpersonal psychology that is "centered in the cosmos rather than human needs and interest, going beyond humanness, identity, self-actualization and the like" (p. iv). It is a sort of scientifically generated idealism and religion for intellectuals. "We need something 'bigger than we are' to be awed by and to commit ourselves to in a new, naturalistic, empirical, non-churchly sense

. . ." (p. iv) he says. We are not endorsing this position, but we present it for illustration.

AUTONOMY AND HEALTH

The evidence presented previously on physiological responses and health when information incongruities are encountered applies as well to autonomous people. They respond to information incongruities in their own information just as the identified do when they find incongruities in the information learned from a communication network. The autonomous people's susceptibility to disease should reflect the situations in which they feel they are capable and have adequate information and those in which they do not. In the case of the autonomous, only knowledge of their particular information repertoire can permit prediction of changes in susceptibility to disease. In the case of the identified member, knowledge of the communication network's information complement offers a means of anticipating changes in members' disease susceptibility. The value for the health scientist in knowing a person's autonomy is that it permits prediction of the influences of information contact and changes on that person's health more accurately than if the autonomous people are included with the identified participants. Changes in the communication network may have little effect on an autonomous person but may be devastating to the identified.

Even though we expect that as a rule the autonomous person is less susceptible to disease than the alienated or the identified members of highly heterogeneous networks, the efforts to maintain autonomy in interaction with identified people, who may try to encroach upon his autonomy, may be a source of continued information incongruity having detrimental physiological influences on him. Costell and Leiderman (1968) used small, five-member laboratory groups in their studies, similar to Solomon Asch's, in which they studied the effects of group pressure when four initiates provided incongruous information on task directions to the experimental subject. They found that the individuals who were independent of the group pressure when faced with a conflict showed significantly higher levels of skin potential (a peripheral electrical measure; see discussion in Chapter IV). The conforming subjects did not differ significantly from controls, "lending support to previous studies suggesting the arousal-reducing function of conforming behavior" (p. 309). The skin potential of the majority tended toward the lowest levels of autonomic arousal more quickly when confronting the conforming subject than when confronting the independent subject. However, even in contact with the independent subject, this tendency toward a lower level of skin potential occurred. Presumably, in the case of the independent subject, the majority either affectively disengaged from the situation, or the ineffective group pressure they attempted to assert promoted greater affiliation among the majority and thereby reduced the significance of the independent subjects' resistance. These processes may reflect the physiological processes to be found when the identified and autonomous interact and try to persuade one another.

Anomie

The concept of anomie found its way into the sociological vocabulary through Emile Durkheim. Durkheim's definition of anomie revolves around his assumption that man has no built-in standards to indicate when he has enough, that he is insatiable. Although animals controlled by instincts can be satisfied when they have obtained some indispensable minimum, in man "a more awakened reflection suggests better conditions" (Durkheim, 1951, p. 247) and enlarges his desires. Durkheim wonders, how is man to determine "the quantity of well-being, comfort or luxury legitimately to be craved by a human being?" (p. 247). He concludes that nothing "appears in man's organic nor in his psychological constitution which sets a limit to such" cravings (p. 247). In addition, Durkheim points out that pursuit of "a goal which is by definition unattainable is to condemn oneself to a state of perpetual unhappiness" (p. 248). Fortunately, society provides the controls man's body does not, setting limits within which man can set attainable goals guided by some standard of appropriateness and sanctions to enforce excesses. Thus man can only be content as long as these social controls continue to be effective. When society is disrupted, men's desires are de-regulated, and this is anomy (Durkheim, 1951, p. 253). The agony and frustration of never being able to find contentment no matter how hard one tries or how much he consumes may even lead to what Durkheim called anomic suicide.

We cannot accept Durkheim's conceptualization of the nature of man. We do not see man as necessarily an insatiable creature. Man's desires are to a very great extent the result of his social relations and do not exist independently of them. Disruption of the social system would alter not only the social controls over desires, but also the desires themselves. Because we cannot adopt his view of man, we cannot utilize his concept of anomie.

Ruitenbeek (1964) laments the lack of work on anomie in the United States, but there have been a few efforts. Merton's (1957, pp. 131–194) discussion of anomie is one of the most well known. Merton's anomie refers to conditions in a society, to the degree to which the norms concerning goals or means are not clearly articulated and shared, and the degree to which access to the means is limited by one's position in the social structure. His famous typology (innovator, ritualist, retreatist, rebel) refers not to personality types but to modes of individual adaptation to situations in which one's social structural position prevents successful utilization of the accepted means (Merton, 1957, p. 152). However, all Merton's modes of adaptation (excepting conformist) or deviance could be placed in our alienation category. The person experiencing conflicts between the goals he has learned to desire and his ability to obtain them is experiencing an information incongruity in our terms. Moreover, these nonconformists know the cultural norms concerning goals and prescribed means. Such people know too much about the communication network to be completely anomic in our terms, although some of them may be partially anomic to the degree that they simply do not know how to obtain the goals or where to find out. Some of Merton's deviant types such as the innovator could even be autonomous by our standards. Our model and Merton's cut the pie up somewhat differently. Merton overemphasizes the influence of disadvantaged positions in society as a source of contact with incongruities, and his model deals with only one general category of the myriad of possible incongruities members of a society may and frequently do encounter.

McIver (cited by Merton, 1957, p. 161) comes somewhat closer to our position. He says, "Anomy signifies the state of mind of one who has been pulled by his moral roots, who has no longer any standards but only disconnected urges. . . ." Srole's (Srole et al., 1962; Leighton, 1963, p. 384) psychological anomie refers to the subjective belief that society as a whole is indifferent to the needs of the individual, and this belief is accompanied by a general sense of the futility of life. Srole's definition could apply to alienation in our terms more readily than to our anomie.

The essence of anomie in our terms and some of the possible sources are discussed in previous sections of this chapter. Essentially, it is the lack of accurate and effective information for a given social milieu. The person does not know the information of a communication network or how to get it. His behavior does not produce the results he desires, and he does not understand why. The norms and values he may bring with him from other networks to the situation may not be congruous enough with the given network to gain entry into the network or to comprehend it. The communication network in which one feels anomic is meaningless to the subject. He is not involved with it.

Anyone can experience anomie with a particular communication network for which he has no information. Because there are a multitude of communication networks in the world, there are many networks that are foreign to any given individual; thus every person might experience anomie in some network or another. In other words, no one is immune to the experience of anomie.

Anomie, unlike identification, alienation, and autonomy, refers to people who cannot function in a given communication network and can only become identified with the network if someone from the network who understands the information of the anomic person introduces and socializes him into the network. Once one has become identified, alienated, or autonomous in a particular communication network, he can never be anomic as long as that network does not change into something strange to him. The anomic are outsiders and, because they are removed from the mainstream of a communication network, the changes in that network have relatively little impact on their encounter with information incongruities. Their self-concepts, norms, and information of the environment come largely from elsewhere, and changes in their health because of information incongruities must be sought in these other information sources that generally are the communication networks with which the person is identified.

We expect that practically everyone is either involved with some communication networks through identification or alienation or has his own norms as in autonomy—and that completely anomic people, having no involvement in any communication network anywhere, are extremely rare. Everyone is anomic in relation to other communication networks for which he has no information. The explanation of the changes in susceptibility to disease, because of information incongruities encountered, for the anomic person lie mainly in those networks with which he does identify. Thus there is little reason to develop anomie as an explanation of disease. The health scientist may group together those people who are anomic in a given network so that they will not contaminate the findings on information processing and susceptibility to disease in that network. The major exception is when anomic people are required to be, or persist in participating, in a network in which they are anomic and when the continued encountering of information incongruities produces changes in disease susceptibility. Communication networks that cluster with other networks for which their information in mainly incongruous, such as foreign language immigrant communities in major cities, provide a sheltered cove for their members, but a cove which depends on the tolerance of the other networks in the cluster. Their members may remain indefinitely anomic in regard to the other networks in the cluster.

ANOMIE AND HEALTH

There is some evidence that anomic people or the degree of anomie a person experiences in a given communication network is related to susceptibility to illness. Christenson and Hinkle (1961) found that managers who had worked their way up from blue-collar workers and mostly had a grammar school education, had the most illnesses of all kinds when compared with managers who were college educated. These more-ill managers were working and living in a social milieu perceived as new, unfamiliar, and full of challenges. Holmes (1956; see also discussion by Cassel, 1970) found tuberculosis rates higher among more marginal people such as ethnic groups who were in the minority in their neighborhood and people who lived alone, who had many occupational and residential moves, and who frequently had broken marriages. He says the tuberculosis patients "were, in essence, strangers attempting to find a place for themselves in the contemporary American scene" (p. 146). They poorly understood their social milieu and felt threatened with being walled off and helpless. They had great difficulty deciding what was expected of them, and their efforts to adjust often involved unrealistic strivings.

Scotch (1963) studied hypertension among Zulus in the rural tribal areas and in urban settings. The apartheid in the Union of South Africa blocks much of the opportunity of the Zulus to learn the new culture of urban societies, increasing the possibility that the Zulu moving to the city will encounter anomie. In the rural tribal areas the Zulu culture is adhered to, and situations experienced are interpreted in terms of it. For example, the traditional extended family relations are important, along with traditional religious and magical beliefs. Having large families is a source of status. For the rural Zulu woman, having children is important for her social status. Consequently, menopause is stressful for the Zulu tribeswoman and is related to hypertension in the rural tribal setting. Age is also a source of status. Thus the Zulu tribeswoman is caught in a break in her status between the time of menopause and aging. In the city, these same values are incongruous with the communication networks of the urban setting. In the city those Zulus having hypertension tended to "live in an extended family, have a lower income, resort to bewitchment to explain illness and misfortune, retain traditional religious beliefs, and have large numbers of children" (Scotch, 1963, p. 1212). Those Zulus having low hypertension in the cities adopted the values of and participated in the communication networks of the city. For example, the low-hypertensive urban Zulu lived in nuclear rather than extended families, had small numbers of children, had higher income, visited European-style medical clinics in preference to traditional tribal medical practices; the women attended Christian churches while the men attended Sunday sports. Among the Zulus the same practices protect one from hypertension in the rural areas and increase one's susceptibility in the urban areas. This tendency can be explained in terms of information incongruities encountered by rural Zulus in the urban setting and the accompanying anomie.

Summary

Social relations can be conceived of as information communication networks composed of a recognizable grouping of communicating and interacting people who transmit a particular configuration of information. Individuals resonate with the information in these networks through interaction and communication media, and the networks resonate with each other through communication channels linking them. Communication networks are without boundaries and cluster with other networks with which communications are exchanged.

Four types of subjective involvement with communication networks are suggested. This typology is based on the degree to which the information one utilizes is taken from a particular communication network and the degree to which this information is found to be accurate and effective by the subject in his milieu. If one finds his information taken from the network is accurate and effective, we suggest that he feels involvement in that communication network. We call this form of involvement identification. If one perceives incongruities between the information he has learned in a network and what he finds to be accurate and effective in the environment, we suggest he feels negative involvement with that network. We call this form of involvement alienation. If one does not take his information as a whole from the communication network but has his own configuration of information and values he finds accurate and effective in his environment and in the given network, we suggest that he is detached in his involvement with that network. We call this form of detached involvement autonomy. If one does not not take his information as a whole from the given communication network and finds that the information he does have is neither accurate nor effective in that milieu or network, we suggest that the person is uninvolved with that communication network. This noninvolvement we call anomie.

Information incongruities can produce changes both in physiological processes and in social involvement. Perceptions of incongruities can produce general physiological responses, can alter susceptibility to disease, and can also lead to alienation from the communication network.

Knowledge of the probability of encountering incongruities in a given communication network and its clustering networks and of the nature of involvement of given individuals with these networks provides the health researcher with some tools for predicting and explaining differences in subjective evaluation of given situations and the related differences in susceptibility to diseases between individuals and groups.

Thus a person is involved in his communication networks to the degree he perceives that the information of these networks is congruous with his perceptions in the environment, and his susceptibility to disease decreases to the degree that his information is congruous with his perceptions of his milieu.

CHAPTER VI

Biosocial Resonation
in Social Change

In the previous chapter we explain how the encountering of information incongruities by the biosocially resonating person can change his subjective involvement with communication networks and increase susceptibility to disease. If enough people in the network, or people strategically placed, experience these incongruities and become alienated, social change may occur. By social change we mean the altering of the information content, possibly including the communication patterns, in a given communication network.

In this chapter we are interested in constructing a broad, conceptual framework for applying biosocial resonation to social change and in suggesting how social change can be generally related to disease susceptibility. As in the last chapter, we are looking for concepts that aid in predicting and explaining disease occurrences among various social categories of people.

Communication Network Change as Resonation

THE INADEQUACY OF THE CONCEPTS OF HOMEOSTASIS, EQUILIBRIUM, AND ADAPTATION IN SOCIAL BEHAVIOR

Three of the most commonly encountered concepts in discussions of social change are adaptation, equilibrium, and homeostasis. Equilibrium or homeostasis refers to the system's processes for preserving continuity, whereas adaptation refers to the changes of the system's processes in such a way that continuity in that milieu is enhanced. These terms have been lifted from biological sciences and freely applied to social phenomena. The use of such organic analogies of society has had heuristic value, but it also has led to assumptions about social phenomena that are, in our opinion, unacceptable.

Ruff and Korchin (1967) define biological adaptation of homeostatic organisms as "a compensatory response which permits continued functioning in spite of the load." In elaboration they say:

> Adaptation can be described in terms of a model of the organism as a system with inputs and outputs of energy and information. Each system tends to maintain steady states of many variables through homeostatic mechanisms. These confine within a limited range the variables which are crucial for continued existence of the system. Inputs which force the variables beyond this range are stressors. Adjustments made to restore equilibrium constitute the process of adaptation. This involves the reorganization of certain subsystems to prevent failure of other subsystems required for survival (p. 297).

The language and style is typical of such definitions by biological scientists. This definition nicely states the major elements of adaptation employed by scientists using a homeostatic model of social systems.

Both disease and stress have been explained in terms of such models. Claude Bernard, the French physiologist (1812–1878) was one of the first to attempt to view diseases as the "outcome of attempts at homeostasis in which adaptive responses to noxious forces, although appropriate in kind, were faulty in amount. The adaptive response to tissue damage, in its intensity, may be more destructive than the original assaults" (Wolff, 1953, pp. vi–vii). Wolff (1953) feels that in stress man's adaptive response may be inappropriate in kind as well as amount. Cassel (1970) also favors the concept of disease initiated by Claude Bernard, later elaborated by Chapman, Hinkle, and Wolff (1960) in which "disease should be viewed as occurring when the adaptive responses of the organism to stimuli are inappropriate in kind or amount or both" (Cassel, 1970, p. 203). Selye's (1956 a) model of stress was based on Cannon's (1932) homeostatic concept.

We question the adequacy of this framework where disease etiology includes social interaction. However, it may be appropriate for strictly physiological changes in response to nonsocial, natural disease agents. As we have mentioned in previous discussions, the arbitrary nature of human evaluations of social behavior makes it impossible to judge when an adaptive social response is inappropriate in kind, amount, or both.

Such models, like Dohrenwend's (see Chapter II), usually end up calling social deviance an illness or stress.

Yet many behavioral scientists are building models of social stress on homeostatic adaptive foundations. Levine and Scotch (1970 b, p. 283) conclude that the collection of articles they present in their book *Social Stress* exhibit a pervasive theme "that stress is not to be viewed as occurring when this or that load, pressure, or stimulus is applied to the individual but instead when there is a failure of the individual's adaptive resources or capacities." Caudill (1958) advocates the homeostatic approach to social systems. Dunbar, originator of the term psychosomatic (1948, 1946) believes that equilibrium is the proper focus for the study of body-mind-social relations. The multitude of coping and problem-solving models of stress (see discussion of Scott and Howard, Lazarus, and others in Chapter II) all reflect devotion to homeostasis as desirable, problem-solving as a means of restoring, and adaptation as a means of modifying various parts of the system to maximize the homeostatic continuity of the whole.

These coping and problem-solving models of social and psychological stress emphasize the importance of previous experience with situations as a source of skills, understanding, and, perhaps, mastery of the problem. This means that previous disruptions of equilibria or homeostasis may have been adaptive or valuable in increasing one's capacity to withstand and prevent future disruptions. Thus one is faced with the near-impossible judgement of whether the current threats of disruption of social-psychological homeostasis is good or bad for the individual and whether this disruption should be prevented or encouraged in order to increase adaptive capacities. This judgement must be made in order to decide if the person's subsequent behavior is adaptive or maladaptive, because restoration of an equilibria that "should" be changed would be maladaptive and failure to restore equilibria that "should not" be changed would also be maladaptive. Whether the behavior is adaptive or maladaptive depends on values and judgements of the researcher. In our opinion, this dependency is far too great for homeostatic-adaptive models to be of any value in the development of a viable model of social behavior and health. Part of the problem is that not everyone means the same thing by equilibrium and homeostasis. In our opinion, the general systems theorists, such as Buckley, have provided the most adequate definitions of these terms.

Equilibrium is seen as a mechanical state of either a balance of energy (entropy), as in the distribution of gas molecules in a closed container (equal pressure on all points), or a steady state in which occurring changes balance each other, as in chemical equilibria where molecules associate at the same rate as others of the same substance dissociate so the total volume of that substance is constant. The application of equilibrium to all systems derives from early mechanistic concepts of science. Clockworks are frequently used as examples, more because historically this was the example used than for any utility of the example (K. Deutsch, 1968).

> Equilibrial systems are relatively *closed* and *entropic*. In going to equilibrium they typically *lose* structure and have a *minimum* of *free energy;* they are affected only by external "disturbances" and have *no internal or endogenous sources of change;* their component elements are *relatively simple* and *linked directly via energy exchange* (rather than information interchange); and since they are relatively closed they have no feedback or other systemic self-regulating or adaptive capabilities (Buckley, 1968, p. 490, emphasis his).

Thus the concept of equilibrium has great utility in the physical sciences but not in the biological or social sciences. The limitations of equilibrium as they pertain to organic systems spurred Cannon (1939) to develop the concept of homeostasis. It is at this point that the concept of feedback becomes prominent.

Cannon saw homeostasis as the body's means of self-regulation through feedback mechanism, using body temperature control and fluid contents maintenance (among others) as examples. Buckley in another of his terse summaries says:

> The homeostatic system (for example, the organism, apart from higher cortical functioning) is open and negentropic, maintaining a moderate energy level within controlled limits. But for our purposes here, the system's main characteristic is its functioning to *maintain the given structure of the system* within pre-established limits. It involves feedback loops with its environment, and possibly information as well as pure energy interchanges, but these are geared principally to *self-regulation* (structure maintenance) rather than adaptation (*change* of system structure) (Buckley, 1968, p. 490, emphasis his).

Homeostasis as developed by Cannon points out that by preserving the steady state of the naturally very unstable organismic system, the system is freed from dependence on the environment, within certain limits. It can maintain optimal operating conditions even in a changing environment, for example, by increasing metabolism to raise body heat when environmental temperature drops. Thus homeostatic mechanisms free the organisms to seek other goals.

There are two general types of homeostasis: homeostasis of materials and of processes. Homeostasis of materials involves mechanisms to ensure adequate supply of necessary materials at any time, especially in emergencies, which is accomplished by various ways including storage. Homeostasis of processes are the ones most commonly discussed, that is, heat regulation, respiration (oxygen supply), and so forth. Cannon (1939, pp. 303–304) said:

> In summary, then, we find the organism liberated for its more complicated and socially important tasks because it lives in a fluid matrix, which is automatically kept in a constant condition. If changes threaten, indicators at once signal the danger, and corrective agencies promptly prevent the disturbance or restore the normal when it has been disturbed. The corrective agencies act, in the main, through a special portion of the nervous system which functions as a regulatory mechanism. For this regulation it employs, first storage of materials as a means of adjustment between supply and demand, and, second, altered rates of continuous processes in the body. These are the result of myriads of generations of experience, and they succeed for long periods in preserving a remarkable degree of stability in the highly unstable substance of which we are composed.

Nevertheless the concept of homeostasis is not adequate for social systems, despite Cannon's attempt to find homeostatic social processes (for example, transportation and other distribution mechanisms such as the market and money) and to point out that the poor quality of feedback indicates evolutionary immaturity of social systems (Cannon, 1932, p. 305).

Von Bertalanffy (1968) believes that a major limitation of the homeostatic concept is that it is essentially a mechanical process designed to return the system to a steady state. He also notes that some authors use homeostasis to refer to any and all kinds of organic regulation and to adaptation in general. We agree with Von Bertalanffy that these latter uses are inappropriate.

In biology there is the general assumption that, as a rule, homeostasis is healthy and indeed necessary. This assumption is carried over into organic analogies of social behavior, but there is no reason to assume that given steady states in social behavior are either healthy, necessary, or good. Certain social steady states, such as slavery or norms of material acquisition as success, could be as easily evaluated as bad, unnecessary, and unhealthy. Homeostatic models must also assume a membrane-enclosed organism, or, in social terms, a social system with boundaries. The notion of adaptation includes assumptions of temporary and permanent changes that are desirable for maintaining homeostatic conditions. The evolution of the species generally is assumed to follow generations of adaptation or the appearance of genetic mutations that increase survival capacity.

We wish to avoid all these assumptions. In the preceding chapter we indicated why we could not accept the notion that boundaries or membranes apply to communication networks. And indeed, if one does not sell his soul to a homeostatic model, there is no reason to assume such a thing. We see no reason to assume evolution of social systems, either as a species or as individual systems that constantly evolve toward some ideal system or the full actualization of its potential. We espouse no idealistic optimism about the human nature of human societies. We see no reason to assume that anything resembling genetically determined homeostatic processes found in organisms occurs in social behavior. We see no reason to discuss social behavior as homeostatic maintaining behavior, or stress as a problem-solving and coping processes to maintain homeostasis or to adapt. In our opinion, social interaction is sufficiently different from organisms to require conceptualizations of its processes as different from homeostasis as homeostasis is from equilibrium.

HOMEOMAISTRE AND RESONATION

Once again we turn to the general system theorists who have clearly observed the limitations of homeostasis and equilibrium as models of social behavior. Buckley argues that for social systems neither equilibrium nor homeostatic concepts are adequate. He suggests the concept of complex adaptive system.

> The complex adaptive systems (species, psychological and socio-cultural systems) are also open and negentropic. But they are *open "internally" as well as externally* in that the interchanges among their components may result in *significant changes in the nature of the components themselves* with important consequences for the system as a whole. And the energy level that may be mobilized by the system is subject to relatively wide fluctuation. Internal as well as external interchanges are mediated characteristically by *information flows* (via chemical, cortical, or cultural encoding and decoding), although pure energy interchange occurs also. True feedback control loops make possible not only self-regulation, but self-direction or at least adaptation to a changing environment, such that the system may *change or elaborate its structure* as a condition of survival or viability (Buckley, 1968, p. 490, emphasis his).

Important here is the emphasis on information and on feedback control loops or cybernetic processes as crucial in self-correction and self-change. Homeostatic systems have feedback, but it is on an elementary level and applies only to regulation of one variable within rather limited ranges. Feedback provides the capacity for change of the structure by the system, something organic homeostatic systems cannot do, and provides the capacity for internal as well as external sources of information to produce change. In our model, resonation is purely an information process and does not involve considerations of energy exchange. Biosocial resonation, a special case of resonation, refers to the body's responses to and creation of information in interaction with the environment and in social interaction. The emphasis is on information.

The science of cybernetics is primarily interested in information control, processing, and transmission. A cybernetic mechanism is self-correcting by means of a feedback loop. Information is picked up, processed, and action directed. It may be a thermostat controlling a furnace or the regulation of body temperature in mammals (Cadwallader, 1968). Buckley (1968, p. 509) says that information in cybernetics is "selective interrelation or mapping" between two or more "subsets of constrained variety" so that information is communicated "as invariant constraint," with one effect being the reduction of uncertainty. Cybernetic systems must have some means of storing and retrieving information, even if it is just the temperature at which the furnace is turned off. Cybernetics is concerned with the continuity of systems in which some kinds of change is necessary for the continuity to be preserved (Cadwallader, 1968).

In Buckley's (1968) complex adaptive system structural change may sometimes be necessary for maintenance of a viable system. He emphasizes that the cybernetic concept must include means of discovering and evaluating alternative goals and methods, particularly when attempts based on existing patterns fail. He suggests that some types of deviance from the systems' patterns may be essential to the continued vitality of the system. Buckley suggests we redevelop our notions of social control to include the developing of new structures, the reinforcing of existing ones, and the destroying and restructuring of older ones, rather than simply the maintaining of a given structure.

From such a perspective, social systems are open cybernetic systems, that are learning and innovating (Cadwallader, 1968). Unfortunately, the general systems theorists tend to see all this in terms of adaptation and tend to develop evolutionary perspectives on social systems. The adaptation of the system is supposed to lead to new, more capable systems, and those which cannot adapt perish (Buckley, 1968; Cadwallader, 1968). According to Von Bertallanffy (1968, p. 18) an open system may "attain a time-independent state independent of initial conditions and determined only by the system parameters." They can be said to have "goals of their own which are reflected in their structure" (p. 18). This structurally implicit goal is the object of their adaptation process and is called equifinality.

We are pessimistic about the value of concepts like equifinality in social behavior. The most we might be willing to believe about communication networks is that they may tend, in the long run, toward a greater congruity between information of the network and the milieu, but we are not convinced they necessarily do or must. There is just as much opportunity to incorporate inaccurate information into the network. If they do tend toward greater congruity, it is not because of the structure of the social system per se but because of the properties of people in social systems. Equifinality might be interpreted as the tendency to reduce uncertainty, but, as we have mentioned, sociocultural systems are frequently sources of uncertainty and may use uncertainty to maintain the loyalty of some members. We are not convinced that communication networks are necessarily bound to reduce uncertainty by their very nature, although this could, indeed, be the consequence of social interaction. Whatever else communication networks do, we suggest they neither evolve nor necessarily progress. Given the malleable and fluctuating nature of the structure of communication networks, it would seem impossible to predict the goal or implicit direction of the system because the structure itself is changing.

One of the key differences between communication networks and homeostatic systems is that homeostatic systems must respond to stimuli and changes as they occur and cannot prevent such changes from occurring in the first place. Usually, homeostatic processes cannot manipulate, alter, or control the source of the external stimuli producing the changes. We do not believe that the usual use of the term adaptation refers to such system mastery, although some carefree scientists use it to mean almost any adjustment to the milieu. Adaptation should refer only to processes of homeostatic adjustment to environmental changes, the development of existing organs to handle increased loads upon the homeostatic system, and the development of new capacities through various means, including mutation and natural selection, for responding to the environment to more adequately maintain the homeostatic systems. A new term is needed to apply to the processes of more goal-directed systems, including social systems.

These systems, which Buckley called complex adaptive systems, exhibit a process with the following properties: if the milieu is congruous with the system's information systems, it resonates with the milieu without changing its own patterns or information; if the information is in some way incongruous with the system's information and patterns, it may either modify the environment to make it more congenial with the system's information or modify its own information and patterns to make them more congruous with the milieu. As we have mentioned, instead of adaptation, this process should be called resonation to distinguish it from homeostatic styles of relating to the environment. Instead of using homeostatic to refer to the continuity-maintaining processes, we offer a new term "homeomaistre" (homeo: Greek for similar; maistre: Old French for master) to call attention to the capacity of these systems to manipulate the environment to which they must adjust rather than to respond only when stimulated. Homeomaistre-resonation processes apply to all the commonly called goal-directed behavioral phenomena of organic systems except the homeostatic.

From our suggested perspective the following key distinctions must be made. Equilibrium is limited to the physical phenomena, and it represents a total lack of capability to maintain a given steady state in the face of environmental change. The structural nature of equilibrium is given by the molecular structure of the substance and is not subject to modification. There is no information content in the process.

Homeostasis is limited to organic phenomena. It is a process able to maintain internal states despite changes of environment (within certain limits), but it cannot control the external environment directly (manipulate). Although there is some information, it involves only the degree of variation from a norm. Usually there is little information exchange between the system and the environment; that is, no new and better ways of coping with problems encountered by homeostatic devices are developed as a result of either success or failure in an encounter. Instead, the structure of homeostatic mechanisms and the form of their behavior is genetically given and is essentially unchangeable. Only through natural selection, mutation, and so forth can improvements take place; no concrete organism can by choice modify its homeostatic mechanisms.

"Homeomaistre" is limited to social phenomena (including social and certain behavioral aspects of animals) and goal-oriented behavior. It is the information content and manipulation by which effective relational patterns or communication networks are maintained (in contrast to Parsons' pattern maintenance, which emphasizes cultural patterns; see Parsons and Bales, 1955). Homeomaistre is the process by which communication networks maintain and improve information congruities and reduce uncertainty. Homeomaistre processes maintain continuity of the complex in some form, either as a network of communication between a particular collection of people or as certain information contents. However, much of the information content need not be preserved in homeomaistre.

Homeomaistre is not a passive response or adaptation to the environment but the active resonation with it, involving adjustments to the environment and the changes in it, the search for information about the environment and prediction of it, and the modification of the structure of the system as changes in the environment require. Only homeomaistre systems can voluntarily change their structure and content to forms that information indicates are more suitable. Homeomaistre systems are tuned-in to their milieu. Individuals perceiving the environment and testing and modifying their information in it are resonating with the environment. Physiological changes occur as part of this resonation. Communication networks resonate with other networks through individuals resonating to each other in interaction. In all of these, information perception, processing, and transmission are the substance of the resonance.

Homeomaistre may involve information, such as social norms and values, that is arbitrarily created by men in interaction. Neither equilibrium nor homeostatic processes, however, can be determined by human decision. They are determined by natural relations or "laws" and by genetic structure. Most of the patterns of the homeomaistre processes in communication networks themselves are manmade, which is why they are so malleable. Consequently, although the nature of homeostatic processes can be predicted in animals of given categories, such as mammals, and although they are essentially the same in all animals of that species and for the life of any given animal, the homeomaistre processes of communication networks must be observed from time to time because they may change in resonation with other networks and the environment.

The homeomaistre processes are mainly changed by the participants as a result of the perception of incongruities and the change in their involvement with the network. Equilibrium and homeostasis take their respective forms independently of the desires of the systems that make them up or of which they are a part. Homeomaistre—its form and occurrence —depends on the desires (not necessarily conscious) of the participants or actors.

Given the malleability of homeomaistre systems and their resonation with the environment, it no longer is of any concern whether a change is adaptive or whether change is prevented and some process returns the system to some previous equilibrium. Continuity becomes simply the continuing ability of participants and others to recognize the communication network as such. Because change is an ordinary element in communication networks, there may always be participants lamenting the loss of the "real" network they originally identified with. These changes are in resonation with the environment and may or may not reduce uncertainty or improve information congruity. They can only be judged as good or bad when arbitrary human values are applied, such as "people shouldn't have to feel uncertain." It is futile to try to judge steady states and changes as good or bad; it is much better simply to observe and predict them.

The processes of homeomaistre in communication networks are information processes, including insulation, isolation, exploration, responsiveness to information incongruities observed by participants, and so forth. Their general form is not systematically developed in this work.

We have developed this discussion not only because we feel that the notion of homeomaistre is useful in the understanding of communication networks and their influence on health, but because so many models purporting to discuss relations between social behavior and health are based on the adaptation-homeostatic model. We believe that this distorts our perception and presents unnecessary assumptions. We have sought to eliminate these difficulties by offering an alternative model dealing with the same dimensions.

The Phases of Change Produced by Encounters with Information Incongruities

THE CONVERGENCE OF SEVERAL PERSPECTIVES ON A GENERAL SEQUENCE IN SOCIAL CHANGE

Social change is the change of the information repertoire of people in their communication networks. Thus social change is the change of people. The individual encounters incongruities that indicate the ineffectiveness and inaccuracy of a communication network's information. If enough people or people in crucial positions in the communication network reject the invalidated information and seek more congruous information, then change in the network's information and communication patterns may occur. To the degree that these patterns and information change and a new consensus is obtained, social change has occurred. All social change, whether it is in a small group of individuals or a society, follows a general sequence which begins in this way.

We are not the first to note this sequence or some of its elements. The work of a number of scientists and theorists of social change converge on and support our notions of a general sequence in all social change, which begins with the invalidation and rejection of a communication network's information.

Marx's suggestion that each economic system contains the seeds of its own destruction in the behavior forms that produce discontent among the people is more than a polemic. The discontent or alienation of the people plays a crucial role in awakening a social system to the inadequacy of its information and communication patterns. Marx conceptualized social change as the outgrowing of the "relations of production" by the "forces of production" (Hook, 1955; Nisbet, 1969; Schumpeter, 1950; Zeitlin, 1968). A social-material environment too complex for the existing information and communication patterns of networks seems likely to favor change. Although we may be inclined to dismiss Marx's materialistic determinism along with Ogburn's (1964) technological determinism

(Hart, 1957), we must not overlook the profound impact of the machine on societies. The behavior patterns resulting from technical advance such as working relations are a major stimulus requiring new formulations of information and communication networks (MacIver and Page, 1967; Mumford, 1963).

Society as an Organism. The most prevalent concepts of society and change in sociology are based on the organic analogy. The birth, growth, maturity, decay, and death sequence of organisms is applied by Spengler (1961) to social change (Smelser, 1968). The growth of the organism to its genetic potential is reflected in Sorokin's (1957) immanent change and Von Bertalanffy's (1968) equifinality. Evolution and embryonic development become the differentiation-integration models of social change of Spencer and Parsons. Parsons (1964; Smelser, 1968) sees societies' evolution as the result of hitting on new patterns that improve adaptive capacities.

There are a number of general problems with the organic analogy. Foremost is the tendency to conceive of societies as cybernetic devices for which change is the consequence of efforts to restore equilibrium after outside disruptions, which we have discussed. Differentiation is apparently a result of adapting to outside conditions.

Although the sequence of differentiation and integration offers some insight into information incongruity-congruity processes in communication networks, we must insist that there are internal sources of change as well as external. Parsons recognizes endogenous as well as exogenous sources of strain that can lead to change. These endogenous sources are never well developed by him, except perhaps in terms of conflicts of subsystems requiring the integration functioning of the system or as the consequence of faulty socialization. His emphasis is mostly on outside sources of change, such as cultural diffusion. This is an inadequate treatment of internal sources of change, and yet there is much in Parsons' writing to suggest the importance of individual alienation in social change. Parsons' arrangement of action systems in a hierarchy suggests that the behavioral organism is likely to be the first to change, being the highest in energy and the lowest in information content; the personality system next; then the social system; and lastly the cultural system, which is lowest in energy, highest in information, and the last to change (Parsons, 1961, 1966 b).

Parson's hierarchy implies that the sequence of change within a concrete system is first the behavior of people, then the social system, followed by the culture. In addition the emphasis Parsons places on legitimation of power and social patterns by the role player suggests that in explaining social change we might watch for situations that produce destruction of subjective legitimation of networks (Parsons, 1966 b). Parsons' concept of institutionalization follows a pattern of disengagement from old norms, transition, and institutionalization, and it roughly approximates his socialization stages. His institutionalization roughly indicates the form of the general sequence of social change, and it considers individual alienation or disengagement from norms as an essential element of change (Parsons, 1955, 1961).

The idea of progress in social change has been whipped by Nisbet (1969). He makes a very good case, and we must conclude with him that it is a historical-theological idea that bears a misleading resemblance to the empirical world. Progress, evolution, and growth, all came from the same roots, and all evaluate change positively as a somewhat inevitable movement toward an optimistically perceived future. We feel that now is the time to discard the idea that change is for the better and to admit that change can be better, worse, or indifferent, depending on one's point of view.

Despite his correction of the bias of progress in social change theory, Nisbet (1966) falls into some of the same errors of the functionalists by insisting that "fixity," not change, is normal. He believes that "significant change is overwhelmingly the result of non-developmental factors; that is to say, factors inseparable from external events and intrusions" (Nisbet, 1969, p. 280). We must discount Nisbet's rejection of internal sources of social change.

The general systems theorists offer a more "alive" model of societies in which change is in part the consequence of active attempts by the system to control the parts of the environment upon which it depends for survival (Buckley, 1968). Toynbee (1961) argues that growth cannot be measured in terms of increased environmental control but in terms of continuing ability to meet new challenges.

Moore (1963) with his tension-management approach has attempted to find the middle ground between the conflict theorists and those who base theories on organic models. He sees tension and conflict as normal but as having many sources, unlike the Marxists. He, like the functionalists, sees social adaptation as a response to disruptive influences, but unlike them he thinks that change may not reduce the tensions but can in fact increase them. Smelser (1968) believes Moore's model is more realistic than those already discussed but has the disadvantage of providing less clearcut clues to causes and consequences of change.

Smelser's synthesis is one of the better modern theories. He captured more of the general sequential form of social change than any other author, although he draws much of his perspective from his mentor Parsons. His main limitations relate to his insistence in maintaining the equilibrium model of social systems and change.

He discusses social control and its influence on change (see his *Theory of Collective Behavior*). He thinks that whether disturbance produces a change that is a beneficial differentiation of the system or whether it permits disorganized collective behavior forms to emerge (for example, riots) depends on the degree of social control maintained.

Smelser postulates a seven-step sequence in social change: (1) dissatisfaction with role prescription or an incumbents' performance; (2) emergence of symptoms of this disturbance: anxiety, hostility," tendencies to glorify the past or build utopian visions of the future. . . . Sometimes these symptoms of disturbance congeal into an ideology, in the name of which one or more social movements rise"; (3) handling and channeling the symptoms of disturbance by the social system involved; (4) "encouragement of new ideas to deal with supposed sources of dissatisfaction," wherein social systems guide investigation of ways to resolve the situation; (5) "attempts to specify institutional forms that will ease the supposed sources of dissatisfaction"; (6) "attempts to establish new institutional forms," with the innovator and entrepreneur taking over for the inventor and creator; (7) "the new institutional forms are consolidated as permanent features of the social structure" (Smelser, 1968, pp. 79–80). This sequence adequately describes the general form of social change from the point of view of social institutions, and although it has been applied to socialization processes as well (Parsons, 1955) it does not adequately consider the role of individual, in our opinion.

Individual Insights as a Source of Social Change. Concepts such as diffusion of culture and other emphases on external events or exogenous sources of change may help explain why a particular communication network changed when it did but not where the information originally came from. Individual insights or creativity has been the subject of several studies of social change.

Barnett (1953) sees creative activity as primarily the recombination of existing ideas in a new fashion. He believes that a recombination must be identified to be useful; that is, the individual must recognize its usefulness. He categorizes wants that provide incentive to innovation, which we do not entirely accept. We do agree that people must want something and feel dissatisfied before they will be innovators; otherwise they will simply let creative thoughts fade away unutilized.

Kroeber's (1944) study of geniuses indicated that isolated geniuses were the exception and that most of the time they occurred in clusters. This finding contributes to the credibility of our own belief that periods of high individual creativity occur during the early periods of social change when old patterns are being discarded and new ones explored. As new patterns begin to crystallize, we can expect creativity to be somewhat reduced in amount and its direction become more channeled in support of the new patterns. Thus we expect geniuses to occur in clusters at periods of pattern change.

Hagen's (1962, p. 86) insights are pertinent: "The interrelationships between personality and social structure are such as to make it clear that social change will not occur without change in personalities." He sees innovation resulting from individual mental processes in two steps: (1) arriving at new mental and aesthetic conceptions and (2) converting the new conceptions into action (for example, technology). Hagen believes that a society cannot simply adopt the patterns of other societies. Even in the modernization of underdeveloped societies, considerable innovation by its membership is necessary. In discussing how these new mental and aesthetic conceptions come to be, he suggests the importance of (discussing his "unanxious creative person") "unconscious alertness that leads the individual to note some aspect of an everyday phenomenon differs from the expected and to appreciate the significance of the difference" (1962, p. 88). This explanation corresponds closely to our own notion of perception of incongruities. Although this perception of difference very frequently can come from exposure to different cultures and ideas or as the result of being a marginal man between two conflicting elements of a given social system, it can also result from individual insight and perception without regard to outside cultural intrusion. Scientific discoveries are frequently an example (Selye, 1964; Watson, 1968).

The social-psychological properties that encourage such creative insight has been the subject of considerable speculation and study. Hagen has offered us a theory based on the following: the child-raising patterns of the previous generation, the degree of authoritarianism, the changing of status positions, and the notion that a society goes into a withdrawal period followed by a creative period. These periods, which he assesses for several historical societies, frequently range over hundreds of years. Although we agree that a creative period follows one of disengagement or withdrawal from the previous social patterns, we think Hagen's time periods are too broad to explain the varieties and prevalence of change we actually observe.

Hart, in refining Ogburn's cultural-lag hypothesis, suggests that in our era of cultural acceleration one should focus on "cultural complexes" (1957, p. 419) such as the family, economy, recreation, and religion. We, of course, agree and suggest that the popular practice—especially in historical and modernization studies (cf. Eisenstadt, 1965, 1968 b; Parsons, 1966 b)—of using whole societies as the unit of analysis has blinded us to the general, sequential pattern of social change. One must look at communication networks of varying levels of size and inclusiveness. The degree of their interdependence provides clues for the consequences of change in one network for another. The overall patterns of change in a society are the cross-section of changes taking place in its component communication networks. Only when a large number of networks or those of central significance to a society change directions does the society-wide change take place. The bias toward using societies as the unit of study is additional evidence of the dominance in theories of change of the organic models that make society the social organism. Once we avoid organic analogies, the society is a no better unit of analysis than some other communication networks, depending on the purposes of the study.

Hart (1957) also sees creative thinking on all levels as primary in social change, not just in regard to technical or material inventions, as Ogburn did. We might think of cultural lag more as the repercussions of change in one communication network upon others, as the problems of developing symbolic concepts to make these repercussions understandable to people, and as the modifying of communication networks to utilize the information.

Although individual discovery can play an important role in some social change, this is only true if the new idea becomes part of the behavior patterns of a group. Rogers (1962) has explored the problem of adoption of new ideas and has described the social and psychological characteristics of innovators, early adopters, early and late majorities, and laggards. He develops five steps in the process of individual adoption of innovation: awareness, interest, evaluation, trial, and adoption. This process catches the fundamental pattern of social change as it relates to the adoption of a new idea presented to the person. It does not, however, handle the problem of individual creativity such as Barnett and Hagen focus upon.

Etzioni presents a model of society that permits the handling of individual creativity and insight much more adequately than the conflict or organic models, and it is compatible with our biosocial resonation model.

> The social entity is not an oppressive reality, hovering above the individual, constraining his acts. It is far more penetrating than this, for it is a part of what he views as his irreducible self, encompassing his streaks of disaffection and rebellion as well as his periods of compliance. The individual more readily can participate in transforming a social entity, making it closer to his image, than he can engage in a fully individualistic act . . . Individuals participate, some even lead others, but the vehicle of change is social grouping (Etzioni, 1968 a, p. 3).

He believes that individuals can innovate and transform the social system by designing new patterns and implementing them. Innovative capacity is related to the actor's consciousness of the environment. Increased societal or elite awareness of existing and alternative patterns is fundamental to change. Because social patterns are in part symbolic, they may be partly changed as a direct result of increased consciousness (Etzioni, 1968 a, p. 240). Etzioni also has some idea of the fundamental form of social change:

> There also seems to be a societal analogy to the psychological proposition that new matters are first reviewed consciously and then routinized and delegated to non-conscious levels and again examined consciously only when deliberate and fundamental changes are attempted (1968 a, p. 240).

Shibutani (1967, p. 169) thinks that in diversified, pluralistic, and continually changing modern societies, changes involve "a loss of responsiveness to the demands of one social world and the adoption of the perspective of another." He says, "It may be hypothesized that the disaffection occurs first on the level of personal relations, followed by a weakening sense of obligation, a rejection of old claims, and the establishment of new loyalties and incorporation of a new perspective."

If one considers all these ideas together, a broad pattern of the sequential form of social change emerges.

THE FUNDAMENTAL SEQUENTIAL FORM OF SOCIAL CHANGE

We have arbitrarily divided the sequence of social change into four phases: invalidation, exploration, innovation, and habituation. These phases are the same for any communication network and for any individual. They are obtained only if the change process is permitted to run its full course. Many things can go wrong in any of these phases and lead to the arresting of the network in that condition, to deflection of the change process, or perhaps to disintegration of the network (Toynbee, 1961).

Invalidation is always the first phase. It involves the encountering of incongruities that invalidate some portion of one's information repertoire and the subsequent rejection of the invalidated information. Until one experiences invalidation of a piece of information, he will not be receptive to alternatives. Contacts with invalidating information do not necessarily produce social change. The second phase of social change begins only when one rejects the invalidated information.

Invalidation may or may not be accompanied by alienation from the communication network from which the invalidated information was obtained. Whether alienation occurs depends on conditions discussed in the preceding chapter. A particular pattern or piece of information in a communication network can be modified with little or no change in members' subjective involvement if the new information can be incorporated into the existing network without requiring fundamental changes in the network's information on which the members' self-concepts, interpretations of the natural world, and norms and values are based. The more the invalidated information is a network's central norms and pronouncements about the natural world, the more alienation is likely to occur as a result of the contact with incongruities that invalidated the information, and the more alienation is necessary for social change of those patterns and information to occur. Whenever alienation occurs, the invalidation phase of social change has occurred; however, invalidation does not necessarily produce alienation. The proportions of members alienated and the strategic location of the alienated members in the communication network determine if network-wide change will be initiated. Still, change may not be obtained, depending on many things including the degree to which change would produce information and patterns incongruous with the other networks in that particular cluster, the responsiveness of the participants to and belief in the existence of acceptable alternatives, and so on. If alienation does occur, the invalidation phase may be a period of awakening and disenchantment in the communication network.

Whether the perception of the invalidating information is the result of experiences in the natural environment, of contact with other networks, or of accepting as participants people who bring with them incongruous information from other networks does not matter much. The argument of whether the source of change is endogenous or exogenous does not apply, except in the sense that some participant is the original source of the information (endogenous) or that the original source is outside the network in some other communication network (exogenous). In all cases, change requires perception of incongruous information by participants in the network.

The second phase is *exploration*. After the invalidated information has been rejected, a search for more accurate and effective alternatives begins. If invalidation was the result of encountering more accurate or effective information, exploration is the search for acceptable, alternative ways of incorporating the new information into the communication network. Even when a satisfactory alternative is provided by experts from outside the network, as when technology is imported, considerable exploration and experimentation is necessary to incorporate the alternative into the network's information.

In those cases in which invalidation has produced alienation sufficient to initiate change of fundamental network information, identification may drain away and the old communication network begins to disintegrate. One's own information can become a more important guide to behavior. Old patterns are reexamined. Relative free play of imagination and exploration of alternative patterns may be encouraged. Emotional expressiveness can be relatively unfettered, permitting new forms of expression to be explored. The degree of freedom depends on the changing communication network's degree of social control and the control that the remaining networks in the cluster can and desire to maintain over the changing area (Smelser, 1968). In general, the more permissive (which is not the same as absence of organization) this period, the more creatively rich it will be. The autonomous may find opportunities for exploration of alternatives, but those who feel set adrift without dependable order may feel very uncomfortable. For the social movements that emerge, it is the period of charisma, "revelation" and "scripture" production (Lang and Lang, 1961; Smelser, 1968). Here are Kroeber's geniuses, the scientific, and aesthetic, and other creative minds running relatively free of restraints from ideologically committed social systems. Here the dialectical process can culminate in the reconciliation of the complexities and conflicts of the previous period. These predictions assume that the change is a successful one leading to a more-satisfied populace. From the participant's point of view, it could of course fail at this point and simply never adequately meet the challenge for yet another synthesis (Toynbee, 1961).

Innovation is the third phase. By innovation we mean the adoption of a new idea and its subsequent utilization (not simply new ideas, as Rogers defines it). This phase is characterized by the spread of adoption of selected alternatives from the exploration period. The new information "catches on" among members of the communication network. The network's information, including interaction patterns, is accommodated to the new information. The range of application of the new information is tested.

This can be a highly productive period, perhaps the period enjoyed by the largest proportion of people, when identification is at its peak. Within the communication network, new networks are developing to utilize the adopted information of the exploration period. Some of the autonomous and other creative people may be delighted to see their creations being put to use, and the more dependent members may be delighted to have an exciting new order with promise of better things to come. The values of the creative period gradually become the property of organizations. Charisma is routinized, and the form of individual rationality predominating may change from substantive-insightful to means-end logic (Hoselitz, 1968; Weber, 1949).

There is, of course, the possibility that a proportion of the people involved or those in clustering networks may not find the innovations congruous and may become alienated from the information and network. Changes are resonating through other networks of the cluster throughout all of these phases.

The fourth phase is *habituation*. Throughout the invalidation and exploration phases within the communication network, there is likelihood of increased responsiveness to the individual. Through the innovation period and peaking in the habituation period, there is an increasing likelihood that the communication network will be less responsive to the individual. Duty and loyalty may become prime virtues. The social movements are now social organizations, probably vested interests (Lang and Lang, 1961). Innovations are now part of the communication network's information: "Everybody does it that way." Creativity and exploration are encouraged primarily to enhance existing social patterns. The exploration period is looked back on as almost sacred or at least classical in the case of change of fundamental information. Emotional expressiveness is limited to acceptable norms. This may be a period of high restriction, regimentation, and routine (Hoselitz, 1968). Identification is likely to be high, as is conformity. This is not necessarily bad, and it may be a very happy period for a very long time; that is, until someone perceives another incongruity and the process begins again.

One must keep in mind that this sequential pattern of social change applies to a change taking place in a particular communication network. One must constantly be on guard so that one focuses on only one network at a time until the change is isolated. Then one can shift to other communication networks in the cluster to examine the ramifications of the change. One might even be able to locate the changing network by looking for the one in which the basic pattern of change is occurring.

AN EXAMPLE OF THE SEQUENTIAL FORM OF CHANGE APPLIED TO THE DEVELOPMENT OF MODERN TECHNOLOGY

"The most novel and pervasive phenomena of our age is not capitalism but mechanization, of which modern capitalism may be merely a by-product" (MacIver and Page, 1967, p. 111). From Mumford's *Technics and Civilization* we have selected some examples of the phases of change as they occurred in the technological communication network. (In this book, of course, we usually focus on much smaller communication networks. The following exposition is, however, quite illustrative of broad changes and their ramifications.)

Mumford recognizes three periods in the development of the machine and technology: the eotechnic, paleotechnic, and neotechnic. These periods divide the change sequence somewhat differently than we have, so that some of our phases occur in more than one of Mumford's periods. The eotechnic ran from about 1000 to 1750 and was a period of fundamental mechanical discoveries on which most later inventions are based. The fundamental source of power was wind and water, and wood was the main material of construction. Because of its roots in antiquity, it is somewhat difficult to see the pattern of social change in the development of the eotechnic period; thus we begin with the paleotechnic period.

The paleotechnic period's *invalidation* and *exploration* phases seem to have run from around the fifteenth to the seventeenth centuries. Disenchantment with Catholic dogma grew, partially because of the inability of scholasticism to describe the world explorers and early scientists were finding. As the old patterns dissolved, the "arts shot up into the air in a hundred pulsing fountains . . ." (Mumford, 1963, p. 45). It was the age of Shakespeare, Michelangelo, and their great contemporaries. Modern science bubbled into life through Bacon, Newton, Descartes, Galileo, and others. Mumford says of the Renaissance:

> Mechanical arts advanced as the humane arts weakened and receded, and it was at the moment when form and civilization had most completely broken up that the tempo of invention became more rapid, and the multiplication of machines and the increase of (mechanical) power took place (1963, p. 112).

Perhaps the greatest product of this creative period was the scientific method, which called for objectivity of the observer; specialization; focus on qualities that could be weighed, measured, or counted; and time-space sequences that could be repeated or predicted.

The *innovation* period was getting underway by the Seventeenth century. Organizational regimentation, modeled after the machine and bound to the clock, spread. The values of Protestantism gained ground and condemned the sensuous, emotional, and intuitive elements of the creative period. Invention and innovation were controlled by the guilds, industrial workers, and capitalists, who paid little attention to science. As early as 1624 in England patent laws were passed that monopolized the control of new departures in the hands of special patent holders (Mumford, 1963, p. 132). Inducements existed for inventions that would extend the industrialists' control. Mumford believes the industrial revolution was completed by the 1750s (England's late entry and dominance is mistakenly called the Industrial Revolution by some). During this innovative phase, coal replaced water and wind, and iron replaced wood. Steam engines soon became the major power device. Mining, not textiles, was the dominant industry. The new patterns were crystallizing.

The *habituation* period followed quite "naturally" when the expenses of steam engines and coal produced monopolies, whereas the abundance of wind and water and wood had permitted widespread small-scale production. With the coming of the railroads, the dominant organizations and cultural patterns were further strengthened. Mumford's work indicates that this habituation period reached its peak in the late-eighteenth and nineteenth centuries, and many of its patterns and values still dominate industry; for example, time, labor, money, space, and matter are to be conquered and exploited, not conserved.

Throughout this phase the emphasis on the well-being of the company, country, church, and other organizations overrode concern for human welfare. As early as the eighteenth century and throughout the nineteenth century, reformers, social critics, and novelists reflected the growing disenchantment with the habituation of technical ideas we call industrialization. Although the content may have changed, concern over the "dehumanizing" qualities of industrial and bureaucratic labor and consumption orientations continues to undermine norms of the habituation phase of the paleotechnic period (Mumford, 1963; Taviss, 1969).

The new period Mumford sees emerging is the neotechnic. Its power is electrical, and its materials are alloys and synthetics. Its invalidation phase, described above, is in full swing, and certain communication networks, such as the electrical, have already passed through the exploration period, but others are lagging behind in the habituation phase of the paleotechnic period. The exploration period of the electrical communication network came in the 1830s to 1850s, when we find a cluster of geniuses: Faraday, Volta, Galvani, Oersted, Ohm, Ampere, and Foureyron. Among their discoveries were the electric cell, the storage cell, the dynamo, electric motors, lamps, spectroscopes, the principle of conservation of energy, and the phenomenon that bear some of their names. By 1910 the influence of electrical innovations was felt in industry, and many recent developments such as television were being discovered or foreshadowed. We suggest that we are in the innovative phase of the change in the electrical communication network, but interdependent networks are in varying stages. What lies ahead in electricity is not creativity in the breakthrough sense but ingenuity in applying and fully developing our knowledge of electricity.

SOCIAL CHANGE AND SUSCEPTIBILITY TO DISEASE

There are some definite advantages to knowing whether a given communication network is changing and, if so, what phase it is in, especially when one desires to predict or explain changes in susceptibility to disease among participants. People who were involved with the prechange network in different ways can be expected to respond differently to the various phases of the change. Changing feelings of involvement with various aspects of emerging networks during later phases must also be assessed.

We have defined alienation as the consequence of encountering an information incongruity of sufficient disruptive capacity to alter one's subjective involvement from identification to alienation. We have also emphasized that the encountering of such incongruities may produce general physiological responses and alter susceptibility to disease. We suggest that the largest proportion of participants having increased susceptibility to disease will occur during the invalidation phase of change in a given communication network, when alienation is most likely to occur. Those most susceptible are the alienated persons, but the probability of the identified members becoming alienated is high if the old information rejected is fundamental to the network and is rejected by ever-increasing numbers of people and if the old communication network dissolves. If the network completely changes, which is rare, everyone who was identified must for a time become alienated. The autonomous person can be expected to fare better than alienated or identified members during the invalidation period, because the change has less significance for him. Those who remain identified may still encounter many incongruities, particularly since they must interact with the alienated, which may increase their susceptibility to disease.

During the exploration phase the alienated and identified participants are still highly likely to be susceptible to disease, with autonomous people less likely to have changes in disease susceptibility. However, the alienated members are more likely to have begun turning to other networks or information, or they may be developing autonomy. Thus the proportion of people alienated and highly vulnerable to changes in disease susceptibility will be somewhat smaller, and thus the overall susceptibility to disease of participants in the network may be expected to be somewhat less during the exploration than in the invalidation phase of change.

The susceptibility to disease of participants of the network should be lowest during the innovation period, when the anticipation and excitement of the development of fresh information and communication networks, including high levels of interaction, rapport, and devotion to causes, could maximize the proportion and vitality of identified participants. During such periods the disparity in earlier phases between autonomous people and the identified and alienated members may be sharply reduced as the proportions of identified increases, and the likelihood of encountering information incongruities by the identified participants is somewhat reduced, assuming that the new information is more accurate and effective.

The habituation period will have a high proportion of identification, which will vary and must be monitored from time to time. There will be a higher proportion of alienation than during the innovation period, a sort of chronic condition in all communication networks. The discussion of the four types of involvement in Chapter V is more or less set in a habituation phase.

Some of the suggestive evidence in Chapter V relating alienation to illness applies here. In addition, Wolff (1953) notes that major changes occurring relatively rapidly, such as over a few years, can diminish a host's resistance to microorganisms. Mutter and Schleifer (1966) studied 42 ill and 45 control children and found that the ill children were exposed to greater numbers of changes in the previous months than the control ones. They believe that change per se was not enough, but changes were more likely to produce illness when the child was lacking in capacities or had other social-psychological predisposing characteristics.

Cassel and Tyroler (1961; Tyroler and Cassel, 1964) have sought evidence concerning the proposition that "recent sociocultural changes will raise the probability of incongruity between the culture of the migrant and the social situation in which he lives" (Cassel and Tyroler, 1961, p. 25) and that the incongruity will lead to increased illness and psychosomatic symptoms. They studied rural mountaineer factory workers and their illness episodes and symptoms reported, defining an illness episode as an absence from work for illness of over 3 days (Cassel and Tyroler, 1961). They studied the degree to which urbanization of the communities and counties of rural folk was related to coronary heart disease. They used death certificates for measuring coronary heart disease and determined urbanization by the size of population of the largest city in the county. They classified the counties of North Carolina in terms of urbanization and measured heart disease twice, once around 1950 and again around 1960 (Tyroler and Cassel, 1964; Cassel, 1970). Rural people living in communities that were urbanizing around them exhibited a dramatic increase in coronary and other heart diseases (Tyroler and Cassel, 1964; Cassel, 1970). Cassel and Tyroler (1964) conclude that there is evidence but not proof for their postulate, but they consider it a useful variable for predicting directions of relations. The incongruities experienced are apparently between the norms and the information of the communication networks the rural and mountain folk were identified with and the new communication networks they were required to participate in or associate with.

Mental health workers have also found change related to changes in health. Wechsler (1961) observed higher rates of hospitalized depressive disorders and suicide in rapidly growing communities, especially among suburban women of childbearing age. Leighton et al. (1963) thinks that the rate and extent of social change have considerable effect on mental health. The disruption of feelings of "belonging to a moral order and feeling right in what one does" (p. 385) and disruption of opportunities for the achievement of love, recognition, and spontaneity are among the most noxious aspects of social disintegration (our invalidation and exploration periods). Leighton et al. point out something frequently overlooked by the worshippers of creativity and freedom from social restrictions. The disintegrated communities were characterized as places where it was easier to do what one liked, unencumbered by social restrictions, but where the numbers of things to do were limited. The choice was limited mainly to sex, aggression, drinking (now we would include drugs), and idleness. There was some opportunity for developing artistic diversions, but with fewer guidelines, rewards, and opportunities "whereby an urge to self-expression can mature into a set of complex and multiple sentiments that are both articulate with the community and satisfactory in the functioning of the personality" (p. 381); in fact, the evidence indicated that social disintegration interfered with much spontaneity and creativity.

Mobility and Susceptibility to Disease. In the preceding we mention that information incongruities can be encountered as a result of normative requirements of the communication network. One way such norms can lead to contact with incongruities is through geographical and social mobility. The norms encouraging higher education and "getting ahead" can produce social mobility, which may produce status incongruities, particularly among the upwardly mobile. These same norms can also encourage one to be geographically mobile in search of better opportunities. One may be socially and geographically mobile for a multitude of reasons, but both mobilities have essentially the same consequence, the movement from participation in one communication network or cluster to different ones; or to different networks in the same larger cluster, such as different congregations of the same church, or different branches of a company; or to different positions within a given network, which may amount to moving to a different network in many ways because information access and communication partners are often different. Both kinds of mobility in various degrees increase the probability of encountering incongruous information, including differences of interpretation of the proper performance of the same information of the same network; differences in the evaluations of the mobile person by the networks he is leaving and entering; differences in the evaluations of the mobile person by the various networks in which he participates; differences in the amount of reward, support, or prestige forthcoming from fellow participants for a given activity in networks he is entering and leaving; encountering networks in which one is anomic or partially anomic but must perform and learn by embarrassing trial and error (especially true of the upwardly mobile).

Smith (1967), in relation to cardiovascular disease, reports that migrants had higher incidence both at their place of origin and destination than nonmigrants and that occupationally, residentially, or socially mobile in a given culture had higher incidence than the nonmobile; those who moved to different cultures but continue to behave according to the old ways had different disease experience than those who adopted the new culture.

Syme et al. (1964) studied coronary heart diseases in both urban and rural settings in North Dakota. They found that white-collar workers of rural backgrounds had coronary heart disease rates two and three times higher than expected when compared with both blue-collar workers from urban backgrounds and agricultural workers from rural backgrounds. Those who were geographically and occupationally mobile had high rates of coronary heart disease. As Cassel (1970, p. 197) puts it, this (and some of Syme's later work) indicates that "those individuals displaying the greatest discontinuity between childhood and adult situations, as measured by occupation and place of residence, have higher rates than those in which less discontinuity could be determined." Similarly, Cassel and Tyroler (1961) found that factory workers from the same North Carolina mountain cove who were the first in their families to work in factories had more illness and symptoms than those who came from families with experienced factory workers.

Cobb et al. (1969) found that women having rheumatoid arthritis are more likely to be from homes where parents have high levels of status inconsistency and are themselves more likely to marry men with whom they have status inconsistencies. The mothers of these women evidently were the source of enormous numbers of information incongruities because they remember their mother's discipline as arbitrary, unreasonable, and severe.

Abramson (1966) found people with status inconsistencies, such as high education and low-status occupation and low education and high-status occupation, have the most emotional disturbances. Jackson (1962) found those whose ascribed status is higher than their achieved status (downwardly mobile) report the highest symptom levels. Stanton and Schwartz (1954) go so far as to suggest that a society in which vertical mobility is not possible might be less traumatic.

Christenson and Hinkle (1961) studied managers and found that the group with the highest numbers of illnesses of all sorts were much more likely to be upwardly mobile than the group experiencing fewer illnesses and episodes of illness. These managers with the higher illness experience were usually sons of men who, on the average, had a grammer school education or less. These managers were more likely to have grown up in moderate or substandard neighborhoods and to have worked as blue-collar workers for a number of years after graduation from high school before attaining their managerial positions. They tended to perceive the milieu in which they were working as new, unfamiliar, and full of challenges, with the same situations providing more threats and demands. The managers with less illness tended to be sons of managers or white-collar workers, from families who have grown up in good neighborhoods with middle to high incomes. Holmes (1956) found tuberculosis related to multiple occupational and residential moves.

All of these findings may well be explained in terms of information incongruities encountered and the subsequent general physiological responses and increased susceptibility to disease.

Summary

Inorganic chemical and physical systems react to environmental energy changes with entropy, reaching a new state of equilibrium. Organic systems have homeostatic processes that involve feedback and respond to environmental change by adapting, either by homeostatic activity, which returns the organic process to some steady state, or by modifying the homeostatic process through mutation, natural selection, and full development of existing genetic capacities to make the organism more effective in the given milieu. Homeostasis assumes the existance of a membrane-enclosed system and a genetically determined steady state maintaining processes that are not subject to change by choice of the animal. Behavioral and social systems resonate with their environment so that they are able to modify themselves and the environment or to preserve existing relations. They may be said to maximize, in general, information congruity and certainty in the milieu and to preserve the continuity of communication networks. We have labeled this process homeomaistre. Equilibrium-entrophy and homeostasis-adaptation models are inappropriate for social phenomena because social phenomena has no boundaries, can modify itself, and essentially involves information (as compared to energy) transmission. A homeomaistre-resonation model of communication networks and social change has been presented.

Conceptual convergences of a number of theories and studies of social change indicate a general sequential form of social change. We have arbitrarily designated the sequential phases as invalidation, exploration, innovation, and habituation. Changes in communication networks can be expected to follow this sequence if the change is not halted or deflected. Perception of information incongruities that indicate some of the network's information is inaccurate or ineffective invalidates that information. If the members subsequently reject the invalidated information, the process of change is initiated, which is the invalidation phase of social change. If the invalidated information is fundamental to the communication network, alienation of members and the subsequent modification of the network may follow. In such cases the autonomous, alienated, identified, and the anomic members fare variously in each of the sequential phases in terms of changes in their susceptibility to health. It is suggested that knowledge of subjective involvement and the current phase of change of the network together improve prediction and explanation of changes of disease susceptibility.

Social and geographical mobility are related to changes in disease susceptibility, and it is suggested that this could be explained in terms of the encountering of information incongruities by the mobile person.

CHAPTER VII

_____

Immunity and Relief
from Information Incongruities
through Social Participation

Communication networks can provide participants with protection from encounters with information incongruities by either preventing such contact in the first place, assisting the member in resolving encountered incongruities, or providing relief from the symptoms of incongruities when they are encountered. We have labeled as social immunity a network's information and communication patterns that prevent encounters with incongruities. We call the network's assistance in resolving encountered incongruities social cure. Relief from the discomfort accompanying the encounter of incongruities without resolving the incongruity itself is termed social therapy.

Social Immunity

If encounters with information incongruities can produce physiological changes that alter disease susceptibility, then social communications that minimize the possibility of encountering incongruities should not only enhance identification with the communication network but also reduce susceptibility to disease. Information and communication patterns for minimizing incongruity contacts vary in configuration and effectiveness in different communication networks. Those who are identified with dif-

215

ferent networks have different disease experiences as a result of variations in the effectiveness of their network's social immunity processes. By examining and comparing social immunity processes in communication networks we should be able to improve our ability to predict and explain variations in disease susceptibility between social groups. We should also be able to improve predictions of the kinds of incongruities more likely to precipitate changes in disease susceptibility of identified and alienated members, especially during times of change.

Autonomous, alienated, and anomic participants derive benefits from social immunity processes only to the degree that they conform with the network's norms or utilize its information. The anomic person benefits very little. The autonomous person may have selectively appropriated some of the information of the network without becoming dependent upon those practices that require continuity of the network. His own resources, skills, and knowledge and those of other networks in which he identifies or participates can amount to considerable protection from incongruities. However, social immunity primarily benefits the identified person. Some aspects of immunity are only effective to the degree to which one is identified and thus conforms and believes.

In physical immunity the term resistance may actually be a more accurate term than immunity because the host is not completely protected from the parasite; immunity refers instead to the relative superiority of the one over the other at the moment (Wilson and Miles, 1964). In communication networks there are some forms of protection from information incongruities that are sufficiently complete to merit being called immunity. However, even these forms are not absolute, existing as they do in a resonating milieu.

Because social immunity is primarily effective for the identified participants, or to the degree one is involved in the network, we have descriptively termed it immunity by identification. Immunity by identification refers to the degree to which the involved participants of a communication network derive protective benefits from the network's accurate and effective information, its information control practices, and the training provided them by the network. It may be partially effective for those not identified with the network who voluntarily conform. Immunity by congruity is the first subcategory of immunity by identification. It refers both to the degree to which incongruities between a particular network's information and the milieu are nonexistent and to the training of members so that the environment encountered can be handled and thus not present information incongruities. Immunity by isolation is the second subcategory of immunity by identification. It refers to the network's norms that prevent participants from coming into contact with information incongruities.

There is also immunity by direct experience, which is not a part of social immunity but which complements it. Immunity by direct experience refers to the development of a participant's understanding and capacities to handle the environment as a result of private trial-and-error experience, exploration, and perceptions of the social and natural milieu. Such experience contributes to the accurate and effective information of a person's information repertoire and thereby reduces the possibility of his encountering incongruities.

There is another form of protection from disease that social participation affords, which does not fall into our category of social immunity, nor does it pertain to information incongruities. We mention it to provide a clearer perspective of our own position. We have applied to this social protection from disease the working title "immunity by socially selected exposure to natural agents of disease." This social selection is sometimes the result of active efforts of a communication network, such as hygiene programs and dietary norms. Norms concerning hygiene of sex organs and sexual relations seem to be important in preventing cervical cancer. Coitus, especially with multiple partners, seems to be a major cause of cervical cancer (Rotkin and King, 1962; Terris and Calmann, 1960; Stocks, 1955; Terris et al., 1967; Martin, 1967), with virgins rarely having cervical cancer (Towne, 1955; Gagnon, 1950). Penile hygiene seems important, with smegma the possible key (Rotkin, 1962; Abou-Daoud, 1967; Aitkin-Swan, 1965; Smith et al., 1961). Network norms that discourage the consumption of alcohol and driving soon after decrease the probability that conformers will have fatal automobile accidents (McCarroll and Haddon, 1962).

Social selection of contact with disease agents is sometimes a latent consequence of social interaction. For example, being poor may protect one from myeloid leukemia: exposure to x-rays increases the risk of myeloid leukemia so that those who can afford better medical care may be more vulnerable to this form of disease (S. Graham, 1970). There is less risk of breast cancer if a woman is of lower socioeconomic status, presumably because of practices encouraging numerous pregnancies, the nursing of children, and early menopause resulting from hysterectomy or ovariectomy, common among such women (S. Graham, 1968). Food consumption practices that discourage irregular eating habits, consumption of alcohol, and high-starch and low-ascorbic-acid diets may decrease the risk of stomach cancer (S. Graham, 1968). Because our interest is limited to the influence of information processing on physiological processes and susceptibility to disease rather than in explaining or predicting contact with disease agents as a result of social behavior, we will not elaborate on immunity by socially selected exposure to natural agents of disease.

IMMUNITY BY IDENTIFICATION

Immunity by congruity is the most desirable form of social immunity because it eliminates the possibility of encountering information incongruities but does not prevent the person from experiencing any part of the environment. Immunity by isolation protects network participants from encountering information incongruities by limiting their contact with the environment, which leaves the person thus protected potentially vulnerable to those incongruities he is not permitted to contact. Immunity by congruity can become the property of the person as he embraces the network's information repertoire, and it may remain effective even if the network should dissolve. But immunity by isolation protects the person only so long as the information control practices of the network are effective, and protection ends when the network dissolves. Immunity by isolation is usually the latent effect of network members' efforts to maintain identification of the network's participants. However, providing congruous information and effective training can have the same positive consequences for member identification without the risk of disillusionment and illness that accompany discovering of information incongruities.

Immunity by congruity has two overlapping elements. One is the correctness of the information taught to network participants about the milieu. The second is the effectiveness of the training provided for network members to assist them in developing skills, capacities, and awareness of resources for handling the environment. The network's information can be correct, but the skills taught its members or its resources may be inadequate to handle the situation. For example, we know a lot about the nature of viruses, but we seem unable to prevent debilitating flu epidemics. We know a lot about pollution of the environment, though as yet we cannot maintain our material security without polluting.

If a member has been taught correct information about the nature of the milieu, that knowledge becomes his and is independent of any communication network from then on. Just the same, the member is likely to develop very positive feelings of involvement with a network that provides him with such knowledge. As far as encountering incongruities about those aspects of the environment is concerned, he is immune because no incongruity exists. Of course, there are large areas of the environment about which man simply does not have the correct information, not even collectively. Consequently, the scope of protection a network can offer in terms of immunity by congruity of information content is limited. One of the major functions of scientists is to increase man's collective information congruity.

Even with correct information, there are many conditions in the environment that require continued manipulation for information congruity to be obtained and for uncertainty to be reduced. Man's food supply is never completely free of such unpredictability, nor his protection from excesses of heat or cold. He must continually work to provide himself a source of warmth, food, and other consumables. His social relations are never static; consequently he must continually exercise social skills to maintain sources of human support and approval. If he is to enjoy immunity by congruity, he must be taught or encouraged to develop skills for handling these environmental conditions. In this case the information congruity is not that the person completely controls his environment but rather that he has learned or developed skills with which he can confidently and adequately satisfy his needs. Such skills must take into account the available resources and how to utilize them, and they must be flexible enough to handle emergent situations.

Subjectively, a person is rarely aware of the limits of his information or of the existance of immunity by congruity. He experiences feelings of well-being in that he understands his milieu and can operate satisfactorily within it.

The more complete one's knowledge and skills and the available resources are, the less likely one is to encounter a situation he does not expect or cannot handle or explain. This is one area we believe could be greatly improved in modern Western societies. The lack of awareness of available resources and how to use them, particularly concerning large organizations, is discouraging. The value of a liberal arts education must be reassessed and serious consideration given to instruction on how to do things such as investing; buying insurance; using the law, courts, and lawyers; utilizing health resources; knowledge of government agencies' services rendered; practicing first aid; practical knowledge of the flora and fauna of the area; awareness of how factories work and the problems of technology; the nature of various substances, including synthetics; raising children; what to expect in marriage; and so forth. The value of a knowledge of ancient history, English literature, and the like must be weighed from our frame of reference against what this will cost in terms of human health if those who learn only these things find they cannot function adequately in the world in which they live. We suspect that more complete and correct instruction on how to live in a modern society would sharply reduce the amount of illness of all kinds and prove a preventive health measure as effective as innoculation.

Just knowing what to expect can prevent or greatly reduce the experiencing of incongruities, even if nothing can be done about it. For example, some patients when struck on the right forearm with a ferule had a urticarial reaction with wheels appearing, and at the same time the capillary tone in the left arm decreased although that arm was not struck. If the ferule were swung as though to strike and stopped short of the right arm, the same decrease in capillary tone occurred in the left arm, but no reaction occurred in the right. If the patient were told of the sham blow to be struck to his right arm, there was no reaction in either arm (Wolff, 1953, citing the work of David Graham). Stern (discussion in Oken, 1967) notes that subjects respond differently to the same degree of electrical shock if they are told that they are going to be shocked or that they will experience a tingling sensation. There seems to be some evidence that subjective distress and fear are reduced if one anticipates an event with the knowledge of what to expect in contrast to anticipation without any accompanying specific information (discussion in Oken, 1967). Brady et al. (1958) note that there are psychophysiological changes associated with the feeling of control over the environment, whether such control is real or illusory.

Janis (1958) studied surgical patients from a psychoanalytic and behavioral point of view. He distinguished a continuum of anticipatory fear and grouped his patients into high, medium, and low along this continuum. He notes that surgery requires passive submission rather than action, and he suggests caution in applying his findings to other situations. He found in general that the absence of preoperative information is related to postoperative disturbances. Those having low anticipatory fear made little use of available information and did not seek it. They were convinced that they would be wholly unaffected by surgery, denying any potential danger and joking with phrases like, "There's really nothing to it." However, after experiencing the pains and disturbances of the operation, they tended to become angry, resentful, irritably grouchy, and occasionally belligerent. They were the most likely not to be cooperative in postoperative proceedings and tended to have strong negative attitudes toward the medical staff, blaming their pain and discomfort on the staff's incompetence. A large majority of these people experienced no preoperative fear because of "environmental circumstances which prevent the person from being exposed to impressive information about the impending stresses of surgery" (p. 401). For this group the actual suffering produced shocked surprise and was interpreted as the failure of those treating them rather than as an unavoidable consequence of surgery. This illustrates not only the importance of immunity by congruity but also some of the dysfunctions of immunity by isolation if it prevents contact with information that although disturbing, prepares one to handle incongruities that must be encountered. Many young people have the same shock in marriage and in college as the low anticipatory fear group did in surgery, probably for similar reasons. "Oh, you'll do just fine" is an all-too-frequent reply to questions about one's preparation for marriage, college, and work.

The moderate anticipatory fear group in Janis' study exhibited minor "part-time" worries, and they asked for and paid attention to information about surgery. They used this information to develop a set of reassuring concepts that took into account some of the realistic dangers and deprivations of the situation and the skill of the medical personnel. They seemed to go over the frightening possibilities ahead of time and to arrive at plausible fear reducing anticipations that assisted in handling the operation. Janis calls this the work of worrying, during which realistic appraisals of the situation were made and solutions imagined. This anticipation seemed to minimize postoperative negative feelings.

The high anticipatory fear group seemed to be unable to sustain an image of themselves as safe and were very agitated before the operation, weeping and requiring heavy sedation. They entered surgery with few effective self-assurances or the ability to handle the operation situation. They were likewise frightened in the recovery period and tended to seek the attention of the medical personnel, trying to be cooperative and having very positive feelings toward the medical staff but still afraid of being hurt. These people seemed to have histories of psychoneurotic predispositions (see also Jenkins and Zyzanski, 1968). Preparation for the situation is important in preventing incongruities and changes in susceptibility from being experienced (Cassel, 1970). Cassel's studies of rural folk going to work in the factory support this notion (cited in previous chapter). Lee and Schneider (1958) suggest that disharmony between the demands of the environment and a person's capabilities may be important in cardiovascular disease. They suggest executives might be trained to judge the amount of stress they can stand and to appreciate the value of outside avenues of expression. Lazarus (1967) found that a disturbing film showing subincision produced less stress reaction when the appraisal of the harmful nature of the events was reduced by the nature of the accompanying discussion.

Of course, there are limitations to the effectiveness of immunity by congruity. Experienced soldiers, although being more skilled and knowledgeable, still felt increasingly uneasy in anticipation of battle (Wolff, 1953). There are some high-risk situations in which no amount of knowledge and skill can reduce the incongruity and accompanying uncertainty to levels benign to health.

Immunity by isolation has two components: (1) the network's norms, which designate proper sources and contents of information to which participants may pay attention and (2) the withholding of information by some members from others for whom they feel it would prove incongruous. Isolation practices are discussed in Chapter V in the section dealing with the maintenance of identification. Isolation practices of a communication network contribute to maintenance of identity and to resistance to disease as long as either the network does not disintegrate or change markedly or the participants do not encounter incongruities that invalidate the network's information. However, when the member does encounter such an incongruity, the disruption of his information repertoire, behavior, and disease susceptibility may be dramatic, as with Janis' low-anticipatory group (see also the discussion of alienation in Chapter V). Thus the participants are always potentially vulnerable to information incongruities unknown to them. Goffman (1965) describes immunity by isolation in the efforts of families to protect handicapped members or those having a stigma from social ridicule through limitations on and definitions of social interaction.

As a rule, participants are not aware of the information process constituting immunity by isolation in their networks and may considerably overestimate their own competence in their milieu, attributing their happiness and success to their own perceived efforts. If they attempt social mobility, they may be sadly dismayed to discover that they are not as effective in other communication networks as they expected.

It should be noted that as the volume of correct information in a network increases, it does not necessarily follow that the network proportionately reduces those processes limiting access to information. Man places arbitrary values on things. These values can continue to be sources of incongruities, even when correct information about the nature of our world has been obtained. In our opinion, many of the most pernicious incongruities in modern societies are those between incompatible ideologies, all of which could be eliminated with little reduction of man's effectiveness in the natural world. Man has the dubious genius of being able to create infinite arrays of incongruous situations having nothing to do with the nonsocial natural environment, or even with effective social relations. Put another way, we have an overabundance of social norms and values in the world when evaluated in terms of the influence of these values on susceptibility to disease.

It is fashionable to believe that open communication on all matters in a network is desirable. In time such communication may lead to greater information congruities, but only if participants are willing to abandon some of their values and norms to produce the congruity. Sudden open communications are more likely to disrupt networks' immunity by isolation and thus to expose people to more incongruities than they can handle. Reaction to open communication can produce violent conflict, polarization, and isolation of the networks involved instead of greater information congruity. The obtaining of increasing congruity between the norms of various networks is an area in which we have a great deal to learn. Communication of some sort is essential, but whether it should be a mammoth dialogue between all the people all the time on every subject or between selected people on selected subjects often without the knowledge of other people is an unsettled question.

Social Cure

Social cure refers to the information of a communication network that is effective in subjectively resolving incongruities encountered. Where social immunity fails, social cure takes over. Social cure processes provide information, resources, redefined situations, and they may alter conditions or even change the network's information repertoire to produce subjective congruity. If social cure processes are effective, a person's encounter with an incongruity is only temporary, having a brief influence, if any, on disease susceptibility. Thus a person's encounter with an information incongruity is cured by social processes resolving the incongruity to the person's satisfaction.

Although the individual may or may not be able to articulate the content of the encountered incongruity, or to recognize the incongruity as the source of his malaise, he often sees the incongruity with sharp clarity. Subjectively, a person frequently seems to express experienced incongruities as problems. Because one does not experience a problem until he encounters an incongruity, he has no problems as long as the social immunity processes of his networks are completely effective, a rare occurrence. The individual's subjective experiencing of problems falls into two large categories concerning the information about and the skills and resources to handle (1) the natural environment and (2) the networks' norms. This distinction is made because questions about the natural environment can, at least in principle, be resolved by direct observation, but questions regarding which norms are right can only be resolved by persuasion of some sort, including force.

The person can cure himself through direct observation of the environment, trial-and-error experimentation, imitation of people conforming to norms, and the like. However, we are primarily interested in the processes and devices of the communication network for handling information incongruities.

Information incongruities pertaining to the *natural environment* can be classified as dealing with information about the properties of natural phenomena or with skills or resources needed to manipulate the phenomena.

The inadequacy of one's *information* about the natural environment includes questions such as "What is it?" "Can it hurt me?" "Why did it do that?" and "Where did it come from?" The communication network has a number of alternative devices for resolving such incongruities. First, it may provide the correct information to the member, if it has it, through people who have had experience with the phenomena in question. This information may be made available through direct personal contact or through written material. If the network does not have the information, or if recognition of the perceived incongruity as correct would invalidate crucial portions of the network's information repertoire, insulating explanations and justifications may be used (see discussion of insulation in Chapter V). Insulating explanations and justifications may not supply correct information, but they can subjectively eliminate the incongruity. The network may also change its information content to correct the information perceived by participants as incongruous, or it may seek the correct information (for example, through scientific experiments).

If the incongruity experienced is one of lack of *skills* for handling the natural environment or the anticipation that one's skills will be inadequate, the communication network may provide demonstration and training by skilled members and an opportunity to test or practice one's skills before being required to rely on them in the environment. If the requisite skills for manipulation are not available in the network, they may be sought from other networks or through network-sponsored research or through the more effective manipulation processes incorporated into the network's information repertoire.

Where correct information is introduced into the network or taught to the participant experiencing the incongruity, social cure is successful, and immunity by congruity results.

When the incongruity experienced is one of inadequate *resources* for manipulating the environment, such as materials and tools, the network's members may provide them and thereby eliminate the incongruity. If the network does not have the resources, it may engage in efforts to acquire them.

If the communication network cannot provide resolutions for a member's inadequate information, skills, or resources for understanding and manipulating the environment, the participant may experience an acute alienation producing incongruity.

When there are incongruities between several networks' information about the environment or their judgements about the more adequate skills and resources for manipulating the environment, the incongruity may be resolved by applying the differing sets of information to the environment, then by observing which is the more effective. Such differences can also be resolved by selection of another, more subjectively authoritative source to indicate the better information.

Problems or incongruities experienced concerning the network's *norms* may be classified as dealing with information about the content of the norms, how to perform them, why the norms are not followed, and disagreements between networks on proper norms.

A network participant may lack knowledge of how normative behavior is defined in that network or about particular norms, as indicated by incongruities between what he expects or desires and experiences when he tries to interact in the network (partial anomie). This lack of clarity about the norms can be resolved by the provision of the information or through socialization by a conforming network member.

If the participant's problem is in deciding what is good or right, the network members may resolve it by persuasion. What is right is established by social consensus or private decison and has nothing to do with the empirical world. In seeking an answer to problems of what is right, the person opens himself up to possible bombardment by the myriad of communication networks advocating their own value systems. He can, of course, limit himself to the values of his existing networks and simply ask for an official interpretation. Or he can cast boldly out upon the bottomless, shoreless, and usually turbulent sea of human values, sailing through one ideology after another and being tossed and buffetted in the storms where they meet and conflict.

When a member knows what the norms are but cannot perform them well enough to obtain the desired or expected results or when he anticipates that he will not perform adequately in a given situation, the network members can resolve the problem by training the member and providing opportunities for practice.

When an individual does not conform to the network's norms, his behavior is experienced as an incongruity by other members. The nonconforming participant may be required by additional norms to resolve this incongruity to the other members' satisfaction if he wishes to remain an accepted member. He can accomplish this by providing acceptable explanations and justifications of the type Scott and Lyman (1968 a) label accounts. Accounts are statements made to explain untoward behavior and to bridge the gap between one's actions and others' expectations. Which accounts one uses depends on what is acceptable to the participants of the networks in which one makes the accounting. The successful tendering of an account and its honoring restores the interaction framework. Scott and Lyman see accounts as, in part, efforts to negotiate identities (self-concepts, in this case) within the speech communities. Scott and Lyman classify accounts as excuses and justifications. Excuses include the claiming of an accident; claiming one was not completely free and that he could not do what he wanted, including the citation of fatalistic forces such as biological drives or social constraint; and in other ways scapegoating by blaming something or someone else ("The devil made me do it!"). Justifications involve the assertion of positive values in one's seemingly incongruous actions in the face of claims to the contrary by others in a community. Justifications include denial that there was any injury resulting from the action; claiming the victim deserved it; the condemnation of the condemners; and the appeal to the network's values asserting that the action was right and calling upon the loyalties of the participants to marshal support. Justifications may include the sad tale and claims that the action was necessary for self-fulfillment. If one's accounts are not honored, he is faced with a vexing incongruity. We might expect those more adept at using accounts to have fewer experiences of incongruity than those who cannot, other things being equal.

When accounts are not accepted or if the participant admits to a normative violation, particularly of a taboo, he may be required to resolve the incongruity through propitiation. Sacrifices, repentance, restitution, and imprisonment are examples.

A participant observing other participants violating the norms may not only require the actions of the violator just mentioned but may request that the network explain or justify such behavior, require propitiation, or eject the offending member from the network, lest the observing member reject the norms in question.

Individuals may experience incongruities between normative requirements within a network or between networks in which they participate. Such incongruities may be permanent conditions, or they may be temporary, occurring only in certain situations. The nature of devices open to the individual who wishes to resolve such incongruities has been illustrated by Toby (1952) in his discussion of role conflict. Toby includes the accident as one of the techniques of handling conflicting expectations between networks in which one participates. The accident prevents the member from fulfilling his obligations. Other socially approved means of handling such role conflicts include arranging various role obligations in a hierarchy so that when a conflict occurs one fulfills the obligations of the role higher in the hierarchy (for example family responsibilities, such as serious illness and death, take precedence over work responsibilities); etiquette, which prescribes proper behavior in commonly encountered incongruous situations; tact or legitimate deception; and the segregation of roles so that one fills one at one time and another at another time (for example to avoid nepotism, one plays role of parent and family man at home and of employer at work, but does not mix the two). There are means of handling the role conflicts that may not meet the approval of the networks involved such as repudiation of one group; playing off one group against the other; stalling until the pressures subside; leading a double-life (so that participants in one network do not know of his participation in another network of which they disapprove); and attempting to redefine the roles so they are compatible (Toby, 1952).

In all of these encounters of normative incongruities is the possibility of change of the network's normative information to improve congruity between the member's information, behavior, and skills and that of other networks' information, thereby producing improved immunity by congruity as a consequence of social cure. For example, normative requirements for achievement, such as the level of education or valued material acquisition, can be reduced, thereby producing congruity for larger numbers of members formerly experiencing incongruities in these areas.

Social cure processes are initiated either by the individual experiencing the incongruity seeking help from the network or by the network itself, perhaps through specialists in the network trained for that purpose. Examples of network-originated social cure include a company's transferring a worker having difficulties with his job to another he can handle; a person who cannot obtain some normatively prescribed goals being told that some other socially approved activity is just as acceptable; or the offering of official explanations of incongruities known to exist or being experienced, which subjectively eliminates the incongruity. The practice of "parentectomy," the removing of asthmatic children from parents, that has been found to lead to the recovery of formerly intractible asthmatics is another example (Robinson, 1967). The amount of effort the individual himself puts into resolving incongruities he experiences may depend in part on the acceptable explanations and justifications in that network. Studies of soldiers indicate that their willingness to actively try to make adjustments to the emotional distress accompanying the incongruities of battle depends on whether the soldiers are encouraged to believe that the causes of their incapacities and fears are a result of childhood and other experiences beyond their control or to believe that their fears and inca-pacities are common to many men and are problems that can be mas-tered (Mechanic, 1966).

Mechanic's (1962) study of the communication network of graduate students preparing for qualifying examinations provides an example of self-initiated efforts at social cure. The students were attempting to han-dle the incongruities between the information available about their pro-fessional capacities and that needed to predict the outcome of the exams. A major social cure device of the student network was an ambiguous defi-nition of the examination situation that permitted the students to utilize an alternative explanation, depending on how things seemed to be going and how they turned out. The examinations were defined as being a test of the student's intellectual capacities on the one hand and as a subjec-tive, arbitrary device for the elimination of personalities considered unde-sirable by the faculty on the other. If things seemed to be going badly, or if they did go badly, the student could explain that it was due to whimsi-cal, inaccurate, and subjective evaluations by the faculty. Those more likely to view the exams as not being objective were those who had failed in earlier attempts.

The student's efforts to establish subjective congruity between his eval-uations of his skills and knowledge and those he believed to be required for passing the examinations included recounting past experiences in which he successfully handled similar exams and making favorable com-parisons between himself and other students who had passed the exams. The students' use of social interaction reflected their search for support that indicated positive evaluation of their capacities. By selective interac-tion with other students and faculty, students were able to maximize fa-vorable information and to avoid information that would invalidate their self-evaluations, thereby resolving at least temporarily, the incongruity. Nevertheless, there was always the risk that in interaction, unfavorable information would be encountered, such as discovering another student who knew a good deal about subjects one knew nothing about. Some stu-dents minimized contact with other students in order to reduce the risk of encountering such information. There was a higher interaction fre-quency between nontenured faculty and students than between the ten-ured faculty and students. The students tended to overestimate the influ-ence that friendly, nontenured faculty could bring to bear to aid the student,

There are also a number of reassuring definitions and magiclike ritu-als, which do not provide information about the situation or one's skills or resources, nor about the normative aspects of the situation. They are incapable of producing immunity by congruity, although they could produce a sort of immunity by self-isolation from the incongruous information. Mostly, they provide only temporary and fragile social cures. For example, some Ph.D. students preparing for exams would concentrate on creating favorable pictures of the future, imagining success as though doing so would somehow magically influence the outcome. Similarly, one student vigorously avoided thinking he would pass the exams because he felt certain that if he thought he would pass he would certainly fail. The students would frequently use joking as a means of subjectively reducing the awesomeness of the exams. Interestingly, Mechanic found the "I don't give a damn" attitude was only effective in the short run, whereas the "it can't happen to me" attitude seemed more effective in handling the subjective incongruity.

There are usually a number of such self-cure routines provided by communication networks that are supposed to assist the person in his own efforts to handle incongruities. These include such things as positive thinking, prayer, some religious and magic manipulations, doing one's duty (for example, give to the poor and to the church and you will never go hungry or without shelter or clothes), astrology, and the like. All of these assist in reducing the feelings of uncertainty that accompany incongruities between what one feels he can handle and what he feels he must face. It must be remembered that incongruities, as we have defined the term, refers to subjective evaluations. Prayer can give one feelings of having access to all the power and resources necessary to handle an incongruity being experienced.

There are also a number of self-cure processes that are not part of the network's information, though perhaps they are the result of and, variously, are sanctioned by it. These primarily involve such efforts to isolate oneself from incongruous information as withdrawal, apathy, dependency, or escape into the sick role (Toby, 1952); day dreaming and irrelevant thoughts (Weiner, 1967); ignoring of information (King, 1962); and psychological processes in which one permits himself to perceive fully the information in only gradually doses he can "take" (Becker, 1942). We expect that in general communication networks do not encourage such behavior.

Social Cure Processes and the Incongruous Experience of Illness. As Selye (1956 a, p. 260) notes, "knowing what hurts you has an inherent curative value." There are a number of social cure processes in various societies for handling illnesses and related uncertainties. Among the Navajo there is a "diagnostician" who does not cure (the medicine man does that) but who primarily tells the patient what is wrong with him and what he can do about it. He also answers questions concerning stolen or lost articles. He uses materials for symbolic reasons and not for their intrinsic value (for example, corn pollen sprinkled over a Gila monster, then saved). The Navajo sees two main causes of illness, obvious causes such as broken bones and unknown influences that, due to previous taboo transgressions by the patient, have waited for a weakened condition to attack the patient (Wyman, 1966). The diagnostician resolves the information incongruity of "What is wrong with me?" and sometimes replaces it with another: "What taboo did I break?" The social cure process for relieving this latter taboo may be sought. All the while social interaction is going on and social sanctions encouraging conformity are being applied.

Respect for taboos may linger on even after the Indians have been "educated" by modern schools, missionaries, and the like. The Hopi Indians have a taboo against treading on the track of a snake. Offenders experience sore ankles and legs, even if the taboo is accidently or necessarily broken. In any case, a medicine man must be consulted. Even educated Indians who have lost faith in the medicine man can still experience sore ankles if they tread on a snake's path (Wolff, 1953). Social change often disrupts social cure processes without adequately replacing them.

Withers' (1966) account of folklore in a small town provides an interesting glimpse of the delicate intertwining of social cure processes, social solidarity, and identification. The experience of illness in the small town was a dramatic occasion. Members of the community were called on to provide help, "medical" advice, and support. Illness episodes were occasions for interaction; they reaffirmed group solidarity, provided feelings of being needed, and reinforced identification, as well as providing social cure. Although some remedies might seem useless or even dangerous, such as cutting off a black cat or chicken's tail and letting the blood drip on sores to cure shingles, or blaming of a wide variety of illnesses on constipation and then taking huge doses of laxatives (up to five times the recommended level) to maintain "regularity," they still provided relief from many of the information incongruities associated with illness (for example, "What have I got? Am I going to get better?"). By doing so they might actually be more conducive to health than materially more sophisticated but haughtily impersonal and noncommunicative modern medical ministrations. In that small town, one knew that people cared.

The small-town people in Withers' study had a number of beliefs about illness that reinforced their distinction from the more urban society around them. For example, germs were viewed as a superstition of city folks, and vitamins were considered to have living qualities and to be of great value. Like most communication networks, this particular small town had some normative information, such as the warning against washing clothes when menstruating lest the woman go insane, that could be eliminated without upsetting the network's effectiveness.

Information control was used in social control as in the practice of giving calomel to children when their elders felt that they were eating too many sweets. The children were told that if they ate something sweet after being given calomel they would be "salivated" and "their teeth will come out in a horrible manner which will leave gaping holes in their cheeks" (Withers, 1966, p. 238). For such threats to be effective the children must not be allowed to know the "truth" about "salivation." (It is, of course, possible that some adults also believe this.)

An unfortunate property of so many social cure processes is that they replace the disturbing qualities of one incongruity with yet another, often artificial one. The old-folk beliefs of "hot" versus "cold" illnesses, remedies, occupations, and people is an example. Hot illnesses required cold remedies, hot people should marry hot people and work at hot jobs. In India the loss or contamination of semen, believed to be carried in the skull and the source of manhood, meant a loss of health and strength. In Mexico, the loss of blood was considered permanent, and thus acquiring blood donations and samples is difficult. In the United States the belief in "tired blood" leads to the use of worthless medicines sold by exploiters of these myths. Voodoo and witchcraft often seem to provide more disturbing incongruities than they protect one from (King, 1962).

Christian Science is an American grown communication network that defines physical illness out of existance. To them the human body is not real and is a distortion of the true nature of man, who is coexisting with God. Illness and death are a lie and can be overcome through elevated consciousness. If one experiences illness, it is because he has not arranged his thinking properly about his true nature, or it is because of mesmeric influences such as "malicious animal magnetism" (Wilson, 1966). Here again, the social cure processes simply substitute one form of disturbing incongruity for another. What could be more frightening than to become ill and to be told that it is due to "malicious animal magnetism" or to one's own inability to think right? Better not to have any idea at all why one is ill or what to do about it, it would seem. At least one can recover and forget an illness, but can one ever get his "thoughts right?" It is desirable that social cure processes be developed to handle the incongruities the participants experience without these processes themselves providing information that could be the source of disturbing incongruities.

Social Therapy

Social therapy processes refer to information and communication patterns of a network that help reduce the symptoms of an incongruity encounter, such as self-doubt, distress, anxiety, and tension, without subjectively effecting the incongruity. A person receiving social therapy may feel better, but he still has an incongruity to deal with, and for that the social therapy processes are of no use.

Social processes that subjectively reduce or eliminate an incongruity are social cure rather than social therapy processes. Social therapy includes therapists whose role in the network is to handle the subjective malaise associated with incongruities. Often this is associated with social control, in which the incongruities may be the result of social norms, such as incapacity to "make it" in a profession or the treading on the path of snakes in the Hopi culture. The therapist's job is to maintain the person as a functioning member of the network without destroying the effectiveness of the socially produced incongruities as a means of sanctioning social loyalties and performances. In addition to therapists, there are usually therapeutic applicances or pacifiers provided by the communication network. These usually take the form of some object, ritual, or saying.

Therapeutic appliances and pacifiers often are distributed by a therapist and bear his aura. They include amulets, good luck charms, drugs, and medicines (in addition to their intrinsic physiological effects), statues, specially sanctioned items of clothing, and so on. The list is nearly endless. A typical example is the South Indian shaman who may give a man a coconut with a "mantra" written on a copper plate nailed to it to protect the man's cattle from illness (Harper, 1966). In modern societies many Mormons wear special underclothing with special markings, referred to as temple garments, which can be worn only after submitting to a special ritual. Some Mormons attribute special protective powers to these garments, such as protection from physical harm or "evil" influences. Some objects take on a socially defined meaning and do not require the therapist as an intermediary, such as copper wire used to prevent rheumatism, a butcher's knife placed under the pillow to "cut" the after pains of childbirth (King, 1962), and many other "folk" remedies that are ineffective in their manifest purpose, but which reduce feelings of uncertainty.

There are many prayers, wise sayings or proverbs, and similar language constructions that may be social cure and/or social therapy devices. The Bible is probably one of the most successful social therapy—and sometimes social cure—devices ever developed.

There is an enormous variety of communication network activities and rituals that have therapeutic value. These activities may be socially sanctioned expressive activities, such as recreation and vacations, or regular community activities providing change and excitement, such as rodeos, carnivals, holidays, and other celebrations. These seem to have a general therapeutic effect not related to any specific incongruity. Part of their value seems to be one of assisting in maintaining a sense of perspective on the seriousness of one's problems and of providing reassurance that there is ample reason to be happy in the world. Religious and other rituals may be more rigid in their enactment, but they have much the same kind of therapeutic effect. Most of these activities create subjective arousal in the participants and give them feelings of belonging to something larger than themselves (discussed under identification in Chapter V). This is by far their most-effective therapeutic influence (Parsons, 1951). There are also many specific rituals, such as the laying on of hands for annointing the sick, funerals, and similar activities, taking place under the auspices of a particular communication network to tender relief to participants during specific kinds of situations.

There are activities approved by some communication networks but practiced as a rule in private, such as believing that the secrets of health and happiness lie in a spartan life of cold showers, open windows, and vigorous breathing; or in exercises like jogging or yoga; or in consuming only organic foods; or the reliance on "meditation" or self-hypnosis. All are believed by their advocates to increase control over an uncertain environment.

Many of these social theapeutic processes have considerable intrinsic value, such as regular exercise, but others have none. In all, the therapeutic value pertains to the process' effects on one's subjective feelings of well being.

The Social Therapist. Modern societies have witnessed a proliferation and increasing specialization in social therapists. Many social roles carry implicitly or explicitly therapeutic consequences. All indications are that this is only the beginning. Psychotherapists, marriage counselors, social workers, physicians, mothers, priests, and teachers are only a few of the roles that can offer social therapy. In many cases, these role incumbents provide support and encouragement for handling incongruities encountered. Sometimes they provide information or skills useful in handling the problem as well.

There are several necessary qualities in a successful social therapist. One important qualification is that he must have status in the eyes of the person he would provide therapy for. The physician is a popular social therapist for that reason; he has considerable status. The social therapist must be able to establish a rapport with the subject, making him feel he is being listened to and understood and offering him support. Among the Javanese this is called *tjotjog* or *fittingness,* in which the success of a cure depends in part on the rapport and the compatibility of personalities of patient and healer or *dukun* (Geertz, 1966). The social therapist must appear to accept the person's problems as meaningful, no mater how trivial or silly the therapist may personally feel they are. The therapist should also not be too eager to reassure but should reflect a realistic appraisal of the difficulties of the situation. Frequently, all that a therapist can do is listen, suggest alternatives, and act as a foil for the person who works out his own problems and makes his own decisions. Any person capable of eliciting respect and trust from others and demonstrating these qualities can be a social therapist. There are hundreds of sensitive friends, neighbors, and relatives who provide social therapy.

It is not always easy to find someone who "cares," even when death is a possibility. Often when patients ask, "Am I going to die?" they are really asking, "Am I going to die alone?" (Marra, 1969). Painfully, they may discover the answer is yes. Quint (1966) studied women having mastectomy (breast removal) to arrest a cancerous growth. She found that the patients experienced considerable difficulty finding anyone to listen to them talk about matters that were of concern to them, such as the possibility of death, unexplained pains and discomfort, and the uncertainty of whether the surgeon "got it all." At home, after a week or so, the family expected the patient to return to a normal routine and were no longer interested in being comforting. The physicians seemed either untrained or unwilling to reassure their patients. They tended to avoid contact and the giving of detailed accurate information, preferring flippant replies to the patient's searching questions. Friends, especially other female friends, were not at all interested in discussing morbid subjects like cancer and death. These patients found themselves progressively isolated emotionally, forced to handle the idea of dying alone. Quint notes the need for social therapists who can permit the patient to talk without being overwhelmed themselves by the individual's problems.

Caudill (1958) suggests a concentric circle model of social therapists in terms of the order sought by an individual. First is the people closest to the person distressed, such as his family; then come friends; then representatives of organizations whom he knows personally, such as his pastor, employer, or physician; and last comes the impersonal support of agencies, such as welfare or public clinics. Of course, there may be times when the impersonal agencies might be sought first, such as when the content of the problem is such that the individual is reluctant to discuss it with people who know him and his family personally. In the community, Caudill suggests that the amount of reciprocity due the person entitles him to support during times of difficulty and reduces the likelihood that the person will seek assistance outside of the community.

The Physician as a Social Therapist. There are a number of medical, paramedical, and pseudomedical practitioners who may be utilized in social therapy, including chiropractors, naturopaths, faith healers, nurses, rehabilitation workers, and even the corner druggist. Parsons and Fox (1952) suggest that because the changes in the modern urban family have produced an isolated, quite-fragile, nuclear family, the hospital may have become a substitute source of emotional support for family members. It appears, however, that the physician is still the major social therapist in the medical milieu. The physician is by training and social definition endowed with a mantle of authority, which for some takes on an aura of superhuman capabilities (Modell, 1966).

> Upon him is conferred a quality, a force which sets him aside from the layman. . . . Regardless of all our medical advances, this quality will be the most potent force at a doctor's command in treating many of his patients through the years (Modell, 1966, p. 369).

This aura is not only of value in social therapy but also in increasing the physician's effectiveness in social cure activities wherein his definitions and assurances are believed.

When information incongruities cannot be handled other ways, the person may focus on the physiological manifestations, which as we have indicated accompanies all encounters with incongruities, and turn to the physician, ostensibly for relief from the physical discomfort experienced (Balint, 1966). The physician is highly visible, and visists to him carry no stigma. Consequently, it is not surprising that when the source of a malaise cannot be articulated by the person but remains vague he may seek the physician in the hope that it is a recognizable physical ailment that can be promptly treated. As Balint (1966, p. 282) points out, "at this initial stage we do not know which is more important, the act of complaining or the complaints that are complained of" when a patient seeks a physician. The social, therapeutic interchange between the patient and physician, after the physician has examined the patient and found nothing physically wrong, is a bargaining one in which the physician offers a series of illnesses that could fit the patient's complaints while the patient makes counter suggestions, until the patient finds one he will accept as the "cause" of his malaise. The physician knows the malaise is of social origins, but the patient usually does not. The patient may then organize his behavior around the assumption that he feels that way because he has such and such an illness, and although this may relieve him subjectively, it makes it even more difficult to get at and correct the social difficulty later. Patients suffering from such malaise may be dissatisfied if the doctor ignores or mishandles the patient's "offers" for a mutually suitable ailment, and he may be displeased if told there is nothing wrong with him (Balint, 1966). Modell (1966) refers to the social therapeutic aspects of patient-physician relations as a placebo effect of the therapeutic encounter.

Of course, the artifacts of a physician, his pills, shots, equipment, and even a little pain, all contribute to the effectiveness of the therapy. Indeed, pain seems to play a part in helping the patient define the encounter as therapy. If the physical and other ministrations were merely pleasant "they might be considered sin rather than therapy" (Modell, 1966, p. 374).

There is considerable evidence that the willingness to seek a physician's assistance and to adopt the sick role is related to the subject's experiencing incongruities and uncertainties in his social milieu (Stoeckle, Zola, Davidson, 1964; Kasl and Cobb, 1964; Mechanic and Volkart, 1960; Parsons, 1966). The willingness to seek a physician over other social therapists, to feel entitled to the sick role, and to accept certain ailments as applying to oneself are all related to one's communication networks' definitions about these matters.

Unfortunately, the physician often underestimates the patient's capacity to understand the details of what is wrong and what must be done, and the physician thus erects unnecessary barriers to communication with the patient and fails to be informative or to explain his terms (Samora, Saunders, and Larson, 1966; Pratt, Seligmann, and Reader, 1966). Of course, sometimes a physician does not give details because he is not sure of what he is doing or whether it will work. If he tells the patient of his uncertainty, his actions will definitely be less effective. At other times he honestly believes it is in the patient's own interest not to be told the details. Understandably, the physician may wish to avoid the emotional burdens of assisting patients in accepting and adjusting to what is physicially or socially ailing them (Davis, 1966). Given the considerable capacity of the physician in modern societies to provide social therapy for a wide range of things from the experiencing of an illness to the social malaise that brings otherwise healthy patients to him, he seems woefully unprepared in terms of training to handle the therapeutic role sensitively, and he receives little support from his colleagues to encourage him in this task. It seems wasteful to squander the social trust currently invested in physicians.

SOCIAL SUPPORT AS A GENERAL SOCIAL THERAPY
AND WELL-BEING FACTOR

Social support provides general social therapy for all types of incongruities one may encounter, soothing and relieving the symptoms of the person encountering the incongruity. The absence of social support seems to be an incongruity of considerable significance for most people. Social support is the subjective feeling of belonging, of being accepted, of being loved, of being needed, all for oneself and not for what one can do. Parsons' (1955) diffuse support concept catches some of the flavor of this property. Social support provides each individual with a communication network that is a safe base. Here he can be accepted whether he succeeds or fails in other networks. Here he can retreat to take stock of himself and prepare to meet "life." Here he is accepted as a "whole person," and all his various qualities, roles, desires, and the like are of interest. He is not simply a role player whose private life is of no concern to others.

The safe base can be one's family, friendships, or some organization like a church. Always the relationships must go beyond the role definitions and include concern and support for that person as a whole; it must involve feelings of closeness and intimacy or rapport.

People who do not receive this kind of support or who are unable to establish such relations because they do not know how to go about establishing or maintaining them may have to resort to instrumental accomplishments of various approved goals of communication networks for their feelings of worth, belonging, and self-esteem. Such accomplishments seem, however, to provide only temporary satisfaction, and one must continue to accomplish successfully in order to maintain one's feelings of well-being and belonging. Those receiving social support are not dependent on accomplishment for their self-esteem (see for example, Rosenberg, 1965). Thus their self evaluations remain more constant. Shibutani says:

> There appears to be increasing consensus among psychiatrists that *the development of an adequate level of self-esteem depends upon one's being the object of disinterested love.* (emphasis his)
>
> A sense of personal worth apparently develops from the spontaneous and unsolicited affection and respect of those with whom one identifies himself (1961, p. 553).

Cassel (1964) sees evidence that membership in groups providing emotional support is related to being less prone to illness. Studies on serum cholesterol, for example, show that those who are not members of such groups have serum cholesterol levels twice as high as those who are members. Much of the disturbance noticed when a loved one is lost (object loss and other notions) can be due to disruption of one's safe base and the elimination of social support without which incongruities become more debilitating. Sandler (1965) found that asthma in children was related to having a mother unable or unwilling to give warmth and emo-

tional support to her child, or who engulfed the child in a consuming relationship that reflected the mother's own needs rather than unqualified
support for the child. In either case, the child would not be accepted if
he did not please mother, and love was often used as a means of discipline, being withdrawn as a punishment. Weis and English (1957) refer
to the "cold" parent who may be a good material provider, socially and
financially successful, but who cannot give the child warmth and affection and may be overindulgent. They see these people as "carrier" parents who, not necessarily disturbed themselves, may produce emotionally
disturbed children. Absence of affection or rejection by mother seems to
be related to rheumatoid arthritis (Scotch and Geiger, 1962). Problems in
engaging in intimate emotional relations, expressing emotions to others,
and feeling one is understood may produce unusually intense startle responses (Moss, 1968). These same problems have been related to cancer
(Blumberg, 1954). The disease marasmus has been found among newborn
babies receiving no loving attention in hospitals. The infants became apathetic and did not develop normally. In hospitals where the mothers
cared for their own children, the children developed much better (Spitz,
1949).

Social support is not necessarily coterminous with identification. Such
support can accompany identification, but one can be identified without
experiencing or being able to establish this sort of social support.

In this chapter we have offered a broad conceptual framework for ap-
proaching the content of the network's information. These concepts
should serve simply as guides to one's attention. The complete cataloging
and analyzing of all the information in a cluster of networks would be an
enormously difficult problem that would never be complete because the
networks are constantly changing. For the working sociomedical researcher to attempt such a cataloging is unnecessary, though if it could
be accomplished it would certainly be a boon. For the most part the concepts we have presented are intended to be used when particular incongruities are being experienced and reported by the network's members.
We wish to determine if and to what degree the network's protective information processes have failed. Such leads may guide us to the communication networks in a cluster and to the network's information and patterns of communication that either are in the process of change or are
beginning to prove inaccurate or ineffective because of other changes. By
discovering such changes in the early stages, we may be able to predict
future changes in the network's protective capacities, in members' involvement, and in the likely direction of changes in disease susceptibility
of its participants. In addition to locating changing information areas, by
noting the persistance and frequency of encounters with particular incon-

gruities we can get some clues to the areas of a communication network's information that could be made more effective and to the nature of such improvements.

Summary

The information content and communication patterns in communication networks have influence on one's susceptibility to disease. We have provided a conceptual framework for categorizing these social information dimensions according to the ways they influence disease susceptibility. We cast our framework in a positive tone, and we call its elements social immunity, social cure, and social therapy. In it we draw attention to some information and communication processes that reduce susceptibility to disease through resolution of information incongruities and relieve the symptoms resulting from the experiencing of incongruities.

We suggest that social immunity is immunity by identification. There are two forms of immunity by identification in which identification with a particular communication network provides one with protection from contact with various information incongruities: immunity by congruity and immunity by isolation. Immunity by congruity refers to conditions in which a communication network has provided correct information about the milieu, training for the development of effective skills in handling the milieu, and adequate resources to implement these skills. Participants in such networks are immune from contacts with information incongruities because none exists. Immunity by isolation refers to social information control practices that prevent network members from coming into contact with information incongruities.

There are two communication and information manipulation processes that are utilized when social immunity fails and incongruities are encountered: social cure and social therapy. Social cure refers to the resolution of the incongruity to the participant's satisfaction. Which procedures are used depends on whether the incongruity deals with the natural environment or with manmade, arbitrary norms. Those dealing with the natural environment can be resolved by providing the correct information, skills, resources, assistance, explanations, or justifications or by sponsoring research to establish the correct information. Incongruities dealing with norms can be resolved by persuasion, instruction, socialization, explanation, justification, propitiation, or elimination of nonconformers. In either case, changes in the network's information repertoire can also be initiated to bring the information into greater congruity with the milieu.

Social therapy refers to the social practices, specialists, and objects that can be utilized to relieve the distressing symptoms accompanying the encounter with an incongruity without resolving the incongruity. Such processes are also useful when social control practices produce incongruities that the network wishes to maintain, such as a negative judgement of a person's capacities, but when the network does not desire to alienate the participant.

We have suggested that the social support of an individual as a whole person, with approval being unconditional and not dependent on performance, is a general-well-being factor having positive influence on health in general.

CHAPTER VIII

Review and Summary

SOME KEY DEFINITIONS

The following list offers a convenient review of the key concepts presented in this study. For the full meaning and discussion of these terms see their development in earlier chapters.

1. *Subjectivity.* The experience of being a functioning organism.

2. *Information.* Relations of energy which stimulate sense organs brought into contact with the environment—the sequential and relational structure of stimulating energy.

3. *Information repertoire.* The total configuration of neural representations of information in the central nervous system.

4. *Perception.* The detection of information by the central nervous system through utilization of sense and somatic organs.

5. *Information incongruity.* Information invalidating part of one's information repertoire, encountered as a mismatch between neural representation of information and current perceptions.

   a. *Information congruity.* Information validating one's information repertoire, encountered as a match between neural representations of information and current perceptions.

6. *Resonation.* The continuing reciprocal influence of interrelated variables.

   a. *Biosocial resonation.* The continuing reciprocal influences of physiological processes and social behavior in social interaction.

7. *General physiological responses.* Autonomic (sympathetic-parasympathetic) neuroendocrine reactions and associated visceral and somatic changes.

8. *Tuning.* The disruption of the sympathetic-parasympathetic balance of the autonomic nervous system, producing dominance by one of the autonomic branches.

9. *Susceptibility to disease.* The likelihood of a person or group contracting a wide array of diseases. (In this work it is used primarily in relation to changes in physiology altering one's ability to resist disease.)

10. *Communication network.* A configuration of interacting people transmitting and modifying a body of information. (This body of information includes language vocabularies—particular conceptions of the natural environment—norms and values, and preferred patterns of interaction.)

11. *Identification.* Positive, subjective involvement with a communication network, on whose information one is dependent for the capacity to understand and handle the environment, as a result of experiencing information congruity.

12. *Alienation.* Negative subjective involvement with a communication network on whose information one has been dependent resulting from rejection of some of its information as a result of perception of incongruities in the network's information.

13. *Autonomy.* Detached participation in a communication network in which the person utilizes information and norms that are his unique synthesis or derived from other networks to guide his behavior and effectively obtain what he desires.

14. *Anomie.* Subjective noninvolvement with a communication network in which one's information repertoire is inadequate to guide behavior or to explain observations.

15. *Homeomaistre.* Communication network's processes for maintaining recognizable continuity in information content, preserving effective interaction patterns while modifying portions of the network's information no longer adequate, and acquiring new information.

16. *Invalidation.* The first phase of the social-change sequence, in which incongruities are encountered that invalidate a portion of a network's information, with the subsequent rejection of the invalidated information.

17. *Exploration.* The second phase of the social-change sequence, in which new information is sought and/or examined and new communication relations tried.

18. *Innovation.* The third phase of the social-change sequence, in which selected information of the exploration period is accepted, refined, and applied, and new communication patterns established.

19. *Habituation.* The fourth and final phase of the social-change sequence, in which the new information becomes established, new communication patterns become more routinized, and the network's control over information is solidified.

20. *Social Immunity.* Communication network information and activities that prevent participants from encountering information incongruities, either by providing correct information or by isolating the participants.

21. *Social Cure.* Communication network information and activities that resolve to the participants' satisfaction encountered information incongruities.

22. *Social Therapy.* Communication network information and activities that relieve participants' symptoms accompanying encounters with information incongruities.

A GENERAL OVERVIEW

We suggest that man is a biosocial resonating being living in a social milieu of resonating communication networks exhibiting homeomaistre, that man is capable of perceiving his environment directly or with the aid of communication networks, and that man can change networks with his insights.

The central element relating man to other men and to his environment in our model is the obtaining, manipulation, application, communication, and evaluation of information. The social milieu is an interlinked cluster of communication networks transmitting various configurations of information. Communication networks resonate to the information and changes of other networks through these information transmission. The information of a communication network exists essentially in the brains of people. Social change is change of people. As long as the information of a communication network is judged by a participant to be effective in handling and accurately describing the environment, he will remain identified or become identified with the network. If sufficient numbers of the participants in the network feel this way, there will be little change in the network.

By conforming to the norms, accepting the information, and participating in the communication patterns of a communication network or a cluster of compatible networks, an individual has less opportunity and less reason to come in contact with members of networks or their information media that present incongruous information. At the same time, the complexity of modern societies and the extent to which component communication networks intertwine make it increasingly difficult to avoid contact with incompatible networks and incongruous information. Individuals can also perceive information directly from the environment, and they may discover inadequacies in the network's information without contact with other networks. The participants of the several networks develop information and communication procedures for avoiding incongruities or explaining and justifying those that cannot be avoided in order to prevent the invalidation and change of the network's information.

If the communication network's information processes cannot successfully prevent the spread of awareness and acceptance of information that invalidates some of the network's information, the network may find itself changing as the information accepted by the people who compose the network changes. Subsequently, new information is developed and eventually accepted.

A number of physiological processes are involved in information processing. Of most interest to us are the changes in the central nervous system and autonomic-neuroendocrine systems. Changes of sufficient intensity and duration in all people but especially in tuned people alter susceptibility to a wide array of disease. Such changes accompanying information processing seem to occur when the individual experiences information incongruities. What constitutes an information incongruity depends on the communication networks in which one participates and the degree to which he is involved in each.

A DIAGRAM OF SOCIAL IMMUNITY

The following figure indicates the points in information obtaining and processing at which social immunity, social cure, and social therapy are influential. The first column outlines the sequence of the process by which information incongruities produce alteration in disease susceptibility. The several lines from social therapy to different intervals in the sequence suggest that a network can have a variety of information and communication processes for relieving the symptoms associated with each particular phase but not resolving the information incongruity.

SOME SUMMARY STATEMENTS

It may be useful to restate some of the general relations of our concepts in more hypothetical form. We do not present these statements as axioms

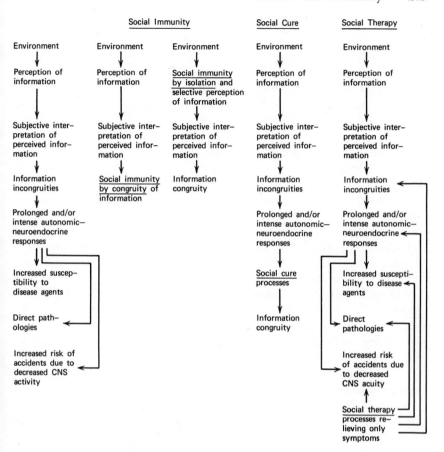

or postulates but as summary statements that can serve as references for formulating testable hypotheses.

1. Perception of information incongruities that are highly salient and/or remain unresolved can produce pronounced, repeated, and/or prolonged general physiological responses that increase susceptibility to disease.

2. Perception of information incongruities that are highly salient and/or remain unresolved can produce pronounced, repeated, and/or prolonged general physiological responses that may establish tuning. Tuned individuals' general susceptibility is greater than that of balanced individuals because general physiological responses are more easily elicited and likely to be more pronounced and prolonged for tuned individuals than for balanced individuals.

3. Perception of information incongruities is more likely to occur and remain unresolved when a communication network's social immunity and social cure are inadequate, thereby increasing the probability of pronounced, prolonged, and/or repeated general physiological responses, increasing participants' susceptibility to disease.

4. A communication network's social immunity, social cure, and social therapy are most effective for identified participants, and they enhance identification for the participants.

5. Alienation results from perception by identified participants of information incongruities that are salient or remain unresolved in a communication network's information. Social change is initiated through such alienation. A communication network's social immunity, social cure, and social therapy are less effective for alienated than identified members, and alienated people are more susceptible to disease than identified.

6. A communication network's social immunity, social cure, and social therapy are mainly ineffective for anomic associates.

7. As a communication network's social immunity, social cure, and social therapy processes improve in effectiveness, identification of members increases and susceptibility to disease decreases; also, alienation decreases, and the likelihood of social change being initiated decreases. Conversely, to the degree social immunity, social cure, and social therapy processes are ineffective and incongruities encountered remain unresolved by the communication network, alienation increases, the likelihood of social change increases, and susceptibility to disease of participants increases.

8. Social change in communication networks when it runs its course follows a sequence from invalidation to exploration to innovation to habituation. When alienation has occurred and has initiated social change, social immunity, social cure, and social therapy are less effective or become ineffective during the invalidation and exploration periods; thus participants identified with the original network experience increased susceptibility to disease during these periods. The autonomous network participants are less likely to experience fluctuations in their susceptibility to disease during these periods of network change than the identified or alienated members. Susceptibility to disease is lowest among network participants during the innovation phase of social change and next lowest during the habituation phase.

9. Social changes in communication networks with which a particular network resonates and direct perception of information incongruities by network participants may alter the effectiveness of a communication network's social immunity, social cure, and social therapy.

In applying this model to research projects the following suggestions may prove useful.

1. The various dimensions of the model are most effectively examined together in the briefest feasible time by focusing the research project on people in a common situation. Some possible study situations would include college freshmen, Ph.D. students taking exams (as Mechanic did), new prison inmates, surgical patients (as Janis did), parents of severely ill children, people recently moving to a new locality, and recently promoted people. The list of possibilities is endless. It is desirable that the situation provide a cross-section of people from different communication networks who exhibit a variety of social properties to permit comparison.

2. The study should focus on illness in general rather than a particular disease, which is done by simply keeping track of all illnesses experienced by the study's subjects during and immediately following involvement in the situation being examined, recording both incidence and prevalence. Only in this way can our suggestion that the encountering of information incongruities is a general risk factor, that increases susceptibility to a wide array of diseases afflicting a variety of organ systems be tested. If there are specific diseases associated with particular situations, they should also emerge, although we doubt that there are any. This factor also permits documentation of illness clustering among those in the situation, when compared with their own illness experience before and after the situation and when compared with control subjects not experiencing the situation. This documentation makes it much easier to differentiate specific causes of the diseases occurring from the general risk factors also present, a highly desirable enterprise if we are to ever be able to predict specific disease causes.

3. Where possible, the participant's subjective interpretations of the situation should be followed through various stages of the experience. It is desirable at least to get the subjects' expectations of the situation before, during, and after the situation. In this way the researcher can monitor whether, when, and under what circumstances subjects experience incongruities, and how incongruities thus encountered are handled.

4. If sufficient funds are available to pay for the equipment and if the situation and subjects under study make it feasible, it is highly desirable that a number of physiological measures be taken concurrent with the experiencing of the situation. Several physiological measures should be used because some do not correlate well with others, and because only in this

way can individual physiological response configurations be discovered and their implications for susceptibility to disease assessed. Such measures also permit observation of occurrences of physiological convergences between interacting participants in a situation. However, even one or two physiological measures are better than none and can be quite innocuous, for example, urine samples.

5. It is advisable always to determine social communication network participation of subjects and the nature of their involvement with each of these networks (for example, identified). At least those networks relevant to the situation being studied should be examined. Knowing communication network participation and involvement provides the key explanations for the subjective interpretations of the situation being studied. It also permits some prediction of the likelihood of the situation proving incongruous and the probable effectiveness of social immunity for given subjects.

6. The effectiveness of the social immunity processes of communication networks to which the subjects belong is brought into sharp focus in particular situations. Here various networks can be compared, and their relative success in handling the encounter of particular incongruities and increased disease susceptibility can be assessed. This comparison also provides insights into the pattern and content of a network's social immunity processes. Without assessment of a subject's social immunity, accurate explanation and prediction of subjective interpretation of information in the situation as incongruous can not be obtained.

7. If the scope of the study permits, it is desirable to determine the phases of change the subject's networks are in, especially if a major network is clearly changing. However, determining the phase of social change of a network usually requires examining the networks themselves and applying some criteria of change. This study shifts the focus of the project from the participants of the situation and can lead to time-consuming, extraneous effort. More frequently it is sufficient to appreciate the fact that aberrations in social immunity provided by a network not explained by individual variation in involvement may be explained as the result of changes in the network itself.

Although we prefer the research orientation described above that focuses on disease in general among people in a common situation, especially if all aspects of the model are to be examined simultaneously, there are other applications of portions of the model that seem promising. For example, instead of focusing on people in a common situation, a researcher might focus on a particular social communication network or cluster of networks. He might examine variations in physiological responses, disease susceptibility, and/or subjective appraisals between members of the network as they experience a variety of situations in interaction together or with members of other networks. The researcher could focus on the differences between members of a given network or cluster in terms of their differences in involvement in the network and differences in their memberships in other networks. This focus would help clarify the nature and effectiveness of a particular network's social immunity processes.

Alternative foci might include examining members of different networks in the same state of involvement, examining changing networks, and examining social immunity processes in various networks.

Portions of this model could, of course, be used without either making physiological measures or examining disease susceptibility. One could examine the relationship between subjective encounters with information incongruities, the modifications of involvement resulting (for example, alienation), and the influence of these conditions on social change in the network.

It is not appropriate to discuss here the practical details of carrying out these studies because practical considerations are different for each concrete project and for each hypothetical problem. However, we believe that our model is basically simple enough and adequately concrete to permit operationalization to a number of problems, and a variety of fruitful and interesting research problems can be derived from it, which, of course, is the purpose for its existence.

References

Abou-Daoud, Kamul. "Epidemiology of the Cervix Uteri in Lebanese Christians and Moslems," *Cancer, 20:* 1706–1714, 1967.

Abramson, J. H. "Emotional Disorder, Status Inconsistency and Migration," *Milbank Mem. Fund Qu., 44:* 23–28, 1966.

Aitken-Swan, Jean, and D. Baird. "Circumcision and Cancer of the Cervix," *Brit. J. Cancer, XIX:* 217–221, 1965.

Alexander, Franz. *Psychosomatic Medicine: Its Principles and Applications.* New York: Norton, 1950.

———. *et al. Psychosomatic Specificity, Vol. I, Experimental Study and Results.* Chicago: University of Chicago Press, 1968.

Allen, Francis R. "Influence of Technology on Communications and Transportation," in Allen, et al. (Eds.), *Technology and Social Change.* New York: Appleton-Century-Crofts, 1957.

Antonovsky, Aaron, and Rachel Kats. "The Life Crisis History as a Tool in Epidemiological Research," *J. Health Soc. Behav., 8:* 15–21, 1967.

Appley, Mortimer H., and Richard Trumbull (Eds.). *Psychological Stress.* New York: Appleton-Century-Crofts, 1967.

——— and ———. "On the concept of Psychological Stress," in Appley and Trumbull (Eds.), *Psychological Stress.* New York: Appleton-Century-Crofts, 1967 b, pp. 1–13.

Arbuckle, Dugald S. "Psychology, Medicine and the Human Condition Known as Mental Health," *Community Ment. Health J., 2:* 129, 1966.

Argyris, Chris. *Personality and Organization.* New York: Harper and Row, 1957.

———. "The Fusion of an Individual with the Organization," *Amer. Soc. Rev. 19:* 267–272, 1954.

251

Arnold, Magda B. "Stress and Emotions," in Appley and Trumbull (Eds.), *Psychological Stress*. New York: Appleton-Century-Crofts, 1967, pp. 123–150.

Bachrach, Arthur J. "Learning" in A. Freedman and Kaplan (Eds.), *Comprehensive Textbook of Psychiatry*. Baltimore: Williams and Wilkins, 1967, pp. 166–171.

Back, Kurt W., and Morton D. Bogdonoff. "Plasma Lipid Responses to Leadership, Conformity, and Deviation," in Leiderman and Shapiro (Eds.), *Psychobiological Approaches to Social Behavior*. Stanford, Calif.: Stanford University Press, 1964, pp. 24–42.

Bakan, Paul. "Thoughts on Hilgard's Paper on 'Levels of Awareness'," in R. B. MacLeod (Ed.), *William Janes: Unfinished Business*. Washington, D.C.: American Psychological Association, 1969, pp. 59–64.

Balinsky, B. I. *An Introduction to Embryology*. Philadelphia: Saunders, 1960.

Balint, Michael. "The Drug, 'Doctor'," in W. R. Scott and E. H. Volkart (Eds.), *Medical Care*. New York: Wiley, 1966, pp. 281–291.

Barnett, H. G. *Innovation: The Basis of Cultural Change*. New York: McGraw-Hill, 1953.

Basowitz, Harold, Harold Persky, Sheldon J. Korchin, and Roy R. Grinker. *Anxiety and Stress: An Interdisciplinary Study of a Life Situation*. New York: McGraw-Hill (Blakiston), 1955.

Beagley, H. A., and J. J. Knight. "The Evaluation of Suspected Non-Organic Hearing Loss," *J. of Laryngol. Otol. 82:* 693–705, 1968.

Becker, Ernest. *The Birth and Death of Meaning*. New York: Free Press, 1962.

Bennett, Edward L., Marian C. Diamond, David Krech, and Mark R. Rosenzweig. "Chemical and Anatomical Plasticity of the Brain," *Science, 146:* 610–619, 1964.

———, and M. R. Rosenzweig. "Brain Chemistry and Anatomy: Implications for Theories of Learning and Memory," in C. Rupp (Ed.), *Mind as a Tissue*. New York: Harper and Row (Hoeber Division), 1968, pp. 63–86.

Berelson, Bernard, and Gary A. Steiner. *Human Behavior: An Inventory of Scientific Findings*. New York: Harcourt, Brace, and World, 1964.

Berne, Eric. *Games People Play: The Psychology of Human Relationships*. New York: Grove Press, 1964.

Biderman, Albert D, "Life and Death in Extreme Captivity Situations," in Appley and Trumbull (Eds.), *Psychological Stress*. New York: Appleton-Century-Crofts, 1967, pp. 242–277.

Bijou, Sidney W. "Modern Meaning of Instincts," in R. B. MacLeod (Ed.), *William James: Unfinished Business*. Washington, D.C.: American Psychological Association, 1969, pp. 31–35.

Bindra, Dalbir. "Emotion and Behavior: Current Research in Historical Perspective," in P. Black (Ed.) *Physiological Correlates of Emotion*. New York: Academic Press, 1970, pp. 3–20.

Black, Perry (Ed.). *Physiological Correlates of Emotion.* New York: Academic Press, 1970.

Blackman, S., and K. M. Goldstein. "Some Aspects of a Theory of Community Mental Health," *Community Men. Health J., 4:* 85, 1968.

Blood, Robert O., Jr., and Donald M. Wolf. *Husbands and Wives: The Dynamics of Married Living.* New York: Free Press, 1960.

Blumberg, Eugene M., Philip M. West, and Frank W. Ellis. "A Possible Relationship Between Psychological Factors and Human Cancer," *Psychosom. Med. 16:* 277–286, 1954.

Bradburn, N. M., and D. Caplovitz. *Reports on Happiness.* Chicago: Aldine, 1965.

Brady, J. V., R. W. Porter, D. G. Conrad, and J. W. Mason. "Avoidance Behavior and the Development of Gastroduodenal Ulcers," *J. Exp. Anal. Behav., 1:* 69–72, 1968.

———. "Emotion and Sensitivity of Psychoendocrine Systems," in Glass (Ed.), *Neurophysiology and Emotion.* New York: Rockefeller and Russell Sage, 1967, pp. 70–95.

Bredemeier, Harry C., and Richard M. Stephenson. *The Analysis of Social Systems.* New York: Holt, Rinehart, and Winston, 1962.

Brown, George W., and J. L. T. Birley. "Crises and Life Changes and the Onset of Schizophrenia," *J. Health Soc. Behav., 9:* 203–214, 1968.

Byrne, W. L. "Molecular Approaches to Learning and Memory," *Science, 158:* 1081–1082, 1967.

Buck, Gary L., and Alvin I. Jacobson. "Social Evolution and Structural-Functional Analysis: An Empirical Test," *Amer. Soc. Rev., 33:* 343–355, 1968.

Buckley, Walter (Ed.). *Modern Systems Research for the Behavioral Scientist.* Chicago: Aldine, 1968.

———. "Society as a Complex Adaptive System," in Buckley (Ed.), *Modern Systems Research for the Behavioral Scientist.* Chicago: Aldine, 1968, pp. 490–513.

———. Lecture given at SUNY at Buffalo, November 1969.

Burke, Kenneth. *Permanence and Change.* New York: Bobbs-Merrill, 1965.

Cadwallader, Mervyn L. "The Cybernetic Analysis of Change in Complex Social Organizations," in Buckley (Ed.), *Modern Systems Research for the Behavioral Scientist.* Chicago: Aldine, 1968, pp. 437–440.

Caffrey, Bernard. "A Review of Empirical Findings," in Syme and Reeder (Eds.), *Social Stress and Cardiovascular Disease. The Milbank Memorial Fund Quarterly,* Vol. XLV, April 1967, p. 119.

———. "A Multivariate Analysis of Sociopsychological Factors in Monks with Mycardial Infractions," *J. Public Health, 60:* 452–458, 1970.

Cannon, Walter B. *The Wisdom of the Body* (revised and enlarged ed.). New York: Norton, 1939.

Caplow, Theodore. *Principles of Organization*. New York: Harcourt, Brace, and World, 1964.

Cassel, J. T. and H. A. Tyroler. "Epidemiological Studies of Cultural Change, I: Health Status and Recency of Industrialization," *Archiv. Environ. Health, 3:* 25–33, 1961.

———. "Social Science Theory as a Source of Hypotheses in Epidemiological Research," *Amer. J. Public Health, 54:* 1482–1488, 1964.

———. "Appraisal and Implications for Theoretical Development." In Syme and Reeder (Eds.), *Social Stress and Cardiovascular Disease. The Milbank Memorial Fund Quarterly*, Vol. XLV, April 1967, p. 41.

———. "Physical Illness in Response to Stress," in Levine and Scotch (Eds.), *Social Stress*. Chicago: Aldine, 1970, pp. 189–209.

Caudill, W. "Effects of Social and Cultural Systems in Reactions to Stress," *Social Sciences Research Council Pamphlet No. 14*, June 1958.

Caws, Peter. "The Structure of Discovery," *Science, 166:* 1375–1380, 1969.

Chapman, Loring F., E. Hinkle, Jr., and Harold G. Wolff. "Human Ecology, Disease, and Schizophrenia," *Amer. J. Psychiat., 117:* 193–204, 1960.

Chauchard, Paul. *The Brain*. New York: Grove Press, 1962.

Christenson, W. N., and L. E. Hinkle, Jr. "Differences in Illness and Prognostic Signs in Two Groups of Young Men," *J. Amer. Med. Assoc., 177:* 247–253, 1961.

Chun, Ki-Taeh, and Theodore R. Sarbin. "Methodological Artifacts in Subception Research," *Psychol. Rec. 18:* 137–149, 1968.

Chusid, Joseph G., and J. J. McDonald. *Correlative Neuroanatomy and Functional Neurology*. Los Altos, Calif.: Lange Medical Publications, 1962.

Clausen, John A. "The Organism and Socialization," *J. Health Soc. Behav., 8:* 243–252, December 1967.

Cleghorn, R. A. "Endocrine Order and Disorder Basic to Mind," in C. Rupp (Ed.), *Mind as a Tissue*. New York: Harper and Row (Hoeber Division), 1968, pp. 313–326.

Cluff, L., A. Canter, and J. B. Imboden. "Asian Influenza," *Arch. Intern. Med., 117:* 159–163, 1966.

Cobb, Sidney, William J. Schull, Ernest Harburg, and Stanislav V. Kasl. "The Intrafamilial Transmission of Rheumatoid Arthritis," *J. Chronic Dis. 22:* 193–296, 1969.

Cohen, Sanford I. "Central Nervous System Functioning in Altered Sensory Environments," in Appley and Trumbull (Eds.), *Psychological Stress*. New York: Appleton-Century-Crofts, 1967, pp. 77–122.

Comte, Auguste. "On the Three Stages of Social Evolution," in Parsons, et al. (Eds.), *Theories of Society, V. II*. New York: Free Press, 1961, pp. 1332–1342.

Corson, Samuel A. "Cerebrovisceral Theory: A Physiologic Basis for Psychosomatic Medicine," *Int. J. Psychiatry, 4:* 234–241, 1967.

Costell, Ronald M., and P. Herbert Leiderman. "Physiological Concomitants of Social Stress: The Effects of Conformity Pressure," *Psychosom. Med. 30:* 298–310, 1968.

Crider, Andrew. "Experimental Studies of Conflict-Produced Stress," in Levine and Scotch (Eds.), *Social Stress*. Chicago: Aldine, 1970, p. 165–188.

Croog, Sydney H. "The Family as a Source of Stress," in Levine and Scotch (Eds.), *Social Stress*. Chicago: Aldine, 1970, pp. 19–53.

Davis, Fred. "Uncertainty in Medical Prognosis, Clinical and Functional," in W. R. Scott and E. H. Volkart (Eds.), *Medical Care*. New York: Wiley, 1966, pp. 311–321.

Davis, Kingsley. "Final Note on a Case of Extreme Isolation," *Amer. J. Sociol. 52:* 432–437, 1947.

Denenberg, V. H. "Stimulation in Infancy, Emotional Reactivity, and Exploratory Behavior," in Glass (Ed.), *Neurophysiology and Emotion*. New York: Rockefeller and Russell Sage, 1967, pp. 161–189.

Deutsch, Cynthia P. "Perception," in Freedman and Kaplan (Eds.), *Comprehensive Textbook of Psychiatry*. Baltimore: Williams and Wilkins, 1967, pp. 152–158.

Deutsch, Karl W. "Toward a Cybernetic Model of Man and Society," in Buckley (Ed.), *Modern Systems Research for the Behavioral Scientist*. Chicago: Aldine, 1968, pp. 387–400.

Deutsch, Martin. "Cognition," in Freedman and Kaplan (Eds.), *Comprehensive Textbook of Psychiatry*. Baltimore: Williams and Wilkins, 1967, pp. 158–166.

———, and R. M. Krauss. *Theories in Social Psychology*. New York: Basic Books, 1965.

Dohrenwend, Barbara S., and Bruce P. Dohrenwend. "Class and Race as Status-Related Sources of Stress," in Levine and Scotch (Eds.), *Social Stress*. Chicago: Aldine, 1970, pp. 111–140.

Dohrenwend, Bruce P. "The Social Psychological Nature of Stress: A Framework for Causal Inquiry," *J. Abnor. Soc. Psychol., 62:* 294–302, 1961.

———. "Toward the Development of Theoretical Models: I," in Syme and Reeder (Eds.), *Social Stress and Cardiovascular Disease. The Milbank Memorial Fund Quarterly*, Vol. XLV, April 1966.

Dubin, Robert. *Theory Building: A Practical Guide to the Construction and Testing of Theoretical Models*. New York: Free Press, 1969.

Dunbar, Flanders. *Emotions and Bodily Changes*, 3rd ed. New York: Columbia University Press, 1946.

——— (Ed.). *Synopsis of Psychosomatic Diagnosis and Treatment*. St. Louis: Mosbey, 1948.

Durkheim, Emile. *Suicide: A Study in Sociology*. Trans. J. A. Spaulding and G. Simpson. Glencoe, Illinois: Free Press, 1951.

Durkheim, Emile. *Sociology and Philosophy*. Trans. D. F. Pocock. Glencoe, Illinois: Free Press, 1953. Also in Coser and Rosenberg (Eds.). *Sociological Theory: A Book of Readings,* 3rd ed. New York: Macmillan, 1969, p. 105.

Easterbrook, W. T. "The Entrepreneurial Function in Relation to Technological and Economic Change," in Hoselitz and Moore (Eds.), *Industrialization and Society*. Unesco-Mouton, 1968.

Eccles, John C. (Ed.). *Brain and Conscious Experience*. New York: Springer-Verlag, 1966.

———. "Conscious Experience and Memory," in Eccles (Ed.), *Brain and Conscious Experience*. New York: Springer-Verlag, 1966, pp. 314–344.

Eisenstadt, S. N. *From Generation to Generation*. New York: Free Press, 1956.

———. "Transformation of Social, Political, and Cultural Orders in Modernization." *Amer. Soc. Rev., 30:* 659–673, 1965.

———. *Comparative Perspectives on Social Change*. Boston: Little, Brown, 1968 a.

———. "Problems of Emerging Bureaucracies in Developing Areas and New States," in Hoselitz and Moore (Eds.), *Industrialization and Society*. Unesco-Mouton, 1968 b, p. 159.

Engel, George L. "Is Grief a Disease?", *Psychosom. Med., 23:* 18–22, 1961.

———. *Psychological Development in Health and Disease*. Philadelphia: W. B. Saunders, 1962.

———. "A Life Setting Conducive to Illness: The Giving-Up–Given-Up Complex," *Ann. Intern. Med., 69:* 293–300, 1968.

Erickson, Erick H. "Identity and the Life Cycle," *Psycho. Issues, Vol. 1,* Monograph 1, 1959, International University Press.

———. "The Problem of Ego Identity," in Stein et al. (Eds.), *Identity and Anxiety*. New York: Free Press, 1960, pp. 37–87.

Etzioni, Amitai. *A Comparative Analysis of Complex Organizations*. New York: Free Press, 1961.

———. *Modern Organizations*. Englewood Cliffs, N.J.: Prentice-Hall, 1964.

———. *The Active Society*. New York: Free Press, 1968 a.

———. "Basic Human Needs, Alienation and Inauthenticity," *Amer. Soc. Rev., 33:* 870–885, 1968 b.

Festinger, Leon. *A Theory of Cognitive Dissonance*. Stanford, Calif.: Stanford University Press, 1957.

———. "The Theory of Cognitive Dissonance," in Schuamm (Ed.), *The Science of Human Communication*. New York: Basic Books, 1963, pp. 17–27.

Flynn, John P. "The Neural Basis of Aggression in Cats," in Glass (Ed.), *Neurophysiology and Emotion*. New York: Rockefeller and Russell Sage, 1967, pp. 40–59.

Foote, Nelson N. "Identification as the Basis for a Theory of Motivation," in J. Manis and B. Meltzer (Eds.), *Symbolic Interaction: A Reader in Social Psychology*. Boston: Allyn and Bacon, 1967, pp. 343–354.

Fredericks, Marcel A., and Paul Mundy. "The Relationship Between Social Class, Stress-Anxiety Responses, Academic Achievement, and Internalization of Professional Attitudes of Students in a Medical School," *J. Med. Educ., 42:* 1023–1030, 1967.

Freedman, Alfred M., and Harold I. Kaplan (Eds.). *Comprehensive Textbook of Psychiatry*. Baltimore: Williams and Wilkins, 1967.

French, J. D. "Neurophysiological Mechanisms Underlying Behavior," in C. Rupp (Ed.), *Mind as a Tissue*. New York: Harper and Row (Hoeber Division), 1968, pp. 55–60.

French, John R. P., Jr. "The Social Environment and Mental Health," *J. Soc. Issues, 19:* 39–56, 1963.

Friedman, Meyer, and Ray H. Rosenman. "Association of Specific Overt Behavior Pattern with Blood and Cardiovascular Findings," *J. Amer. Med. Assoc., 169:* 1286–1296, 1959.

———, R. H. Rosenman, and S. O. Byers. "Serum Lipids and Conjunctival Circulation after Fat Ingestion in Men Exhibiting Type-A Behavior Pattern," *Circulation, 29:* 874, 1964.

Fromm, Erich. *Escape From Freedom*. New York: Holt, Rinehart, and Winston, 1941.

Gagnon, F. "Contribution to the Study of Etiology and Prevention of Cancer of the Cervix of the Uterus," *Amer. J. Obstet. Gynec., 60:* 516–522, 1950.

Galbraith, John K. *The New Industrial State*. Boston: Houghton Mifflin, 1967.

Galdston, Iago (Ed.). "Social Medicine: Its Derivations and Objectives," *The New York Academy of Medicine Institute on Social Medicine, 1947*. New York: The Commonwealth Fund, 1949.

Geertz, Clifford. "Curing, Sorcery, and Magic," in W. R. Scott and E. H. Volkart (Eds.), *Medical Care*. New York: Wiley, 1966, pp. 17–37.

Gellhorn, Ernst, and G. N. Loofbourrow. *Emotions and Emotional Disorders*. New York: Harper and Row, 1963.

———. *Principles of Autonomic-Somatic Integrations*. Minneapolis: University of Minnesota Press, 1967.

———. *Biological Foundations of Emotion*. Glenview, Ill.: Scott, Foresman, 1968.

———. "Attempt at a Synthesis: Contribution to a Theory of Emotion," in Gellhorn (Ed.), *Biological Foundations of Emotion*. Glenview, Ill.: Scott, Foresman, 1968, pp. 144–153.

George, F. H. "Models and Theories in Social Psychology," in L. Gross (Ed.), *Symposium on Sociological Theory*. New York: Harper and Row, 1959, p. 311.

Gerard, Harold B. "Physiological Measurement in Social Psychological Research," in Leiderman and Shapiro (Eds.), *Psychobiological Approaches to Social Behavior*. Stanford, Calif.: Stanford University Press, 1964, pp. 43–58.

Geschwind, Norman, and Ira Sherwin. "Language-Induced Epilepsy," *Arch. Neurol., 16:* 25, 1967.

Gibbs, Jack P., and Walter T. Martin. *Status Integration and Suicide.* Eugene, Ore.: University of Oregon Press, 1964.

Gibson, James J. *The Senses Considered as Perceptual Systems.* Boston: Houghton Mifflin, 1966.

Gibson, Eleanor J. *Principles of Perceptual Learning and Development.* New York: Appleton-Century-Crofts, 1969.

Glaser, Barney G., and Anselm L. Strauss. *The Discovery of Grounded Theory: Strategies for Qualitative Research.* Chicago: Aldine, 1967.

Glass, David C. (Ed.). *Neurophysiology and Emotion.* New York: Rockefeller Press and Russell Sage, 1967.

Goffman, Erving. *The Presentation of Self in Everyday Life.* Garden City, N.Y.: Doubleday, 1959.

————. *Encounters.* Indianapolis, Ind.: Bobbs-Merrill, 1961.

————. *Behavior in Public Places.* New York: Free Press, 1963.

————. *Stigma.* Englewood Cliffs N.J.: Prentice-Hall, 1965.

Goode, William J. "A Theory of Role Strain," *Amer. Soc. Rev., 25:* 483–496.

Gouldner, Alvin W. "Reciprocity and Autonomy in Functional Theory," in Demerath and Peterson (Eds.), *System, Change, and Conflict: A Reader on Contemporary Sociological Theory and the Debate over Functionalism.* New York: Free Press, 1967.

Graham, David T., et al. "Physiological Response to the Suggestion of Attitudes Specific for Hives and Hypertension," *Psychosom. Med., 24:* 159–169, 1962.

———— and Ian Stevenson. "Disease as Response to Life Stress," in Lief et al. (Eds.), *The Psychological Basis of Medical Practice.* New York: Harper, 1963.

————. "Health, Disease, and the Mind-Body Problem: Linguistic Parallelism," *Psychosom. Med., 29:* 52–65, 1967.

Graham, Saxon. "New Clues to the Causes of Cancer," *Transaction,* January–February, 1968, pp. 43–48.

———— et al. "Religion and Ethnicity in Leukemia," *Amer. J. Pub. Health, 60:* 266–274, 1970 a.

————. "Behavioral Factors Associated with the Etiology of Physical Diseases." Paper presented at the American Public Health Association Meetings, October 29, 1970 b.

Grastyan, Endre. "Comments," in Gellhorn (Ed.), *Biological Foundations of Emotion.* Glenview, Illinois: Scott, Foresman, 1968, pp. 114–127.

Gray, Henry. *Anatomy of the Human Body.* 27th ed. C. M. Goss (Ed.). Philadelphia: Lea and Feibiger, 1959.

Gray, S. J., et al. "Adrenal Influences upon the Stomach and the Gastric Response to Stress," in Selye and Heuser (Eds.), *Fifth Annual Reports on Stress, 1955–56.* New York: MD, 1956, pp. 138–160.

Green, J. E., and F. Dunn. "Correlation of Naturally Occurring Infrasonics and Selected Human Behavior," *J. Acous. Soc. Amer., 44:* 1456–1457, 1968.

Grinker, Roy R., and John P. Spiegel. *Men Under Stress.* Philadelphia: Blakiston, 1945.

Gross, Edward. "Work, Organization, and Stress," in Levine and Scotch (Eds.), *Social Stress.* Chicago: Aldine, 1970, pp. 54–110.

Gross, Llewellyn. "Society, Maternal Behavior and Gastrointestinal Disorders," *Psychiat. Q. Suppl. 29:* 23–37, 1955.

———— (Ed.). *Symposium on Sociological Theory.* New York: Harper and Row, 1959 a.

————. "Theory Construction in Sociology: A Methodological Inquiry," in L. Gross (Ed.), *Symposium on Sociological Theory.* New York: Harper and Row, 1959 b.

————. "System-Construction in Sociology," *Behav. Sci., 5:* 281–290, 1960 a.

————. "An Epistemological View of Sociological Theory," *Amer. J. Soc.,* March 1960 b, p. 445.

————. *Sociological Theory: Inquiries and Paradigms.* New York: Harper and Row, 1967.

————. "Intellectual Journey," *Amer. Behav. Sci., 12:* 19–25, 1968.

Gunther, Max. *Writing the Modern Magazine Article.* Boston: The Writer, 1968.

Gurin, G., J. Verhoff, and S. Feld. *Americans View Their Mental Health.* New York: Basic Books, 1960.

Guyton, Arthur C. *Textbook of Medical Physiology,* 2nd ed. Philadelphia: W. B. Saunders, 1961.

Hagen, Everett, E. *On the Theory of Social Change.* Homewood, Illinois: Dorsey, 1962.

Halpern, B., C. Druidi-Aaracco, D. Bessirard, and F. Martineau. "Brain Monomamines and Thyroid Hormones on the Emotional Stress Induced by Sympathomimetic Agents in Aggregated Animals," in Jamin (Ed.), *Endocrine Aspects of Disease Processes.* St. Louis: Green, 1968, pp. 47–73.

Hansen, Donald A. "Personal and Positional Influence in Formal Groups: Propositions and Theory for Research on Family Vulnerability to Stress," *Soc. Forces, 44:* 202–210, 1965–1966.

Harlow, Harry F. "William James and Instinct Theory," in R. B. MacLeod (Ed.), *William James: Unfinished Business.* Washington, D.C.: American Psychological Association, 1969, pp. 21–30.

Harper, Edward B. "Shamanism in South India," in W. R. Scott and E. H. Volkart (Eds.), *Medical Care.* New York: Wiley, 1966, pp. 344–353.

Hart, Hornell. "The Hypothesis of Cultural Lag: A Present-Day View," in Francis H. Allen, et al. (Eds.), *Technology and Social Change.* New York: Appleton-Century-Crofts, 1957, p. 417.

Hart, Hornell. "Social Theory and Social Change," in Gross (Ed.), *Symposium on Sociological Theory*. New York: Harper and Row, 1959, p. 196.

Hebb, D. O., and W. R. Thompson. "The Social Significance of Animal Studies," in G. Lindzey and E. Aronson (Eds.), *The Handbook of Social Psychology*, 2nd ed., Vol. 2. Reading, Mass.: Addison-Wesley, 1968.

Heinz, H. C., E. J. Dennis, and H. Pratt-Thomas. "The Possible Role of Smegma in Carcinoma of the Cervix," *Amer. J. Obstet. Gynec., 76:* 726–735.

Herzberg, F., and R. M. Hamlin. "A Motivation-Hygiene Concept of Mental Health," *Ment. Hygiene, 45:* 394–401, 1961.

Hilgard, Ernest R. "Levels of Awareness: Second Thoughts on Some of William James' Ideas," in R. B. MacLeod (Ed.), *William James: Unfinished Business*. Washington, D.C.: American Psychological Association, 1969.

Hinkle, Lawrence E., Jr., and Harold G. Wolff. "Ecological Investigations of the Relationship Between Illness, Life Experiences and the Social Environment," *Ann. Inter. Med., 49:* 1373–1888, 1958 a.

———— et al. "An Investigation of the Relation Between Life Experience, Personality Characteristics, and General Susceptibility to Illness," *Psychosom. Med., 20:* 278–295, 1958 b.

———— et al. "II. An Examination of the Relations Between Symptoms, Disability and Serious Illness, In Two Homogeneous Groups of Men and Women," *Amer. J. Public Health, 50:* 1327–1336, 1960.

————. "Ecological Observations of the Relations of Physical Illness, Mental Illness, and the Social Environment," *Psychosom. Med., 23:* 289–296, 1961.

————. "Relating Biochemical, Physiological, and Psychological Disorders to the Social Environment," *Arch. Environ. Health, 16:* 77–82, 1968.

Hobsbawm, E. J. *The Age of Revolution: 1789–1884*. New York: Mentor, 1962.

Hofstadter, Richard. *Anti-Intellectualism in American Life*. New York: Knopf, 1963.

Holmes, T. H. "Multidiscipline Studies of Tuberculosis," in P. J. Sparer (Ed.), *Personality, Stress, and Tuberculosis*. New York: International Universities Press, 1956, pp. 65–152.

Homans, George C. *Social Behavior: Its Elementary Form*. New York: Harcourt, Brace and World, 1961.

Hook, Sidney. *Marx and the Marxists*. Princeton: Van Nostrand, 1955.

Horwitz, Murray, David Glass, and Agnes M. Niyekawa. "Muscular Tension: Physiological Activation or Psychological Act?," in Leiderman and Shapiro (Eds.), *Psychobiological Approaches to Social Behavior*. Stanford, Calif.: Stanford University Press, 1964, pp. 59–91.

Hoselitz, Bert F. "Main Concepts in the Analysis of the Social Implications of Technical Change," in Hoselitz and Moore (Eds.), *Industrialization and Society*. Paris: Unesco, 1963.

Howard, Alan, and Robert A. Scott. "A Proposed Framework for the Analysis of Stress in the Human Organism," *Behav. Sci., 10:* 141–161, 1965.

Hughes, H. Stuart. *Consciousness and Society*. New York: Vintage, 1961.

Imboden, John B., Arthur Canter, and Leighton Cluff, "Separation Experiences and Health Records in a Group of Normal Adults," *Psychosom. Med.*, *25:* 433–440, 1963.

Jackson, Elton F. "Status Consistency and Symptoms of Stress," *Amer. Soc. Review*, *27:* 469–480, 1962.

Jahoda, Marie. *Current Concepts of Positive Mental Health*. New York: Basic Books, 1958.

Janis, Irving L. "Problems of Theory in the Analysis of Stress Behavior," *J. Soc. Issues*, *10* (#3): 12–25, 1954.

———. *Psychological Stress*. New York: Wiley, 1958.

———. "A Behavioral Study of Psychological Stress Among Surgical Patients," in W. R. Scott and E. H. Volkart (Eds.), *Medical Care*. New York: Wiley, 1966, pp. 321–335.

Jasmin, Gaetan (Ed.). *Endocrine Aspects of Disease Processes*. St. Louis: Green, 1968.

Jenkins, C. David. "Appraisal and Implications for Theoretical Development," in Syme and Reeder (Eds.), *Social Stress and Cardiovascular Disease, The Milbank Memorial Fund Quarterly*, Vol. XLV, April 1967.

———, and Stephen J. Zyzanski. "Dimensions of Belief and Feeling Concerning Three Diseases: Poliomyelitis, Cancer, and Mental Illness: A Factor Analytic Study," *Behav. Sci.*, *13:* 372–381, 1968.

———. "Psychologic and Social Precursors or Coronary Disease," *N. Engl. J. Med.*, *284:* 244–255, 307–317 February 4, 1971; February 11, 1971.

John, E. Roy. "Neurophysiological Correlates of Learning and Memory," in Freedman and Kaplan (Eds.), *Comprehensive Textbook of Psychiatry*. Baltimore: Williams and Wilkins, 1967, pp. 149–151.

Kahn, R. L., E. M. Wolfe, R. P. Quinn, and J. D. Snoek. *Organizational Stress: Studies in Role Conflict and Ambiguity*. New York: Wiley, 1964.

Kaplan, Howard B., Neil R. Burch, and Samuel W. Bloom. "Physiological Covariation and Sociometric Relationships in Small Peer Groups," in Leiderman and Shapiro (Eds.), *Psychobiological Approaches to Social Behavior*. Stanford, Calif.: Stanford University Press, 1964, pp. 92–109.

Kaplan, H. S., and H. I. Kaplan. "Current Concepts of Psychosomatic Medicine," in Freedman and Kaplan (Eds.), *Comprehensive Textbook of Psychiatry*. Baltimore: Williams and Wilkins, 1967, p. 1039.

Kasl, Stanislav V., and Sidney Cobb. "Some Psychological Factors Associated with Illness Behavior and Selected Illnesses," *J. Chronic Dis.*, *17:* 325–345, 1964.

Kety, Seymour S. "Psychoendocrine Systems and Emotion: Biological Aspects," in Glass (Ed.), *Neurophysiology and Emotion*. New York: Rockefeller and Russell Sage, 1967, pp. 103–107.

King, Stanley, and Sidney Cobb. "Psychosocial Factors in the Epidemiology of Rheumatoid Arthritis, *J. Chronic Dis.*, *7:* 466–475, 1958.

King, Stanley, and Sidney Cobb. *Perceptions of Illness and Medical Practice.* New York: Russell Sage Foundation, 1962.

Klein, George S., Donald P. Spence, Robert R. Holt, and Susannah Gourevitch. "Cognition Without Awareness: Subliminal Influences Upon Conscious Thought," *J. Abnor. Soc. Psychol., 57:* 255–256, 1958.

Kleiner, R. J., and S. Parker. "Goal-Striving, Social Studies, and Mental Disorder: A Research Review," *Amer. Soc. Review, 28:* 189–203, 1963.

————. "Goal-Strivings and Psychosomatic Symptoms in Migrant and Non-Migrant Population," in Kantor (Ed.), *Mobility and Mental Health.* Springfield, Ill.: Charles C Thomas, 1965, pp. 78–85.

Kornhauser, Arthur. *Mental Health of the Industrial Worker: A Detroit Study.* New York: Wiley, 1965.

Kopa, J., I. Szabo, and E. Grastyan. "A Dual Behavioral Effect From Stimulating the Same Thalamic Point with Identical Stimulus Parameters in Different Conditional Reflex Situations," in Gellhorn (Ed.), *Biological Foundations of Emotions.* Glenview, Ill.: Scott, Foresman, 1968, pp. 107–114.

Krech, David. "Brain Chemistry and Anatomy: Implications for Behavior Therapy," in C. Rupp (Ed.), *Mind as a Tissue.* New York: Harper and Row (Hoeber Division), 1968, pp. 39–54.

————. "Does Behavior Really Need a Brain? In Praise of William James: Some Historical Musings, Vain Lamentations, and a Sounding of Great Expectations," in R. B. MacLeod (Ed.), *William James: Unfinished Business.* Washington, D.C.: American Psychological Association, 1969, pp. 1–11.

Kroeber, A. L. *Configurations of Culture Growth.* Berkeley: University of California Press, 1944.

Kuhn, Manford H., and T. S. McPartland. "An Empirical Investigation of Self-Attitudes," *Amer. Soc. Rev., 19:* 68–76, 1953.

————. "The Reference Group Reconsidered," in Manis and Meltzer (Eds.), *Symbolic Interaction: A Reader in Social Psychology.* Boston: Allyn and Bacon, 1967, pp. 171–184.

Lacey, John I. "Somatic Response Patterning and Stress: Some Revisions of Activation Theory," in Appley and Trumbull (Eds.), *Psychological Stress.* New York: Appleton-Century-Crofts, 1967, pp. 14–42.

Lang, Kurt, and Gladys E. Lang. *Collective Dynamics.* New York: Crowell, 1961.

Lazarus, Richard S. *Psychological Stress and the Coping Process.* New York: McGraw-Hill, 1966.

————. "Cognitive and Personality Factors Underlying Threat and Coping," in Appley and Trumbull (Eds.), *Psychological Stress.* New York: Appleton-Century-Crofts, 1967, pp. 151–181.

Lebedev, B. A. "Corticovisceral Psychosomatics," *Int. J. Psychiat., 4:* 241–246, 1967.

Lee, Richard E., and Ralph F. Schneider. "Hypertension and Arteriosclerosis in

Executive and Nonexecutive Personnel," *J. Amer. Med. Assoc., 167:* 1447–1450, July 19, 1958.

Lehr, Eugene L. "Carbon Monoxide Poisoning: A Preventable Environmental Harzard," *Amer. J. Public Health, 60:* 289–293, 1970.

Leiderman, P. H., and David Shapiro (Eds.). *Psychobiological Approaches to Social Behavior.* Stanford, Calif.: Stanford University Press, 1964.

Leighton, D. C., et al. *The Character of Danger* (vol. 3). New York; Basic Books, 1963.

Lennard, Henry L. "A Proposed Program of Research in Sociopharmacology," in Leiderman and Shapiro (Eds.), *Psychobiological Approaches to Social Behavior.* Stanford, Calif.: Stanford University Press, 1964, pp. 127–137.

Lerner, Daniel. "Toward a Communication Theory of Modernization: A Set of Considerations," in Eisenstadt (Ed.), *Comparative Perspectives on Social Change.* Boston: Little, Brown, 1968, p. 133.

Le Shan, Lawrence. "An Emotional Life-History Pattern Associated with Neo-Plastic Disease," *Ann. N.Y. Acad. Sci. 125:* 780–793, January 1966.

Levinson, H. "What Is Mental Health," *Think,* March–April 1965, p. 28.

Levine, Sol, and Norman A. Scotch. "Toward the Development of Theoretical Models: II" in Syme and Reeder (Eds.), *Social Stress and Cardiovascular Disease. Milbank Memorial Fund Quarterly,* Vol. XLV, April 1967, pp. 163–174.

————— and —————. *Social Stress.* Chicago, Illinois: Aldine, 1970 a.

————— and —————. "Social Stress," in Levine and Scotch (Eds.), *Social Stress.* Chicago, Illinois: Aldine, 1970 b, pp. 1–18,

————— and —————. "Perspectives in Stress Research," in Levine and Scotch (Eds.), *Social Stress.* Chicago: Aldine, 1970 c, pp. 279–290.

Libet, B. "Brain Stimulation and the Threshold of Conscious Experience," in J. C. Eccles (Ed.), *Brain and Conscious Experience.* New York: Springer-Verlag, 1966.

Lichtheim, George. *The Concept of Ideology and Other Essays.* New York: Vintage, 1967.

Lieban, Richard W. "Sorcery, Illness, and Social Control in a Philippine Municipality," in W. R. Scott and E. H. Volkart (Eds.), *Medical Care.* New York: Wiley, 1966, pp. 222–232.

Lilienfield, Abraham N. "Epidemiological Methods and Inferences in Studies of Noninfectious Diseases," *Public Health Rep.* (Review) *72:* 51–60, January 1957.

Lindesmith, A., and A. L. Strauss. *Social Psychology.* New York: Holt, Rinehart, and Winston, 1968.

Locy, William A. *Biology and Its Makers,* 3rd ed. New York: Holt, Rinehart, and Winston, 1935.

McCall, George, J., and J. L. Simmons. *Identities and Interactions.* New York: Free Press, 1966.

McCarroll, James R., and William Haddon, Jr. "A Controlled Study of Fatal Automobile Accidents in New York City," *J. Chronic Dis., 15:* 811–826, 1962.

MacIver, R. M., and C. H. Page. "Technology and Social Change," in Hunt and Darlin (Eds.), *Society Today and Tomorrow,* 2nd ed. New York: MacMillan, 1967, p. 111.

Mackler, Bernard, and E. Bernstein. "Contribution to the History of Psychology: II. Phillipe Pinel: The Man and His Time," *Psychol. Rep., 19:* 703–720, 1966.

MacLeod, Robert B. (Ed.). *William James: Unfinished Business.* Washington, D.C.: American Psychological Association, 1969.

McPartland, T. S., and J. H. Cummings. "Self-Conception, Social Class, and Mental Health," *Hum. Organ. 17:* 24–29, Fall 1958.

Malmo, Robert B. "Physiological Concomitants of Emotion," in A. Freedman, and H. Kaplan (Eds.), *Comprehensive Textbook of Psychiatry.* Baltimore: Williams and Wilkins, 1967, pp. 1044–1048.

Mandler, George. "The Conditions for Emotional Behavior," in Glass (Ed.), *Neurophysiology and Emotion,* New York: Rockefeller and Russell Sage, 1967, pp. 96–102.

———. "Acceptance of Things Past and Present: A Look at the Mind and the Brain," in R. B. MacLeod (Ed.), *William James: Unfinished Business.* Washington, D.C.: American Psychological Association, 1969, pp. 13–16.

Manis, Jerome G., and Bernard N. Meltzer (Eds.). *Symbolic Interaction: A Reader in Social Psychology.* Boston: Allyn and Bacon, 1967.

Marks, Renee U. "A Review of Empirical Findings," in Syme and Reeder (Eds.), *Social Stress and Cardiovascular Disease. Milbank Memorial Fund Quarterly,* Vol. XLV, April, 1967, p. 51.

Marra, Edward, M.D., Chairman, Department of Preventive Medicine, University of Buffalo School of Medicine, private communicate, January 15, 1969.

Martin, Clyde E. "Marital and Coital Factors in Cervical Cancer," *Amer. J. Public Health, 57:* 803–814, 1967.

Marx, Karl, and F. Engles. "On Alienation," in Mills (Ed.), *Images of Man.* New York: Braziller, 1960, p. 486.

Maslow, A. H. *Motivation and Personality.* New York: Harper, 1954.

———. *Toward a Psychology of Being,* 2nd ed. Princeton, N.J.: D. Van Nostrand, 1968.

Mason, John W., and Joseph V. Brady. "The Sensitivity of Psychoendocrine Systems to Social and Physical Environment," in Leiderman and Shapiro (Eds.), *Psychobiological Approaches to Social Behavior.* Stanford, Calif.: Stanford University Press, 1964, pp. 4–23.

May, Rollo. "William James' Humanism and the Problem of Will," in R. B.

MacLeod (Ed.), *William James: Unfinished Business*. Washington, D.C.: American Psychological Association, 1969, pp. 73–91.

Mead, Margaret. "Culture, Change and Character Structure," in Stein et al. (Eds.), *Identity and Anxiety*. New York: Free Press, 1960, pp. 88–98.

Mechanic, David, and Edmund H. Volkart. "Illness Behavior and Medical Diagnoses," *J. Health Hum. Behav. 1:* 86–94, 1960.

———. *Students Under Stress*. New York: Free Press, 1962.

———. "The Influence of Mothers on Their Children's Health Attitudes and Behavior," *Pediatrics, 33:* 444–453, 1964.

———. "Perception of Parental Responses to Illness: A Research Note," *J. Health Hum. Behav., 6:* 253–257, 1965.

———, and Margaret Newton. "Some Problems in the Analysis of Morbidity Data," *J. Chronic Dis. 18:* 569–580, 1965.

———. "Response Factors in Illness: The Study of Illness Behavior," *Soc. Psychiat., 1:*11–20, 1966.

———. *Medical Sociology*. New York: Free Press, 1968.

Meier, E. G. "An Inquiry into the Concepts of Ego Identity and Identity Diffusion," *Soc. Casework, 45:* 63–70, 1964.

Meltzer, Bernard M. "Mead's Social Psychology," in Manis and Meltzer (Eds.), *Symbolic Interaction: A Reader in Social Psychology*. Boston: Allyn and Bacon, 1967, pp. 5–24.

Melzack, Ronald. "Brain Mechanisms and Emotion," in Glass (Ed.), *Neurophysiology and Emotion*. New York: Rockefeller and Russell Sage, 1967, pp. 60–69.

Merton, Robert K. *Social Theory and Social Structure,* (rev. ed.). New York: Free Press, 1957.

Michaux, William W., K. H. Gansereit, O. L. McCabe, and Albert A. Kurland. "The Psychopathology and Measurement of Environmental Stress," *Community Ment. Health J., 3:* 358–372, 1967.

Miller, Neil. "Some Reflections on the Law of Effect Produce a New Alternative to Drive Reduction," *Nebraska Symposium on Motivation*. Lincoln: University of Nebraska Press, 1963.

Milner, Peter. "Do Behaviorists Really Need a Brain Drain?" in R. B. MacLeod (Ed.), *William James: Unfinished Business*. Washington, D.C.: American Psychological Association 1969, pp. 17–19.

Mills, C. Wright. "Situated Actions and Vocabularies of Motive," in Manis and Meltzer (Eds.), *Symbolic Interaction: A Reader in Social Psychology*. Boston: Allyn and Bacon, 1967.

Mills, Theodore. "Equilibrium and the Process of Deviance and Control," *Amer. Soc. Rev., 24:* 671–679, 1959.

Modell, Walter. "Placebo Effects in the Therapetuc Encounter," in W. R. Scott and E. H. Volkart (Eds.), *Medical Care*. New York: Wiley, 1966, pp. 368–380.

Moore, W. E., and M. M. Tumin. "Some Social Functions of Ignorance," *Amer. Soc. Rev., 14:* 787–795, 1949.

———. *Social Change.* Englewood Cliffs, N.J.: Prentice-Hall, 1963.

Mordkoff, Arnold M., and Oscar A. Parsons. "The Coronary Personality: A Critique," *Psychosom. Med., 29:* 1 (January–February) 1967.

Moss, Gordon E. "The 'Jumpers' of Maine: A Sociological Appraisal," *J. Maine Med. Assoc., 59:* 117–121, 1968.

Mowrer, O. H. *The New Group Therapy.* Princeton, N.J.: D. Van Nostrand, 1964.

Mumford, Lewis. *Technics and Civilization.* New York: Harcourt, Brace, and World, 1963.

Murphy, E. B. M. "Personality and the Vermiform Appendix," *J. Health Hum. Behav., 7:* 153–161, 1966.

Mutter, Arthur Z., and Maxwell J. Schleifer. "The Role of Psychological and Social Factors in the Onset of Somatic Illness in Children," *Psychosom. Med., 28:* 333–343, 1966.

Myers, Jerome K., Jacob J. Lindenthal, and Max P. Pepper. "Life Crises, Health Status and Role Performance: Some Preliminary Findings," Paper delivered at the 63rd Annual Meeting of the American Sociological Association, Boston, Mass., August 27, 1968.

Nardini, J. E. "Survival Factors in American Prisoners of War of Japanese," *Amer. J. Psychiat., 109:* 241–248, 1952.

Naylor, J. C., and C. H. Lowshe. "An Analytical Review of the Experimental Basis of Subception," *J. Psychol., 46:* 75–96, 1958.

Nisbet, Robert A. *The Sociological Tradition.* New York: Basic Books, 1966.

———. *Social Change and History.* New York: Oxford University Press, 1969.

Notterman, Joseph M., and Richard Trumbull. "Note on Self-Regulating Systems and Stress," in Buckley (Ed.), *Modern Systems Research for the Behavioral Scientist.* Chicago: Aldine, 1966, pp. 351–353.

Ogburn, W. F. *Social Change with Respect to Culture and Original Notes.* Gloucester, Mass.: Peter Smith, 1964.

Oken, Donald. "The Psychophysiology and Psychoendocrinology of Stress and Emotion," in Appley and Trumbull (Eds.), *Psychological Stress.* New York: Appleton-Century-Crofts, 1967, pp. 43–76.

Opler, Marvin K. "Cultural Induction of Stress," in Appley and Trumbull (Eds.), *Psychological Stress.* New York: Appleton-Century-Crofts, 1967, pp. 209–240.

Osofsky, Howard J., and Seymour Fisher. "Psychological Correlates of the Development of Amenorrhea in a Stress Situation," *Psychosom. Med., 29:* 15, 1967.

Ostfeld, Adrian M. "The Interaction of Biological and Social Variables in Cardiovascular Disease," in Syme and Reeder (Eds.), *Social Stress and Cardio-*

vascular Disease. The Milbank Memorial Fund Quarterly, Vol. XLV, April 1967, p. 13.

Parsons, Talcott. *The Social System.* New York: Free Press, 1951.

————, and Robert F. Bales. *Family, Socialization and Interaction Process.* New York: Free Press, 1955.

————. "Definitions of Health and Illness in the Light of American Values and Social Structure," in E. G. Jaco, (Ed.), *Patients, Physicians and Illness.* New York: Free Press, 1958, pp. 165–187.

————, and Neil J. Smelser. *Economy and Society.* New York: Free Press, 1956.

————. "An Outline of the Social System," in Parsons et al. (Eds.), *Theories of Society: Vol. I.* New York: Free Press, 1961, p. 30.

————, and Renee Fox. "Illness, Therapy, and the Modern Urban American Family," *J. Soc. Issues, 8:* 31–44, 1952.

————. "Evolutionary Universals in Society," *Amer. Soc. Rev., 29:* 339–357, 1964.

————. "Illness and the Role of the Physician: A Sociological Perspective," in W. R. Scott and E. H. Volkart (Eds.), *Medical Care.* New York: Wiley, 1966, pp. 271–280.

————. *Societies: Evolutionary and Comparative Perspectives.* Englewood Cliffs, N.J.: Prentice-Hall, 1966 b.

Payne, Anthony M. M. "The Limitations of Limitation," in Syme and Reeder (Eds.), *Social Stress and Cardiovascular Disease, The Milbank Memorial Fund Quarterly,* Vol. XLV, April 1967, p. 183.

Peele, Talmage L. *The Neuroanatomic Basis for Clinical Neurology.* New York: McGraw-Hill, 1961.

Peiptone, Albert. "Self, Social Environment, and Stress," in Appley and Trumbull (Eds.), *Psychological Stress.* New York: Appleton-Century-Crofts, 1967, pp. 182–208.

Petroni, Frank A. "The Influence of Age, Sex, and Chronicity in Perceived Legitimacy to the Sick Role," *Sociol. Soc. Res., 53:* 180–193, 1969.

Pratt, Lois, Arthur Seligmann, and George Reader. "Physicians' View on the Level of Medical Information Among Patients," in W. R. Scott and E. H. Volkart (Eds.), *Medical Care.* New York: Wiley, 1966, pp. 302–311.

Pribram, Karl H. "Emotion: Steps Toward a Neuropsychological Theory," in Glass (Ed.), *Neurophysiology and Emotions.* New York: Rockefeller and Russell Sage, 1967, pp. 3–39.

Quint, Jeanne C. "Mastectomy—Symbol of Cure or Warning Sign?" in J. R. Folta and E. S. Deck (Eds.), *A Sociological Framework for Patient Care.* New York: Wiley, 1966.

Rahe, Richard H., and Ransom J. Arthur. "Life-Change Patterns Surrounding Illness Experience," *J. Psychosom. Res., 11:* 341–345, 1968.

Rapoport, Anatol. "Uses and Limitations of Mathematical Models in Social Science," in L. Gross (Ed.), *Symposium an Sociological Theory*. New York: Harper Row, 1959.

Reisman, David. *The Lonely Crowd*. New Haven: Yale, 1961.

Rennert, Helmit. "A Unitary Conception in International Psychiatry," *Inter. J. Psychiat., 4:* 246–249, 1967.

Robert, A. "Endocrine Factors in the Etiology of Peptic Ulcer," in Jasmin (Ed.), *Endocrine Aspects of Disease Processes*. St. Louis: Green, 1968, pp. 175–200.

Robinson, George. "The Interrelationship of Anxiety and Guilt: Some Physiologic Correlations," *J. Asthma Res., 5:* 115–121, December 1967.

Roessler, Robert, and Norman S. Greenfield. "Incidence of Somatic Disease in Psychiatric Patients," *Psychosom. Med., 23:* 413–419, 1961.

Rogers, E. M. *Diffusion of Innovations*. New York: Free Press, 1962.

Rose, Arnold M. "Varieties of Sociological Imagination," *Amer. Soc. Rev., 34:* 623–630, 1969.

Rosen, George. "The Philosophy of Ideology and the Emergence of Modern Medicine in France," *Bull. Hist. Med., 20:* 328, 1946.

———. "What is Social Medicine? A Genetic Analysis of the Concept," *Bull. Hist. Med., 21:* 674–733, 1947.

———. *A History of Public Health*. New York: MD Publications, 1958.

———. "The Evolution of Social Medicine," in Freeman, et al. (Eds.), *The Handbook of Medical Sociology*. N.J.: Prentice-Hall, 1963, pp. 17–61.

Rosenberg, Morris. *Society and the Adolescent Self-Image*. Princeton, N.J.: Princeton University Press, 1965.

Rosenman, Ray H., and Meyer Friedman. "Behavior Patterns, Blood Lipids, and Coronary Heart Disease," *J. Amer. Med. Assoc., 184:* 934–938, 1963.

———., et al. "Coronary Heart Disease in the Western Collaborative Group Study," *J. Amer. Med. Assoc., 195:* 86–92, 1966.

Rosovold, H. E. "The Prefrontal Cortex and Caudate Nucleus: A System for Effecting Correction in Response Mechanisms," in Rupp, C. (Ed.), *Mind as a Tissue*. New York: Harper and Row (Hoeber Division), 1968, pp. 21–38.

Rotkin, I. D., and R. W. King. "Environmental Variables Related to Cervical Cancer," *Amer. J. Obstet. and Gynecol., 83:* 720–729, 1962.

———. "Relation of Adolescent Coitus to Cervical Cancer Risk," *J. Amer. Med. Assoc., 179:* 486–491, 1962.

Ruff, George E., and Sheldon J. Korchin. "Adaptive Stress Behavior," in Appley and Trumbull (Eds.), *Psychological Stress*. New York: Appleton-Century-Crofts, 1967, pp. 297–323.

Ruitenbeek, Hendrik M. *The Individual and the Crowd: A Study of Identity in America*. New York: Mentor (New American Library), 1964.

Rupp, Charles (Ed.). *Mind as a Tissue*. New York: Harper and Row (Hoeber Division), 1968.

Samora, Julian, Lyle Saunders, and Richard F. Larson. "Medical Vocabulary Knowledge Among Hospital Patients," in W. R. Scott and E. H. Volkart (Eds.), *Medical Care*. New York: Wiley, 1966, pp. 292–302.

Sandler, Louise. "Child-rearing Practices of Mothers of Asthmatic Children," *J. Asthmatic Res.*, Part I, 2: 109–142, 1964; Part 2, 2: 215–256, 1965.

Schachter, Stanley, and Jerome E. Singer. "Cognitive, Social, and Physiological Determinants of Emotional State," *Psychol. Rev., 69:* 379–399, 1962 a.

—— and Ladd Wheeler. "Epinephrine, Chlopromazine, and Amusement," *J. Abnormal Soc. Psychol., 65:* 121–128, 1962 b.

————. "The Interaction of Cognitive and Physiological Determinants of Emotional State," in Leiderman and Shapiro (Eds.), *Psychobiological Approaches to Social Behavior*. Stanford, Calif.: Stanford University Press, 1964, pp. 138–173.

————. "Cognitive Effects on Bodily Functioning: Studies of Obesity and Eating," in Glass (Ed.), *Neurophysiology and Emotions*. New York: Rockefeller and Russell Sage, 1967, pp. 117–144.

Schaefer, H. "Psychosomatic Problems of Vegetative Regulatory Functions," in J. C. Eccles (Ed.), *Brain and Conscious Experience*. New York: Springer-Verlag, 1966, pp. 522–547.

Schick, Allen. "The Cybernetic State," *Transaction, 7:* 14–26, 1970.

Schmale, Arthur, and Howard P. Iker. "The Affect of Hopelessness and the Development of Cancer," *Psychosom. Med., 28:* 714–721, 1966.

Schroder, Harold M., Michael J. Driver, and Siegfried Streufert. *Human Information Processing*. New York: Holt, Rinehart, and Winston, 1967.

Schumpeter, J. A. *Capitalism, Socialism and Democracy,* 3rd ed. New York: Harper Torch, 1950.

Scotch, Norman, and H. Jack Geiger. "The Epidemiology of Rheumatoid Arthritis: A Review with Special Attention to Social Factors," *J. Chronic Dis. 15:* 1037–1067, 1962.

————. "Sociocultural Factors in the Epidemiology of Zulu Hypertension," *Amer. J. Public Health, 53:* 1205–1213, 1963.

————. "Inside Every Fat Man," in Glass (Ed.), *Neurophysiology and Emotion*. Rockefeller and Russell Sage: New York, 1967, pp. 155–166.

Scott, J. P., and F. H. Bronson. "Experimental Exploration of the Et-epimeletic or Care-Soliciting Behavioral System," in Leiderman and Shapiro (Eds.), *Psychobiological Approaches to Social Behavior*. Stanford, Calif.: Stanford University Press, 1964, pp. 174–193.

————. "Biology and the Emotions," in Glass (ed.), *Neurophysiology and Emotions*. New York: Rockefeller and Russell Sage, 1967, pp. 190–200.

Scott, Marvin, and Stanford Lyman. "Accounts," *Amer. Soc. Rev., 33:* 46–61, 1968 a.

————. "Paranoia, Homosexuality, and Game Theory," *J. Health Soc. Behav., 9:* 179–187, 1968 b.

Scott, Richard W., and Edmund H. Volkart (Eds.). *Medical Care*. New York: Wiley, 1966.

Scott, Robert, and Alan Howard. "Models of Stress," in Levine and Scotch (Eds.), *Social Stress*. Chicago: Aldine, 1970, pp. 259–278.

Sechenov, I. *Reflexes of the Brain*. trans. by S. Belsky. Cambridge, Mass.: MIT Press, 1965 (first published 1893).

Segall, Marshall H., David T. Campbell, and Melville J. Herskovits. *The Influence of Culture on Visual Perception*. Indianapolis, Ind.: Bobbs-Merrill, 1966.

Selye, Hans. *The Stress of Life*. New York: McGraw-Hill, 1956 a.

———. "Synopsis of Physiology and Pathology of Stress," in Selye and Heuser (Eds.), *Fifth Annual Reports on Stress, 1955–56*. New York: MD Publications, 1956 b, pp. 25–104.

———. "Recent Progress in Stress Research, with Reference to Tuberculosis," in Sparar (Ed.). *Personality, Stress and Tuberculosis*. New York: International University Press, 1956 c, pp. 45–64.

———, and Gunnar Heuser (Eds.). *Fifth Annual Reports on Stress, 1955–56*. New York: MD Publications, 1956 d.

———. *From Dream to Discovery*. New York: McGraw-Hill, 1964.

———. "The Stress Syndrome," *Amer. J. Nursing, 65:* 97–99, 1965.

———. *In Vivo. The Case for Supramolecular Biology*. New York: Liveright, 1967.

Shapiro, David, and P. Herbert Leiderman. "Acts and Activation: A Psychophysiological Study of Social Interaction," in Leiderman and Shapiro (Eds.), *Psychobiological Approaches to Social Behavior*. Stanford, Calif.: Stanford University Press, 1964, pp. 110–126.

Sheldon, Richard C. "Some Observations on Theory in the Social Sciences," in Parsons et al. (Eds.), *Toward A General Theory of Action*. New York: Harper, 1965, p. 30.

Sherif, Muzafer, and O. J. Harvey. "A Study in Ego Functioning: Elimination of Stable Anchorages in Individual and Group Situations," *Sociometry, 15:* 272–305, 1952.

Shevrin, H., W. H. Smith, and D. E. Fritzler. "Repressiveness as a Factor in the Subliminal Activation of Brain and Verbal Responses," *J. Nerv. Ment. Dis., 149:* 261–269, 1969.

——— et al., "Subliminally Stimulated Brain and Verbal Responses of Twins Differing in Repressiveness," *J. Abnorm. Psychol., 76:* 39–46, 1970.

Shibutani, T. *Society and Personality*. Englewood Cliffs, N.J.: Prentice-Hall, 1961.

———. "Reference Groups as Perspectives," in Manis and Meltzer (Eds.), *Symbolic Interaction: A Reader in Social Psychology*. Boston: Allyn and Bacon, 1967, pp. 159–170.

Silverman, Lloyd H., and Robert H. Spiro. "Some Comments and Data on the

Partial Ace Controversy and Other Matters Relevant to Investigations of Subliminal Phenomena," *Percept. Mot. Skills, 27:* 325–336, 1967.

Simmons, Leo W., and Harold G. Wolff. *Social Science in Medicine.* Russell Sage Foundation, New York: 1954.

Singer, Jerome L. "Some Experimental Studies of the Stream of Thought," in R. B. MacLeod (Ed.), *William James: Unfinished Business.* Washington, D.C.: American Psychological Association, 1969, pp. 65–72.

Smelser, Neil J. *Theory of Collective Behavior.* New York: Free Press, 1962.

———. *Essays in Sociological Explanation.* Englewood Cliffs, N.J.: Prentice-Hall, 1968.

Smith, I. H., E. N. McKay, and A. H. Sellers. "A Symposium on Cancer of the Cervix Uteri," *Can. Med. Assoc. J., 84:* 351–359, 1961.

Smith, Thomasina. "A Review of Empirical Findings," in Syme and Reeder (Eds.), *Social Stress and Cardiovascular Disease. The Milbank Memorial Fund Quarterly,* Vol. XLV, April 1967, pp. 23–39.

Sontag, L. W. "Determinants of Predisposition to Psychosomatic Dysfunction and Disease: Problem of Proneness to Psychosomatic Disorder," in Dunbar (Ed.), *Synopsis of Psychosomatic Diagnosis and Treatment.* St. Louis: Mosley, 1948, p. 39.

Sorokin, Pitirim A. *Social and Cultural Dynamics.* Boston: Porter Sargent, 1957.

———. *Social and Cultural Mobility.* London: Free Press, 1959.

Sparer, P. J. (Ed.). *Personality, Stress and Tuberculosis.* New York: International University Press, 1956.

Spengler, Oswald "On The Style-Patterns of Culture," in Parsons et al. (Eds.), *Theories of Society: Vol. II.* New York: Free Press, 1961.

Spitz, Rene. "The Role of Ecological Factors in Emotional Development in Infancy," *Child Dev., 20:* 145–155, 1949.

Srole, Leo, et al. *Mental Health in the Metropolis.* New York: McGraw-Hill, 1962.

Stanton, A. H., and M. S. Schwartz. *The Mental Hospital.* New York: Basic Books, 1954.

Stein, Marvin. "Some Psychophysiological Considerations of the Relationship Between the Autonomic Nervous System and Behavior," in Glass (Ed.), *Neurophysiology and Emotion.* New York: Rockefeller and Russell Sage, 1967, pp. 145–154.

Stinchcombe, Arthur L. *Constructing Social Theories.* New York: Harcourt, Brace, and World, 1968.

Stocks, P. "Cancer of the Uterine Cervix and Social Conditions," *Br. J. Cancer, 9:* 487–494, 1955.

Stoeckle, John D., Irving K. Zola, and Gerald E. Davidson. "The Quantity and Significance of Psychological Distress in Medical Patients: Some Preliminary Observations About the Decision to Seek Medical Aid," *J. Chronic Dis., 17:* 959–970, 1954.

Strodtbeck, Fred L., and J. F. Short, Jr. "Aleatory Risks Versus Short-Run Hedonism in Explanation of Gang Action," *Soc. Probs., 12:* 127–140, 1964.

Suchman, Edward A. *Sociology and the Field of Public Health.* New York: Russell Sage Foundation, 1963.

———. "Sociomedical Variations Among Ethnic Groups," *Amer. J. Soc., 70:* 319–331, 1964–65.

———. "Stages of Illness and Medical Care," *J. Health Hum. Behav., 6:* 114–128, 1965.

Suchman, Edward A. "Appraisal and Implications for Theoretical Development," in Syme and Reeder (Eds.), *Social Stress and Cardiovascular Disease. The Milbank Memorial Fund Quarterly,* Vol. XLV, April 1967.

Swanson, Guy E. "Mead and Freud: Their Relevance for Social Psychology," in Manis and Meltzer (Eds.), *Symbolic Interaction: A Reader in Social Psychology.* Boston: Allyn and Bacon, 1967, pp. 25–45.

Sweetser, Dorrian Apple. "How Laymen Define Illness," *J. Health Hum. Behav., 1:* 219–225, 1960.

Syme, S. L., M. M. Hyman, and P. E. Enterline. "Some Social and Cultural Factors Associated with the Occurrence of Coronary Heart Disease," *J. Chronic Dis., 17:* 277–289, 1964.

——— and Leo G. Reeder (Eds.). *Social Stress and Cardiovascular Disease. Milbank Memorial Fund Quarterly,* Vol. XLV, April 1967.

———. "Implications and Future Prospects," in Syme and Reeder (Eds.), *Social Stress and Cardiovascular Disease. Milbank Memorial Fund Quarterly,* Vol XLV, April 1967, p. 109.

———. Lecture given at SUNY at Buffalo, April 1970.

Traviss, Irene. "Change in the Form of Alienation: The 1900's vs. the 1950's," *Amer. Soc. Rev., 34:* 46–47, 1969.

Terris, Milton, and Margaret C. Oalmann. "An Epidemiologic Study of Carcinoma of the Cervix," *J. Amer. Med. Assoc., 174:* 1847–1851, 1960.

———, Fitzpatrick Wilson, Harold Smith, Evelyn Spring, and J. H. Nelson, Jr. "The Relationship of Coitus to Carcinoma of the Cervix," *Amer. J. Public Health, 57:* 840–847, 1967.

Thomas, William I., and Florian Znaniecki. "On Disorganization and Reorganization," in Parsons et al. (Eds.), *Theories of Society, Vol. II.* New York: Free Press, 1961, pp. 1292–1297.

Thurlow, H. John. "General Susceptibility to Illness: A Selective Review," *Can. Med. Assoc. J., 97:* 1397–1404, 1967.

Timiras, P. S. and A. Vernadakis. "Brain Plasticity: Hormones and Stress," in Jasmin (Ed.). *Endocrine Aspects of Disease Processes.* St. Louis: Green, 1968.

Toby, Jackson. "Some Variables in Role Conflict Analysis," *Soc. Forces, 30:* 323–327, 1952.

————. *Contemporary Society*. New York: Wiley, 1964.

Towne, J. E. "Carcinoma of the Cervix in Nulliparous and Cellibate Women," *Amer. J. Obstet. and Gynecol., 69:* 606–613, 1955.

Toynbee, Arnold. "The Disintegration of Civilizations," in Parsons et al. (Eds.), *Theories of Society: Vol. II.* New York: Free Press, 1961, p. 1355.

Trumbull, Richard, and Mortimer H. Appley. "Some Pervading Issues," in Appley and Trumbull (Eds.), *Psychological Stress.* New York: Appleton-Century-Crofts, 1967.

Tulchinsky, Dan, and Baruch Modan. "Epidemiological Aspects of Cancer of the Stomach in Israel," *Cancer, 20:* 1311–1317, 1967.

Turner, Ralph H. "Role-Taking, Role Standpoint, and Reference-Group Behavior," *Amer. J. Soc., 61:* 316–328, 1956.

Tyroler, H. A., and J. C. Cassel. "Health Consequences of Culture Change: The Effect of Urbanization on Coronary Heart Mortality in Rural Residents of North Carolina," *J. Chronic. Dis., 17:* 167–177, 1964.

Udry, J. Richard. *The Social Context of Marriage.* New York: J. B. Lippincott, 1966.

Van Duzer, Charles Hunter. *Contributions of the Ideologues to French Revolutionary Thought.* Baltimore: Johns-Hopkins Press, 1935.

Vernon, Glenn M. *Human Interaction.* New York: Ronald, 1965.

————. private Communication with the author, 1969.

Vickers, Geoffry. "The Concept of Stress in Relation to the Disorganization of Human Behavior," in Buckley (Ed.), *Modern Systems Research for the Behavioral Scientist.* Chicago: Aldine, 1968 a, p. 354–358.

————. "Is Adaptibility Enough?" in Buckley (Ed.), *Modern Systems Research for the Behavioral Scientist.* Chicago: Aldine: 1968 b, pp. 460–473.

Von Bertalanffy, Ludwig. "General System Theory: A Critical Review," in Walter Buckley (Ed.), *Modern Systems Research for the Behavioral Scientist.* Chicago: Aldine, 1968, pp. 11–30.

Wahler, H. J. "The Physical Symptoms Inventory: Measuring Levels of Somatic Complaining Behavior," *J. Clin. Psychol., 24:* 207–211, 1968.

Walker, Charles B. *Technology, Industry, and Man: The Age of Acceleration.* New York: McGraw-Hill, 1968.

Warshay, Leon H. "Breadth of Perspective and Social Change," in G. K. Zollschan and W. Hirsch, (Eds.), *Explorations in Social Change.* Boston: Houghton Mifflin, 1964, pp. 319–344.

Watson, James D. *The Double Helix.* New York: New American Library (Signet), 1968.

Weber, Max. *The Theory of Social and Economic Organization.* (trans. Henderson and Parson). New York: Free Press, 1949.

Wechsler, Henry. "Community Growth, Depressive Disorders, and Suicides," (abstract) *Amer. J. Soc., 67:* 9–16, 1961.

Weiner, Herbert. "Schizophrenia, III: Etiology" in Freedman and Kaplan (Eds.), *Comprehensive Textbook of Psychiatry*. Baltimore: Williams and Wilkins, 1967, pp. 603–621.

Weiss, E., and O. S. English. *Psychosomatic Medicine*, 3rd ed. Philadelphia: W. B. Saunders, 1957.

Werner, David. "Healing in the Sierra Madre," *Nat. Hist., LXXIX:* 60–67, 1970.

Weybrew, Benjamin B. "Patterns of Psychophysiological Response to Military Stress," in Appley and Trumbull (eds.), *Psychological Stress*. New York: Appleton-Century-Crofts, 1967, pp. 324–362.

White, A., P. Handler, E. Smith, and D. Stetten, Jr. *Principles of Biochemistry,* 2nd ed. New York: McGraw-Hill, 1959.

White, R. W. "Competence and the Psycho-Sexual Stages of Development," in Jones (Ed.), *Nebraska Symposium on Motivation*. Lincoln, Neb.: University of Nebraska Press, 1960, pp. 97–141.

Whiting, John W. M. "Analysis of Infant Stimulation," in Glass (Ed.), *Neurophysiology and Emotion*. New York: Rockefeller and Russell Sage, 1967, pp. 201–204.

Whorf, Benjamin Lee. "Science and Linguistics," *Techn. Rev., 42:* 229-231, 247–248, 1940.

———. *Language, Thought, and Reality: Selected Writings of Benjamin Lee Whorf;* J. B. Carroll (Ed.). Cambridge and New York: M.I.T. and Wiley, 1956.

Whyte, William H., Jr. *The Organization Man*. New York: Simon and Schuster, 1956.

Wilkins, Walter L. "Group Behavior in Long-term Isolation," in Appley and Trumbull (Eds.), *Psychological Stress*. New York: Appleton-Century-Crofts, 1967, pp. 278–296.

Wilson, Bryan. "The Religious Teachings and Organizations of Christian Science," in W. R. Scott and E. H. Volkart (Eds.), *Medical Care*. New York: Wiley, 1966, pp. 41–50.

Wilson, Sir Graham S., and A. A. MILES. *Topley and Wilson's Principles of Bacteriology and Immunity,* 5th ed., vol. 2. Baltimore: Williams and Wilkins, 1964.

Withers, Carl. "The Folklore of a Small Town," in W. R. Scott and E. H. Volkart (Eds.), *Medical Care*. New York: Wiley, 1966, pp. 233–246.

Wittkower, E. D., and L. Solyom. "Models of Mind-Body Interaction," *Intern. J. Psychiat., 4:* 225–33, 1967.

Wolf, Stewart. "Life Stress and Patterns of Disease," in Lief, et al. (Eds.), *The Psychological Basis of Medical Practice*. New York: Harper and Row, 1963, pp. 109–114.

——— and Helen Goodell (Eds.). Harold G. Wolff's *Stress and Disease,* 2nd ed. Springfield, Ill.: Thomas, 1968.

Wolff, Carl, et al. "The Relationship Between Ego Defenses and the Adrenal Response to the Prolonged Threat of Loss: A Predictive Study," (abstract), *Psychosom. Med., 25:* 497, 1968.

Wolff, Harold G. *Stress and Disease.* Springfield, Ill.: Charles C Thomas, 1953.

Woodburne, Russell T. *Essentials of Human Anatomy.* New York: Oxford University Press, 1961, esp. pp. 23–32.

Wooley, D. "Involvement of the Hormone Serotonin in Emotion and Mind," in Glass (Ed.), *Neurophysiology and Emotion.* New York: Rockefeller and Russell Sage, 1967, pp. 108–116.

Wrong, Dennis H. "The Oversocialized Conception of Man," *Amer. Soc. Rev., 26:* 185–193, 1961.

Wyman, Leland C. "Navaho Diagnosticians," in W. R. Scott and E. H. Volkart (Eds.), *Medical Care.* New York: Wiley, 1966, pp. 8–16.

Zajonc, Robert B. "Cognitive Theories in Social Psychology," in Lindzey and Aronson (Eds.), *The Handbook of Social Psychology,* Vol. I. 2nd ed. Reading, Mass.: Addison-Wesley, 1968, pp. 320–411.

Zeitlin, Irving M. *Ideology and the Development of Sociological Theory.* Englewood Cliffs, N.J.: Prentice-Hall, 1968.

Zetterburg, Hans L. *On Theory and Verification in Sociology,* 3rd ed. Totowa, N.J.: Bedminster Press, 1965.

Zollschan, G. K., and W. Hirsch (Eds.). *Explorations in Social Change.* Boston: Houghton, Mifflin, 1964.

Zyzanski, S. J., and C. David Jenkins. "Basic Dimensions Within the Coronary-Prone Behavior Pattern," *J. Chronic Dis., 22:* 781–795.

Index

pituitary, 27, 101
Glucocorticoids, 27, 55

Habituation, 206
    definition of, 243
Heart disease, cardiovascular, 16, 30, 34,
    171, 212, 221
    coronary, 1, 14, 16, 61, 210, 212
    rheumatic, 16
Hemorrhage, 35
Hernia, 16
Hippuric acid, 36
Homeostasis, 12, 187, 190
Homeomaistre, definition of, 192, 194, 242
Hypertension, 1, 16, 108, 121, 184
Hypertensive heart disease, 2
Hyperthyroidism, 122
Hypothalamus, 62, 100, 113

Identification, definition of, 141, 242
    development of, 144–156
    health and, 155
    in involvement typology, 141
    preservation of, 150
    self in, 145–148
Ideologues, 5–7
Illness clustering, 16, 155, 170, 184
Immunity, 119–124
Immunity, social, 215
    by congruity, 216, 218–221
    definition of, 243
    diagram of, 245
    by direct experience, 217
    by identification, 216, 218
    by isolation, 216, 222–223
    by socially selected exposure to natural
        agents of disease, 217
Inconsistent statuses, 170, 171
Inflammation, 28
    definition of, 241
    nature of, 78, 82–84
Information congruity, definition of, 241
Information incongruities, 133–137
    in adolescence, 168
    in careers, 167
    categories of, 134–135
    in communication network norms, 225
    definition of, 241
    in families, 168
    handling of, 224

in lack of, skills, 224
    resources, 224
    probability of encountering, 152
    social change and, 197
    uncertainty and, 137
Information repertoire, 132, 141, 241
Innovation, definition of, 205, 243
Insulation, from information incongruities,
    152
Invalidation, definition of, 203, 241
Involvement typology, 141
Ischemia, 35
Isolation, from information incongruities,
    151

Justifications, a form of insulation, 153, 224,
    225

Language, 87–89
    and the brain, 71
Learning, 68, 72
    perceptual, 86
Leukemia, myeloid, 217
Lymphatic tissue, 120

Manic-depressives, 13
Marasmus, 238
Memory, 68, 84
    neurological aspects of, 65
Mental disease, 1, 230
Mental health, 210
Mind, 4
Mineralcorticoids, 27
Mobility, and disease, 211–213
Murders, 16

Nasal disorder, 34
Nausea, 122
Nephritis, 16
Nervous system, autonomic, 98–100, 111,
    113–116, 121–124
    in ergotropic responses, 113–116
    methods of measuring, 105
    parasympathetic, 98
    sympathetic, 98
    in trophotropic responses, 113–116
    tuning of, 114–116, 121, 242
Nervous system, central, 61, 68, 123
    development of knowledge of, 7
Network, communication, see Communica-
    tion network